Another Possible World

RECLAIMING LIBERATION THEOLOGY

Another Possible World

Edited by

Marcella Maria Althaus-Reid
Ivan Petrella
Luiz Carlos Susin

scm press

British Library Cataloguing in Publication data

A catalogue record for this book is available
from the British Library

978 0 334 04094 1

First published in 2007 by SCM Press
13–17 Long Lane,
London EC1A 9PN

www.scm-canterburypress.co.uk

SCM Press is a division of
SCM-Canterbury Press Ltd

Typeset by Regent Typesetting, London
Printed and bound in Great Britain by
William Clowes Ltd, Beccles, Suffolk

Contents

Acknowledgements

With thanks to the sponsors of
the 2005 World Forum for
Liberation and Theology:

Adveniat, Adviescommissie Missionaire Activiteite, Centraal Missie Commissariaat (AMA–CMC)

Broederlijk Denle, Brot für Alle, Christian Aid, Church of Sweden, Comité Catholique contre la Faim et pour le Développement (CCFD), Cordaid, Desarollo y Paz, Dreikönigsaktion der Katholischen (DKA)

Evangelisches Missionswerk in Deutschland (EMW), Fastenopfer, Internationales Katholisches, Missionswerk MISSIO e.v., Lee Cormie, Misereor, Misioneros de Maryknoll, Mission 21, Missionszentrale der Franziskaner Bonn, Nordelbisches Zentrum für Weltmission (NMZ)

Presbyterian Church in Canada, Scottish Catholic International Aid Fund (SCIAF), Secours Catholique Caritas France (SCCF), The Catholique Agency for Overseas Development (CAFOD), United Church of Canada, World Council of Churches (WCC/CMI)

Series Editors' Preface

Liberation theologies are the most important theological movement of our time. In the twentieth century their influence shook the Third and First Worlds, grass-root organizations and the affluent Western academy, as well as the lives of priests and laypeople persecuted and murdered for living out their understanding of the Christian message. In the twenty-first their insights and goals remain – unfortunately – as valid as ever.

Liberation theologies are born from the struggles of the poor and the oppressed, struggles that were translated into an epistemological break with the whole of the Western theological tradition; that is, they are not one theological school among others in the canon. Instead, they sought and seek a new understanding of theology itself. The basis of that new understanding is the attempt to do theology from the perspective of the oppressed majority of humankind. Here lies the epistemological break: Liberation theology – whether Latin American, black, womanist, African, feminist, queer, etc. – realizes that theology has traditionally been done from a standpoint of privilege. Western theology is the product of a minority of humankind living in a state of affluent exception and enjoying gender, sexual and racial dominance. Oppression and poverty remain the norm for the majority of the world's population. By grounding themselves in the perspective of the oppressed, therefore, liberation theologies come as close as possible to being the first truly global theologies.

This series recovers the heart and soul of liberation theology by focusing on authors that ground their work in the perspective of the majority of the world's poor. This need not mean that the authors are solely located in the Third World; it is widely recognized that the First World/Third World distinction is today social as well as geographical. What matters is not the location of one's physical space but the perspective from which theology is done. *Reclaiming Liberation Theology* is the first to present the writings of a new generation of thinkers grounded in the liberationist tradition to the wider public. As such, this is the venue for the most radical, innovative and important theological work produced today.

Liberation theologies were born with the promise of being theologies that would not rest with talking about liberation and instead would actually further liberation. Let us hope that they will one day soon no longer be necessary.

Marcella Althaus-Reid
Ivan Petrella

List of Contributors

Marcella Althaus-Reid is an Argentinian theologian and Professor of Contextual Theology at the University of Edinburgh, Scotland. She is the author of numerous books and articles on Liberation Theology and sexuality, among them *Indecent Theology* (2000); *The Queer God* (2004) and *Liberation Theology and Sexuality* (2006). She is a member of the Theological Advisory Group of the Metropolitan Community Church and Director of the International Association for Queer Theology. With Ivan Petrella, she co-edits the SCM series *Reclaiming Liberation Theology*.

Tissa Balasuriya is a Sri Lankan priest of the order of the Oblates of Mary Immaculate and the founder of the Centre for Society and Religion in Colombo. He has written extensively, most notably *The Eucharist and Human Liberation* (1979; *Planetary Theology* (1984) and the controversial *Mary and Human Liberation* (1997), which resulted in excommunication by the Vatican in the same year. The excommunication was subsequently lifted in 1998.

Leonardo Boff is Professor Emeritus of Ethics, Ecology and Philosophy of Religion in the Universidad Estatal de Río de Janeiro, Brazil. He is the author of more than 60 books, among them *Jesus Christ Liberator* (1978); *Ecclesiogenesis: The Base Communities reinvent the Church* (1986) and *Church, Charisma and Power* (1985), which earned him condemnation to a year of silence by the Vatican. Boff is a member of the Earth Charter Commission and received The Right Livehood Award, the alternative Noble Prize for Peace, in 2001.

Wanda Deifelt is Professor of Systematic Theology at the Escola Superior de Teologia da Igreja Evangelica de Confissao Luterana no Brasil. She has served as a member of the editorial board of *Concilium* and as theological advisor to the Council of the Lutheran World Federation in the Standing Committee of Ecumenical Affairs. A member of the board of the Ecumenical Institute in Strasbourg, Wanda has published on issues such as women in the Church, theological studies, leadership, and church and community.

Ulrich Duchrow is Professor of Theology at the University of Heidelberg and co-founder of Kairos Europe and also of Attac-Germany. He is a very prolific author and among his many books we can mention *Global Economy: A Confessional Issue for the Churches?* (1987); *Total War Against the Poor: Confidential Documents of the 17th Conference of American Armies* (with Hippler and Eisenbürger 1990); *Alternatives to Global Capitalism. Drawn from Biblical History, Designed for Political Action* (1995; 1998) and *Property for People, Not for Profit: Alternatives to the Global Tyranny of Capital* (with F. Hinkelammert 2004).

Claude Geffré, OP, a Dominican, is Honorary Professor at the Catholic Institute in Paris and one of Europe's foremost theologians. He was Director of the École Biblique et Arquélogique Française de Jérusalem (1996–99). Among his many books published we can mention *Le Christianisme au risqué de l'interprétation* (1988); *Profession Théologien. Quelle pensée Chrétienne pour le XXIéme Siécle?* (1999) and *Croire et Interpréter* (2001).

Rosino Gibellini is a theologian and editor of several important works on the figures and movements in contemporary theology such as *Frontiers of Theology in Latin America* (1979); *The Liberation Theology Debate* (1987) and *Paths of African Theologies* (1994). He is Director of *Queriniana* and publisher of the Italian edition of the Roman Catholic Journal *Concilium*.

Dwight Hopkins is Professor of Theology at the University of Chicago, part of the USA minorities section of the Ecumenical Association of Third World Theologians (EATWOT) and a member of Trinity United Church of Christ in Chicago. He is the author of numerous books including *Down, Up, and Over: Slave Religion and Black Theology* (2000); *Introducing Black Theology of Liberation* (1999) and *Shoes That Fit Our Feet* (1993). His most recent book is *Being Human: Race, Culture and Religion* (2005).

Deenabandhu Manchala is the Executive Secretary of the Executive Secretary of programme on Unity, Mission, Evangelism and Spirituality of the World Council of Churches, Geneva. He is the editor of

Nurturing Peace: Theological Reflections on Overcoming Violence (2005)

Emmanuel Martey is Associate Professor of Theology at the Trinity Theological Seminary, Legon in Ghana. He is also the Secretary of the Conference of African Theological Institutions (CATI) and author of *African Theology: Inculturation and Liberation* (1993).

James Massey is Director of the Centre for Dalit/Subaltern Studies (CCCC), New Delhi, India, and Privatdozent in the Faculty of Protestant Theology in the Johann Wolfgang Goethe-University, Germany. He is the author of numerous books and articles such as *Indigenous People* (1994); *Towards a Dalit Hermeneutics* (1994) *and Minorities and Religious Freedom in a Democracy* (2003).

Jung Mo Sung is Korean by birth, nationalized Brazilian. Professor of the post-graduate programme in Religious Science at the Methodist University of Sao Pablo (UMESP) and the Pontíficia Universidade Católica do Rio de Janeiro, he is the author of numerous articles and of 11 books, among them *Teologia e Economia; Repensando a Teologia da Liberaçao e as Utopias* (1994); *Desejo, Mercado e Religiâo* (1998); *Sujeito e Sociedades Complexas* (2002, translated into Spanish) and *Sementes de Esperanca: A Fé em um Mundo en Crise* (2005). Many of his books have been translated into Spanish, Korean and English.

Ivan Petrella is Assistant Professor in the Department of Religious Studies at the University of Miami. He is author of *The Future of Liberation Theology: An Argument and Manifesto*, editor of *Latin American Liberation Theology: The Next Generation* and with Marcella Althaus-Reid co-editor of the *Reclaiming Liberation Theology* book series with SCM.

Luiz Carlos Susin is a member of the Order of Capuchin Fathers and Professor of the Institute of Theology and Religion of the Pontíficia Universidade Católica of Porto Alegre, Brazil. He is a member of the Editorial Board of *Concilium*, and a founder member and ex-president of the Society of Theology and Religious Sciences (SOTER) of Brazil. He has written extensively in books and articles on theology, philosophy and spirituality. Among his many publications are *A Criação de Deus* (2003); *Terra Prometida. Movimento Social, Engajamento Cristão e Teologia* (2001); *Sarça Ardente. Teologia na América Latina* (2000). He edited *Mysterium Creationis* (1999), which was nominated for the prize 'Jabuti' of the Brazilian Chamber of Books.

Juan José Tamayo Acosta is Director of the Theology and Religious Science Program, and the Ignacio Ellacuría Chair at the Carlos III University in Madrid, Spain. His many publications include *Presente y Futuro de la Teología de la Liberación* (1994); *Hacia la Comunidad* (2000); *Nuevo Pardigma Teológico* (2003) and *Fundamentalismos y Diálogos entre Religiones* (2006). He is the General Secretary of the Asociación de Teólogos Juan XXIII in Spain.

Elsa Támez is President of the Latin American Biblical Seminary and researcher at the Departamento Ecuménico de Investigaciones in San Jose, Costa Rica. She is the author of many books and articles including *The Amnesty of Grace* (1993); *When the Horizons Close: Re-reading Ecclesiastes* (2000) and *The Scandalous Message of James* (2002). Her work has been translated into many languages.

Felix Wilfred is Professor at the School of Philosophy and Religious Thought, The University of Madras. He has been a member of the International Theological Commission of the Vatican and Secretary of the Theological Advisory Commission of the Federation of The Asian Bishops' Conferences, Hong Kong. His publications include *On the Banks of Ganges* (2002); *Asian Dreams and Christian Hope. At the Dawn of the Millennium* (2000) and the edited collection *The Struggle for the Past* (2002).

1 A World Forum for a Global Liberation Theology

FR LUIZ CARLOS SUSIN

Contemplating our small and precious planet from outer space in the images sent by space exploration provokes in our generation a new feeling: we inhabit a common house which is part of a collective destiny, even though our common house suffers the consequence of a conflictive human family. This World Forum of Theology and Liberation is part of this feeling and takes place in the context of the World Social Forum in January 2005. It was sparked by the theme 'Another World is Possible'. To understand the current state of its aims, it is worth briefly recalling its past.

During the third meeting of the World Social Forum, in January 2003, in Porto Alegre, which included the contribution of a number of theologians, an exchange of ideas between Sergio Torres and Leonardo Boff turned into a proposal for a connection between the World Social Forum and a forum of liberation theology organized globally, and becoming part of the new world context of ecological sensitivity, religious pluralism and social movements. That same year in Sao Pablo, Brazil, a conference took place on Christianity in Latin America, and on this occasion, at a meeting of the organizing committee, the first ideas for this sort of joint forum were agreed upon. They then searched for other entities which could come together to form an organizing committee. It was in this way that the Latin American Amerindian Network, the Association of Third World Theologians (Asset/Easwot), the Association of Theology and Sciences of Religion (SOTER), and, from Brazil, the Ecumenical Centre of Service to Evangelization (CESEP), the Pastoral Centre of the Pontifical Catholic University of Río Grande do Sul (PUCRS), the Ecumenical Centre of Evangelization, Training and Council (CECA), the High School of Theology (EST) and the Humanitas Institute of the University Vale do Rio dos Sinos (UNISINOS), all came together.

A local executive committee was then set up with people from the four religious entities, and the secretary of the forum was established in the Pastoral Centre of the Pontifical Catholic University (PUCRS), which became more and more connected to all the preparation for and execution of the forum, with the support of the presidency of that university and with the involvement of the office of the vice-rector for university extension. At the same time they tried to contact renowned people whose prestige would reinforce the particular committees and whose quick and cordial agreement we gratefully acknowledge. They also established contact with theologians from different continents to support the initial project.

During the World Social Forum of 2004, which took place in Mumbai, India, Sergio Torres extended the group of contacts, both at the forum itself and during his travels throughout Europe and North America, coming into contact with ecclesiastical institutions which could provide financial help. These institutions generously supported our dream and project, and for this we are wholeheartedly grateful. Their names are to be found in the Acknowledgements.

The meetings and preparation work for the forum were organized around determined objectives with the aim of a forum that could become a constitutional assembly for the future. For this first forum, still in the initial stages, we can recall the aims of the project such as they have been set out so far:

1 A forum of mutual understanding and dialogue between Christian theologians of different regions of the planet. There is less and less a central point or separate zones in our world, as if each continent formed a world on its own. More and more, a transparent network is formed. It makes no sense to elaborate contexts and contextual theologies without taking into account the other side of religious affirmations which are precisely the insertion into a global web.
2 A forum to establish contacts and relations between different experiences and liberation theological reflections found in different continents and the most varied social and ecclesial movements.
3 Provide reasons for our active hope as Christian theologians in a world of a pluralism of possibilities in dialogue and co-operation as well as in fundamentalisms and violence between religions.

From a more formal point of view, this forum was designed and projected as a debate between those invited. For this reason, and after the first day communications, a programme was prepared with only one major presentation per day, followed by two panels in which at least half the time was reserved for debate. A work-group prepared a series of notes for team systematization for synthesis the following day. The last afternoon was dedicated to preparing details about the future of the forum.

The local executive committee faced some limitations and difficulties while preparing the forum, for example, achieving a representative level of participants. Many invitations could not be accepted due to semester engagements in the northern hemisphere and other previous commitments.

It is important to clarify that while based on a pluralistic and global representation, it was not focused on an ecclesial or ecclesiastical or academic institutions representation. That would have involved a most complex, costly and difficult organizing process. It is a forum of people who are involved in theology and who have a wide horizon such as the one that the World Social Forum opens up, and which develops in the demand that 'Another World is Possible'. The different ecclesial homes obviously contributed to the richness that each theologian provided. But our identities can confront and add here to the efforts for the transformation of our planet and in this way generate a truly liberating theological project.

The executive committee, together with the secretary for the Pastoral Centre of PUC, is honoured to have been able to prepare this forum and put all its energy and its gifts towards the good fruits achieved. We join with the organizing committee in seeking your understanding for all the failures and limitations in a process whose size and originality knows no past experience. But above all it is an invitation to join efforts and creativity in overcoming difficulties and resistance, so as to find ourselves together on the true path of value and benefit for this small and so complex round and blue world. *The road is paved as we walk!*

2 Two Urgent Utopias for the Twenty-first Century

LEONARDO BOFF

We live in the midst of a crisis of civilizations of planetary proportions. Every crisis offers us the opportunity of a transformation and at the same time the risk of a devastating failure. In crisis there is a mixture of fear and hope. To reinforce hope, utopias are born. By their nature, utopias are never wholly realized. But they keep us on the way. They are stars. We never reach them. But they bewitch our night and guide navigators. As Mario Quintana, a poet from Porto Alegre says:

> If things become unattainable, pray!
> There is no reason not to wish them.
> How sad the way if it were not for
> The magic presence of stars![1]

In the current context of crisis I see two utopias emerging that are natural to liberation theology. The utopia to safeguard our common home – planet Earth; and the utopia to preserve the human family. Let's consider the first one.

The utopia to safeguard the common home

Liberation theology was born upon hearing the cry of the oppressed. Its merit is to have provided a central place to the impoverished, making them subjects of their history, as well as the starting point from which the nature of God as the God of life, the mission of Jesus as promoter of life in fullness and the nature of the Church as sacrament, that is, as instrument and sign of liberation, is best understood.

But it is not only the poor who cry out. The waters cry out, forests cry out, animals cry out, ecosystems cry out, the Earth cries out. All

---

1 Mario Quintana, 'Das Utopias'. Available online at http://www.casado-bruxo.com.br/poesia/m/utopia.htm.

of them are victims of the same logic that creates impoverishment. This is why the Earth and nature are exploited and devastated. In the preferential option for the poor and against poverty and for liberation – trademark of liberation theology – we include the Great Poor which is the Earth, the only common home we have to live in. A theology of liberation will only be integral if it incorporates into its reflection and practice the liberation of the Earth as a system of systems, as a living super-organism of which we are all sons and daughters together with the other living organisms, our brothers and sisters, produced by and fed by Mother Earth.

In the same way that the encounter with the poor allowed for an original and originating spiritual experience, which became the base for a liberating practice and reflection, now the encounter with the ecological issue leads towards a new experience of the sacred and of the *Spiritus Creator* which acts in creation and encourages alternative practices in relation to nature and our lifestyles. From this experience and this practice the utopia of safeguard of the Earth projects itself.

This utopia includes a sense of urgency because our civilization has built up its principle of self-destruction. There are 25 different ways to destroy the human planetary project and to seriously injure the biosphere. Over 40,000 years ago, long before the Neolithic (about 10,000 years ago), there began a systematic assault on the biosphere because instruments which really started the domination of nature were developed. In a few thousand years, hunters made mammoths, giant monkeys and other prehistoric animals extinct.

Currently this process has been aggravated in a terrifying way. There is a basic rate of extinction, which is normal in a process of evolution: about 300 species a year. But nowadays, one species definitively disappears every 13 minutes, due to the production and consumerist voracity of human beings. This dramatic script led Arnold Toynbee (d. 1975), the great historian, to write in his biographical essay *Experiences* (1969): 'I have lived to see that the end of history has turned into a intra-historic possibility capable of being realized not by God, but rather by human beings.'[2] Carl Sagan, the renowned cosmologist, shared these thoughts when shortly before his death four years ago he said that the directing forces of nature and the universe no longer guarantee the future on Earth. This now depends on the political will of human beings. To survive we need to wish this collectively. Finally, no one has expressed the current drama in a better way than

---

2 Arnold Toynbee, *Experiences*, New York and London, Oxford University Press, 1969.

the Earth Charter; this document was the result of global reflection on safeguarding the planet and UNESCO has adopted it to be taught in all schools:

> we face a critical moment in the history of Earth, a time in which humanity must choose its future. The option is the following: create a global alliance to save the Earth and care for each other or risk our destruction and the devastation of the diversity of life.[3]

We can now understand how well founded is the utopia of safe-guarding the Earth. This time there will be no Noah's Ark to save some and let others perish. We are all saved, or we all perish. Such urgency creates a new centre. The question no longer is what future does the civilization of techno-science have in the current globalized world, or what future does Christianity have, or even liberation theology have. The question is what future do the Earth and humanity have and in what way do our techno-science, the Church and liberation theology contribute to secure a future of hope for all.

For this reason we need a new paradigm that will re-establish an alliance for lasting peace with the Earth. Its name is the ecological paradigm. Ecology here is not reduced to a technique for managing scarce natural resources; it implies a new vision of nature, a perception in which there is no environment, rather what really exists is a great life community in which we are all members together, our singularity being that we are ethical and spiritual beings with the mission of being guardians of creation caring for all that exists and lives, because all that exists and lives deserves to exist and live. It implies understand-ing, as the native people understood, and as the leading scientists of today understand, that the Earth is not inert, it is not a coffer of unlim-ited resources. The Earth is alive; it balances all physical-chemical-ecological resources in the subtle and integral manner that only a living organism can do. For this reason it is called a living super-organism, Gaia or Pacha-Mama. And men and women proceed from humus (fertile land), as Adam proceeds from *adamá*, fertile land, and human beings, rather than sons and daughters of Earth, are the same Earth, which in a certain moment of evolution began to feel, think, love, care and venerate.

There is no space here to expand on the principles that sustain the Earth utopia. Our culture has sent them into exile, but currently they

---

3 *Toward a Sustainable World: The Earth Charter in Action*, Preamble, p. 1. Available online at http://www.earthcharterinaction.org/assets/pdf/charter/charter_eng.pdf.

are returning and building the base for a geo-society. It is care, which is a loving reality; it is care that constitutes a basic ethic which preserves life and guarantees coexistence. It is the dimension of the soul, of the feminine in man and woman, which makes us sensitive to the whole, opening us up to grasp the messages that all realities radiate and which confers centrality to life and co-operation, overcomes competitiveness and a merely utilitarian vision of nature. Finally, it is spirituality, as a moment of conscience, which feels bound and binds to the whole, and which lives on non-material values, such as compassion, love, solidarity and dialogue with the original source of all being. These principles allow us, as the great Portuguese poet Fernando Pessoa once said 'to imagine life as it never was.'[4]

The utopia of safeguarding the unity of the human family

The second utopia consists in safeguarding the unity of the human family. There is a real danger that the human family will divide into those who benefit from the technological advances and biotechnology and have at their disposal all possible media for life and welfare, nearly 1,600 million people who can prolong life till the age of 130, which corresponds to the age of cells, and another humanity, the other 4,400 million human beings, dehumanized, left to their own luck, who can live, at most, to be 60 or 70 with conventional technology in a frame of perverse poverty, abject misery and social exclusion.

This abyss results from the economic horror that has dominated the history under the axis of globalized economy. It considers itself triumphant against socialism, whose defeat came at the end of the 1980s, aggravating principles such as competition, individualism, privatization and the defamation of all forms of politics, in addition to the demonization of the state, which is reduced to a minimum. Two hundred mega-companies have an economic power equivalent to 180 countries; they direct the world economy, together with capitalist organizations such as the International Monetary Fund, the World Bank and the World Trade Organization, under the principle of competition with no sense of co-operation. In Brazil there are 8 million families who are creditors of the government, which disposes of 700,000 million reales (1 per cent of the rich posses 42 per cent of national wealth). In this system all is commodified, from sex to mysticism, from water to human organs, in a voluptuousness of wild accumulation of riches and

---

4 Fernando Pessoa, 'Quero Dormir'. Available online at http://nescritas. nletras.com/fpessoa/poesiafpessoa/archives/1911_09.html.

services, at the expense of the devastation of nature and the unlimited precariousness of jobs.

The danger lies in that they create a world only for themselves, reducing human rights to a human necessity to be attended to by the mechanisms of the market (in this sense, only those who pay have rights, it is not enough simply to be a person); they make those who are different, unequal, and those who are unequal, other, people no longer belonging to the human species and thus worthy of rights.

In the West – where this globalization process dominates – the idea of equality never triumphed politically. It was always limited to the religious-Christian discourse of utopian content. This deficit of an egalitarian culture suppresses the bonds that would prevent the divergence of the human family. An age of world darkness, which plunges over humanity in its totality, can triumph.

The urgent utopia is to maintain the unity of the human family living in the same common home. All are Earth, sons and daughters of the Earth, created in the image and likeness of the Creator, made brothers and sisters in Jesus Christ and temples of the Holy Spirit. All have the right to be included in the common home and participate in its gifts.

For this utopia to take shape we need to recuperate values linked to solidarity and compassion. It is important to remember that it was solidarity and compassion that allowed our ancestors, millions of years ago, to make the jump from animality to humanity. When out collecting food, they did not eat it individually, as the superior animals did; rather they would gather their fruits and what they had hunted, then they would take it to their groups of peers and they would share fraternally between each. From this primordial gesture was born solidarity, language and human singularity. Even today, it will be unrestricted solidarity, beginning from below, and compassion that becomes sensitive when faced with the suffering of others that will guarantee the human character of our identity and our practices. Shamefully this was what was missing in the great international creditors, when after the tragedy of the South East Asia tsunamis, they did not cancel the several billion dollars of total external debt of the countries which suffered the tragedy, but rather only delayed payment for one year.[5] Without a Good Samaritan gesture that renounces entering nirvana for love of the suffering or the wounded animal or the shattered branch, we will hardly be strong enough to overcome the daily barbarism which is being installed in the world.

---

5 See World Bank Report, available online at http://web.worldbank.org/wbsite/external/datastatistics.

I conclude these fragmentary thoughts. From an astronaut's perspective, someone who is privileged to see the Earth from beyond the Earth, Earth and humanity form a unity with no distinctions; dynamic, radiant and open. They are now both under threat; both share a same destiny, and both are summoned together for the future. Their safeguard is the greatest content of a unique great utopia, the utopia of the twenty-first century.

If our theologies do not help us dream this dream and lead people to live it, we will not have fulfilled the mission the Creator reserved for us in the community of beings, that of being the good master and not the Satan of the Earth, nor will we have listened to or followed the One who said 'I have come to bring life, and life abundant'. Sisters and brothers, let us grow up, in the conscience of our responsibility, knowing that no concern is more important that to care for the common home we have, and to achieve that the whole human family may live united in this common home with care, solidarity, fraternity, compassion and reverence, which produce a simple happiness for the short time we have received to spend on this small planet.

3 Religion for Another Possible World

TISSA BALASURIYA

The present world

First of all, what is the present world we are in and what do we mean by another possible world? Is it a world that is desirable in itself, is it feasible, or not such as a utopia would be?[1] Second, is it a feasible world towards which human groups could strive in a given period of time? Third, is it the world that is likely to be if the present processes of development and relationships of people are continued in the next 25 years, half century or during the twenty-first century? And finally what is likely to be the change if some of the more active agents of transformation both for good and for bad evolve without much interaction of forward-looking human groups?

There are also the imponderables such as the advancement of sciences and technology and the impact of deadly diseases like AIDS, both of which can radically transform human relationships in the world even in the next 25 years.

In the present world there is a great imbalance in the division of resources among peoples, beginning with the land and capital and in the resources of technological advancement and scientific education. From this perspective we could refer to the likely changes that will take place in the distribution of population in the world in the coming 25 or 50 years or even the whole century, according to present possibilities of population projection. The population changes are challenges to world justice.

---

1 The concept of 'utopia' has been used among Liberationists with different connotations. Among Latin Americans, the term is usually used in a positive sense (cf. Leonardo Boff's chapter in this book). Examples of its positive use can be found in Gustavo Gutiérrez, *A Theology of Liberation*, London, SCM Press, 1973, p. 136; also Juan Luis Segundo, *La Cristiandad: Una Utopia?* Vol. 1: Los Hechos, Montevideo, Mimeográfica Luz, 1964 [Editor note].

Population: some data on growth, movements and prospects

Most of Europe was sparsely populated in 1820, inhabitants being mainly in the villages. By 1900 the European population more than doubled. European migrants went to the Americas, Australasia, Southern Africa and Siberia. The population of these areas increased from 5.7 million to over 200 million between 1810 and 1910.

Between 1810 and 1840 only 1.5 million left Europe, mainly to the USA. Between 1841 and 1886 the figure leapt to 8.15 million, and between 1880 and 1910 to 25 million. 'Between 1800 and 1930 the White proportion of the world's population expanded from 22 to 35%.'[2] See, for example the figures in the following tables:

European population growth 1800–1910 (excluding Russia).[3]

1800	123 million
1810	140 million
1830	156 million
1840	170 million
1850	170 million
1860	194 million
1870	210 million
1880	225 million
1890	244 million
1900	267 million
1910	294 million

Migration data

Percentage of population increase that has permanently emigrated (calculated from data on gross immigration in Australia, Canada, New Zealand and the United States).

* The periods from 1950 to 1960 pertain to emigration only to the United States.
** Emigration only to the United States.[4]

Period	Europe	Asia*	Africa	Latin America*
1851–1880	11.7	0.4	0.01	0.3
1881–1910	19.5	0.3	0.04	0.9

2 *Times History of the World Atlas*, New York, Harper Collins, 1999, p. 209.
3 *Times History of the World Atlas*, p. 208.
4 The World Bank Report, 1984, p. 69 ref. 18.

Period	Europe	Asia*	Africa	Latin America*
1911–40	14.4	0.1	0.03	1.8
1940–60	2.7**	0.1	0.01	1.0
1960–70	5.2	0.2	0.10	1.9
1970–80	4.0	0.5	0.30	2.5

Overseas migration from Europe between 1846 and 1924

Austria-Hungary	4,878,000
Belgium	172,000
Denmark	349,000
Finland	342,000
France	497,000
Germany	4,533,000
Great Britain and Ireland	18,030,000
Italy	9,474,000
Netherlands	207,000
Norway	804,000
Portugal	1,633,000
Russia	8,000,000
Spain	4,314,000
Sweden	1,145,000
Switzerland	307,000

Between 1846 and 1924 55 million people migrated from Europe. In this period Chinese, Indians and Japanese also moved, much less and often as labourers.[5]

Between 1960 and 2000 there have been very substantial changes in the world population distribution. The population projections are in millions.[6]

Year	1960	2000
Developed market economies	633	857
Eastern Europe and USSR	313	429
Developing countries	1,367	3,558
China and Asian planned economies	704	1,400
World total	3,019	6,251

---

5 *Times History of the World Atlas*, pp. 209, 225, 245.
6 United Nations, *Global Outlook*, 2000, p. 227.

These projections, which have been more or less realized, indicate that out of an increase of world population by 3,232 million, the developing world has to provide for about 2,930 million, whereas the developed countries have to provide for 224 million and the Eastern European bloc including Siberia for 116 million. This is the biggest gap in the world structure.

World population prospects in millions

	World	Asia	Europe	N. America	L. America	Aus/NZ
2000	6,057	3,672	727	314	519	23
2050	9,322	5,428	603	437	805	31

The change from 2000 to 2050 is:

+3,265	+1,756	−124	+123	+306	+8

Total world population in millions

	2000	2050
World	6,091.3	9,366.7
More developed	1,171.4	1,151.7
Less developed	4,515.7	8,204.9

The world system of land distribution is consolidated more or less as in 1945 after five centuries of colonial expansion and the end of World War Two. Thus countries such as China and India have limited land despite a very high population in relation to land.

Without a just and peaceful remedy for this imbalance there will be no guarantee of life and security for the billions who are poor, nor will the rich countries be able to prevent an overflow of population from the South to their under-cultivated areas. Capitalistic globalization not only does not provide solutions for this problem, it makes the situation worse by the policies of structural adjustment and the World Trade Organization (WTO). Neither is the United Nations Organization (UNO), as it is presently conceived and structured, capable of finding meaningful solutions for this imbalance.

It would be good for present peoples of European origin to reflect on how they were able to migrate in the nineteenth century when their population was increasing, and they had problems like the Irish potato famine.

[Handwritten annotations in top margin: "Justice", "transparency: race, ethnicity, political morality...", "nationality", "thesis and antithesis", "True justice of the Kingdom"]

[Handwritten annotation in left margin: "But who is to blame for what has happened in the past?"]

Having gone to those lands, marginalizing or even exterminating the previous indigenous inhabitants, now they are sealing off these lands and their own lands in Europe to the rest of humanity, except mainly when it benefits them. What is the ethical justification for this? How does international law regard this situation? How would international law, in so far as it exists, have to be reformed in terms of a global ethic that is rational and humane, not to say civilized?

The situation is more intriguing and challenging when we reflect that most of the peoples of European origin are considered to be of Christian civilization and peoples of the poor countries who cannot now move to the free land spaces of the world are of other religions. The issue becomes more complex when thought of against the background of the Islamic/Christian conflicts of the late Middle Ages, and early modern period and the so-called clash of civilizations today.

Foundational injustice of the world system

This imbalance of population to land is in a sense the foundational injustice of the whole world system today, coming down from the colonial period. It was consolidated after World War Two with the setting up of the UN and the Security Council basically to preserve this distribution as what is considered the just world order. Its preservation is thought of as the maintenance of peace and law in the world. This may be called global apartheid and is one of the biggest structural evils that continue from generation to generation. A reflection on it would give some of its characteristics:

1 It is a result of violence, consolidated by the victors in terms of territorial frontiers and carried on from generation to generation. It is based on 'might is right'.
2 It is racism of an extreme form, leads to the fear of the disadvantaged races by the possessors of land and hence to defensive militarism.
3 It is the most basic form of inequality and deprivation from which others such as of incomes, wealth and resources flow.
4 It deprives people in need of the opportunities of work, food and livelihood.
5 It causes economic depression by decreasing production of food.
6 It leads to waste of resources by neglect, by non-cultivation and perhaps over-fertilization.
7 It is maintained by unjust immigration laws, leads to illegal immigration and conflicts; it is a basic cause of social conflicts in the countries and contributes to the expenditure on arms.

8 It helps increase land, water and air pollution; it is against the principle of 'the free market' and of liberal values that would exalt freedom of movement. It is the result of the Western land grab of the past 500 years; it makes people insensitive to the needs of others and to the evils of the past; it is a centennial form of injustice for which no adequate solution is in sight, for it influences the mindsets of the dominant.

9 It goes against the core values of the religions, which advocate that the whole Earth be available to all humankind and teach sharing to be a principal virtue.

10 It is a basic problem for the liberation of the elite, challenging them to respond to the advantages that are from birth.

This problem is neglected by most economists, political scientists, politicians, planners, international lawyers and theologians. It is not generally studied by universities and international foundations. It is not within the scope of the religions either, especially Christianity. Since the demographic data indicate a worsening situation in the course of the twentieth century, it is a challenge for the youth of today to participate in making the world more just by bringing about changes in mindsets as well as in the global structure of the world system. Most solutions presently discussed for development, justice and peace are piecemeal and reformist, keeping the foundational system intact. It may be called the original sin of the modern world.

4 Difficulties and Opportunities for Theology in Today's World

ULRICH DUCHROW

Thesis 1

At first sight, the difficulties and opportunities presented for theology by today's world seem to be quite clear. The difficulties are caused by an extremely asymmetrical power system, economically ('total' market), ideologically (entrenched in the hearts and minds of people as in the ideological institutions) and politically (the empire). Here theology faces similar problems to those confronting Judaeo-Christian faith groups during the Hellenistic-Roman empires in facing the powers.[1] The opportunities are mainly linked to the emergence of social movements worldwide. However, what are the conditions required for them to successfully implement alternatives?

As long as the workers' movements were strong and competition with real socialism in its various forms challenging enough (in spite of the latter's shortcomings), capitalism in its national forms had to accept some social obligations. This was the time after the great recession in 1929 until the 1970s. In conjunction with the globalization of industrial and financial capital, the introduction of dictatorships in the South, which opened up the markets to transnational capital, and the growing hegemony of the neo-liberal ideology, the economy was stripped more and more of these obligations and began to serve only

---

1 See Walter Wink's trilogy on the powers: *Naming the Powers: The Language of Power in the New Testament*, Minneapolis, Augsburg Fortress Publishers, 1984; *Unmasking the Powers: The Invisible Forces that Determine Human Existence*, Minneapolis, Augsburg Fortress Publishers, 1986; and *Engaging the Powers: Discernment and Resistance in a World of Domination*, Minneapolis, Augsburg Fortress Publishers, 1992. Also Ulrich Duchrow, *Alternatives to Global Capitalism, Drawn from Biblical History, Designed for Political Action*, Dublin, International Books, 1996.

the maximization of profits. At the same time the state was stripped of its welfare functions and left with its security functions for capital owners. After the breakdown of real socialism in the 1990s, capitalism in conjunction with the ever more overt imperialism of the USA and its allies supplemented its normal methods of exploitation with methods of direct expropriation.[2] This development – resulting in extreme concentration of power and wealth for a minority, on the one hand, and exclusion and impoverishment of the world's majority and destruction of nature, on the other – has been researched and described by numerous scholars.

For theology and churches this raises the basic question of whether the prevailing system as such, including its justifications, has to be rejected and resisted like National Socialism and apartheid.[3] In the terminology of the Reformation traditions the question is whether neo-liberal capitalism constitutes a *status confessionis*. This means that the gospel itself and the being of the Church are at stake. Christians and the churches are obliged to corporately confess God's taking sides for the victims in word and deed and consequently resisting the system that produces these victims structurally, while themselves living out alternatives. The necessity to become confessing churches as under Hitler and apartheid can, of course, be expressed in other terms. The historical peace churches speak of the necessity to follow Jesus in *faithful discipleship* in spite of suffering persecution. Eastern Orthodox theology speaks of liturgy after the liturgy, meaning you cannot participate in the Eucharist without *sharing* in daily life. Similarly, the Lutheran World Federation recently highlighted the meaning of *communion* over against an excluding system. In Baptist and Reformed tradition the language of *covenant* prevails. You cannot claim to live in God's covenant without being committed to observe the life-giving rules of this covenant, biblically speaking the Torah. Recently the World Council of Churches expressed the same by referring to the language of *AGAPE*, traditionally translated as 'love' or 'solidarity' and now interpreted as an acronym for 'Alternative Globalization Addressing People and Earth'. Christians and churches cannot say they proclaim the God of love if they co-operate with or legitimize a system which by its very nature excludes and destroys.

Biblically the Hellenistic-Roman empires constituted a similar context. Here faithful theology developed the apocalyptic writings

---

2 See Christian Zeller, *Die globale Enteignungsökonomie*, Münster, West-fälisches Dampfboot, 2004.

3 See Ulrich Duchrow, *Global Economy: A Confessional Issue for the Churches?*, Geneva, WCC, 1987.

(starting with the book of Daniel) as an underground theology, nurturing resistance and, in the figure of Jesus, additionally empowering people in community to become human in the midst of inhumanity and to launch alternatives.

In a situation like this, the biblical method is not to start a dialogue with the powerful but to empower the powerless. In today's world this is happening in and through the social movements. So the chief opportunity open to theology and churches is to work with them. However, the problem is how to overcome the injustices and the violence of empire effectively; and how to ensure that, after overcoming the dominant system the new one will not fall back into the old pattern, co-opting the biblical message as happened after Constantine in the fourth century AD. So we have to look at many more dimensions of response by social movements than mere resistance.

Thesis 2

While the economic and political powers produce their own crises, the ideological power remains rather strong. The neo-liberal hegemony was prepared systematically by transnational networks of theoreticians strategically building up think tanks and infiltrating universities, media, political institutions, etc.[4] How can theology help in building up interdisciplinary theoretical work on alternatives to the neo-liberal hegemony? One key issue is the question of property. While private ownership of the means of production is a key pillar of ruling capitalism, and state ownership has failed, what are the (legal and practical) alternatives for reappropriating the resources of the Earth for sustainable use of all people?[5] Here the Bible offers a range of options.

Since the Asian crisis in 1997 it should have become clear to everyone that, in economic terms, the neo-liberal system is not sustainable. According to the ideologists of the system, China and India show that only capitalism leads to prosperity. Yet China's economy is not growing because of deregulation but by its control of capital flows and the currency exchange rate. And the growth itself is producing more and more

---

4 See R. Cockett, *Thinking the Unthinkable. Think-Tanks and the Economic Counter-Revolution 1931–1983*, London, Harper Collins, 1994 and Bernhard Walpen, *Die Offenen Feinde und ihre Gesellschaft. Eine Hegemonietheoretische Studie zur Mont Pelerin Society*, Hamburg, VSA Verlag, 2004.

5 See Ulrich Duchrow and Franz J. Hinkelammert, *Property for People, Not for Profit: Alternatives to the Global Tyranny of Capital*, London, Zed Books, 2004; also Zeller, *Die globale Enteignungsökonomie*.

inequality, plus social and particularly ecological problems. It remains to be seen what the integration of China into the WTO will do to its economy and society. Also the chaos created by the imperial war waged by the USA against Iraq shows that the more an empire builds on pure violence and military force the more vulnerable it becomes.

However, at the ideological level the system is still going strong. The majority of economists in universities, institutes and government service as well as the capital-controlled media continue to disorient people in their hearts and minds. Here new research shows how strategically the ideology has been planted and made hegemonic by transnational networks, think tanks and foundations,[6] while the left has neglected to develop coping strategies. Yet around the world there are respectable NGOs, institutes and organizations trying to develop alternatives at theoretical levels. Social movements have also developed consulting groups for scientific advice (cf. Attac in France and Germany, trade unions, etc.). Could theology play a role in helping to strengthen interdisciplinary research and alternative models?

The Costa Rican economist Franz Hinkelammert and myself have taken up one of the central theoretical issues that has a strategic role in critiquing neo-liberal capitalism as well as developing alternatives: the issue of property.[7] We looked at the roots of an economy built on private property and money mechanisms in eighth-century Greece, at incipient forms of resistance and alternatives in biblical traditions, at the history of modern capitalism and possibilities for a new 'property order from below', including legal, economic and social aspects. Recently Christian Zeller (2002) has continued this line by formulating the task of a reappropriating strategy of the people as a post-capitalist perspective.[8] In our book we follow the Bible which, on the basis of the theological thesis that the Earth belongs to God (Psalm 24.1) and therefore must not be commercialized (Leviticus 25.23), limits property to its use value in an 'economy of the enough for all' (see Exodus 16, the Manna story) and rejects property as exchange value for wealth creation of the owners. The Bible also provides for mechanisms of restoration when things went wrong (Sabbath and Jubilee regulations, e.g. in Deuteronomy 14 and 15) – a perspective that is placed at the centre by the US–Mexican network 'Jubilee Economics Ministry' and the scholarly 'Sabbath Economics Collaborative' in Los Angeles.

---

6 See Cockett, *Thinking the Unthinkable* and Walpen, *Die Offenen Feinde und ihre Gesellschaft*.

7 Duchrow and Hinkelammert, *Property for People, Not for Profit*.

8 Christian Zeller, 'Project teams as means of restructuring research and development in the pharmaceutical industry', *Regional Studies* 36.3 (2002): 275–89.

Thesis 3

Another problem is the weakened power of the labour movement in comparison to globally mobile capital. Here the question is the building of alliances between the labour movement and other groups or movements affected in different ways by the consequences of neo-liberalism. What are their means of struggle besides the strike capacity of the workers? Consumer boycotts? Withdrawing the money from the commercial markets through alternative banking? What else? Here the theological challenge is how to motivate the churches to live viable examples and to build alliances with the social movements. A sign of hope is the ecumenical process on alternatives to neo-liberal globalization animated by the World Council of Churches, the World Alliance of Reformed Churches and the Lutheran World Federation.

However, the globalization of mobile capital and the territorial limitation of the workers' capital can militate against them. In addition, the development of information technology has replaced a lot of simpler forms of work. Both factors weaken the power of the labour movement to tame capitalism. On the other hand, neo-liberal policies subject the whole of life to the destructive logic of capital accumulation so that all groups in society are affected. Potentially all of them could be part of the countervailing power if they built alliances for resistance and the development of alternatives. Of course, the production process and thus the workers remain key actors. But the consumers also have potential powers, for example by boycotting TNCs or specific products and by giving preference to organic and fair-trade products. Another strategy is the withdrawal of money from the commercial banking system and the use of alternative credit and banking systems.[9]

Here, too, theology can draw guidance from biblical traditions and contribute to the mobilization of Christians and churches. A sign of hope is the ecumenical process on alternatives to neo-liberal globalization. Started by the assemblies of the World Alliance of Reformed Churches (WARC; Debrecen 1997) and the World Council of Churches (WCC; Harare 1998) a coalition has been formed, meanwhile including the Lutheran World Federation (LWF) and regional councils of churches. Regional consultations have prepared the ground for grassroots work in all continents and the next assemblies at global level. The LWF and WARC held assemblies again in 2003 and 2004, pro-

---

9 See Richard Douthwaite, *Short Circuit: Strengthening Local Economies for Security in an Unstable World*, Dublin, Lilliput Press, 1996 in relation to strengthening local economies.

ducing respectable and even revolutionary resolutions. The WCC has produced a study paper for the preparatory process of the churches preceding the assembly planned for Porto Alegre in 2006.

In all of these documents Christians and the churches are being called to recognize the irreconcilability of neo-liberalism and the Christian faith and to join the social movements struggling for alternatives. The key task now is also to win the Roman Catholic Church to join this ecumenical process. The Christian Church in its four social forms (local congregations, discipleship groups, worldwide ecumenical structures, regional church) has the unique role in this struggle of being a network at all levels, from local to global. Its criteria and therefore its partners are those who respond to the basic needs of people (Matthew 25.31ff.).

Thesis 4

Liberation theology has so far mainly looked at structural, gender and cultural issues. What about strengthening the psychological and anthropological perspectives? The losers are being traumatized by the dominant system, while the winners are addicted to success and the middle classes fearful of becoming losers. What are the conditions and strategies for liberating these groups from their specific captivity and assisting them to become human beings in solidarity with each other and with nature as well as to join the struggle? How can we deal with the two poles of self-assertion and co-operation? How can we develop a theology of the liberating Spirit?

In the context of the total market and totalitarian empire the first step is to critique the dominant structures and develop viable economic and political alternatives. Looking at the subjects of change it is also crucial to analyse the cultural and gender perspective (indigenous movements, women's movements, etc.). But it is also necessary to look at the psychological factors, which is seldom done. Neo-liberalism by its very nature divides people into losers and winners. Between them is the middle class in various forms.[10] According to new research, all of these groups are characterized by different psychic captivities. The losers suffer from traumas. This has been researched particularly in the case of unemployment. The winners are captives to addiction. They

---

10 See Pierre Bourdieu, *Gegenfeuer. Wortmeldungen in Dienste des Widerstands gegen die neoliberale Invasion*, Konstanz, Universitätsverlag Konstanz, 1998.

must win and win and win in order not to lose in competition. The middle class is split into a majority of losers and a minority of winners. As it is upwardly oriented it is filled with fear of decline. Because of early child patterns it idealizes the higher authority and projects the bad side of it at scapegoats beneath itself (foreigners, Jews, etc.). This in turn is instrumented by the upper classes to stop any coalition-building between lower and middle classes. But alliance building is the key strategy in regaining political space in order to overcome the dominance of the capitalist economy. Therefore the liberation of at least part of the middle classes in order to win them as partners for the struggle is crucial for building up alliances with the underclass as countervailing power.

Biblically, the liberation of slaves is at the root of the history of faith in Yahweh. In the same way the strategy of Jesus is to liberate and heal the marginalized and build new communities with them. The conversion of rich people, addicted to wealth, is something he regards as humanly impossible but possible by God. Only one rich person can be motivated by Jesus to restore justice and share his wealth, and that is Zacchaeus (Luke 19.1ff.). However, after Pentecost Luke reports in Acts that people do not claim their resources are private property, they share what they have (Acts 4.32ff.) so that there are no poor in their communities. This would also apply to middle classes of today which did not exist in antiquity. So the key theological task would be to revitalize the perspective and experience of the spirit of Pentecost. This means to de-individualize the teaching of the Holy Spirit. After all, it is in just relationships that the new psychology and biblical theology implement liberation and healing. It is in building new communities with new human beings that social change begins. So structural change for a new society can, and must, be linked with the renewal of human beings as they become truly human.

5 Class, Sex and the Theologian: Reflections on the Liberationist Movement in Latin America

MARCELLA ALTHAUS-REID

I do not mean to imply that there are easy and evident continuities between Evita and the libertarian and Gay rights movements or between Evita the power Queen and gay sensibility. Rather, what I mean to understand is how the surpluses of meaning generated by . . . Evita lend themselves to multiple appropriations . . .

David Foster[1]

The poverty of sexuality and the sexuality of the poor

I want to start these reflections on liberation theology, sexuality and poverty by referring to Evita. Deliberately I am mentioning Evita, 'the woman-metaphor' and not Eva Perón, the historical figure. Liberation theology and Evita may have many things in common: to start with, liberationists shared some of the romanticism of the Evita saga: the call to the poor and marginalized but also her pragmatism and determination (using Segundo's concept)[2] to find the right ideology in order to achieve the utopia of the Kingdom among us. Also, as Foster mentions, Evita becomes a gendered metaphor for different possibilities towards an alternative way of living. This is true economically but also in terms of relationships outside social class constructs, for instance, and a window for reformulating sexual transgressions in the years to

---

1 David Foster, 'Evita Perón, Juan José Sebreli and Gender', in Susana Chávez-Silverman and Librada Hernández (eds), *Reading and Writing the Ambiente. Queer Sexualities in Latino, Latin American and Spanish Cultures*, Wisconsin, University of Wisconsin Press, 2000, pp. 218–39 (p. 221).

2 See Juan Luis Segundo's concept of attainable utopia in his discourse of means and ends in ideology in Segundo, *The Liberation of Theology*, New York, Orbis, 1976, p. 116.

come among the gay community in Argentina. And this is precisely the starting point of my reflections. Liberation theology needs to be understood as a romantic and pragmatic movement with, at the same time, a strong vocation towards the marginalized and with an emphasis on praxis informed by a framework of multiple suspicions.

Each different generation of liberationists in Latin America has been somehow opening new windows and discovering different paths towards the utopia of the kingdom: social-economic and racial justice being as important and mutually interdependent as sexual justice. However, it would be unfair to say the first wave liberationists were unconcerned with sexual or gender justice, and I am excluding here the obvious pioneer work done by the feminist liberation theology movement. Allow me to repeat what I have elaborated in more detail elsewhere.[3] Liberationists were too sophisticated to be homophobic but also too indebted to patriarchal Christianity, and specifically, to hetero-patriarchy, to be able even in the best of cases to go beyond a gender-tolerance model. That is, there was a model of inclusion of gender and perhaps even sexual differences (although seldom made explicit) in the theological movement and militant churches without further in-depth questioning. And that takes us to the kernel of the problem, because the 'questioning further' is what separates the theological goats from the sheep in our present century. Either our theological enquiries are concerned with multiple structures of oppression and their interdependence or they are subsumed into that hermeneutics of consequences which Latin Americans have so strongly criticized.

It is precisely the hermeneutics of consequences that aims to modify behaviour (of public or private morality) without attempting to consider the structure or hidden conformation behind the problematic issues we want to deal with theologically. And that requires a reflection on the interrelation of the parts that make up what liberationists have called the structures of sin. The construction of sexuality, I would like to affirm, is not then a secondary issue but a central one: it redefines the ideological constructions and interrelationships in our theological as well as social and economic justice model. In fact, an alternative world outside the restriction of global capitalism may depend more on sex, than on class.

---

3 Cf. Althaus-Reid, 'Let Them Talk . . .! Doing Liberation Theology from Latin American Closets', in M. Althaus-Reid (ed.), *Liberation Theology and Sexuality*, London, Ashgate, 2006, pp. 10–13.

The problem with inclusion

There were two main projects at the genesis of liberation theology. One was the project of the alternative kingdom and integral salvation from private and structural sins such as hunger and political persecution. The other was the hegemonic project from the dictatorial regimes that flourished during the Cold War, which curiously mixed the national security doctrine with their own theological discourses. The project from liberation theology was expressed in the idea of an inclusive church. The metaphor of a broad and ethical eucharistic table, surrounded with enough chairs for everybody, offers not just a fraternal image but an economic metaphor of inclusiveness concerned with the creation of an alternative model of a participatory society.[4] That is, a society where bread and wine will not be the product of exploitative labour conditions, as Enrique Dussel has rightly pointed out,[5] but on the contrary, the fruit of the liberating work of communities in which bread and wine on the table will be a right. I have deliberately said before that the liberationist project was one for an inclusive church and society. Yet it may be that this was not the case. In a way, we can say that liberation theology had this message of inclusivity, but from another perspective, we may say that it did not. This is a hard comment to make, but let us consider the issue of inclusivity in Latin America with theological honesty.

In the same way that my years of experience working with poor communities taught me how many subtleties and nuances of the everyday realities of the liberationist Christian praxis cannot be expressed in theological discourses, the same can be said about the metaphors of inclusiveness. Liberationists from the 1970s and 1980s in Latin America[6] had a discourse which is sometimes lacking reality. In fact

---

4 I'm taking this metaphor, well known to many in Latin America, from the last sermon of Father Rutilio Grande on 13 February 1977, just days before he was assassinated. See Jon Sobrino, *Jesus in Latin America*, Maryknoll, NY, Orbis, 1989, p. 18.

5 Cf. Enrique Dussel's unpublished paper delivered to the Conference 'In Search of a Larger Christ', Edinburgh, 1985. For a nineteenth-century tradition of Eucharist among landowners and oppression, cf. H. Brito, 'La Organización de la Iglesia', in CEHILA, *500 Años de Cristianismo en Argentina*, Buenos Aires, Nueva Tierra, 1992, p. 56.

6 I'm referring here to the historical period from where the main corpus of the Latin America liberation theology was conceived and formed/informed by the praxis of the militant churches during times of political oppression in the continent. These discourses have produced the canon or normativity of liberation theology, or to say in other words, they have made of liberation theology a dogma.

the liberationist praxis in Latin America, from where the richness of doing a theology in community comes, has been and still is a contested area. Anyone who has sat in a militant church around a table together with the poorest of the poor of our brothers and sisters knows that the bad smell left in the room by those who never have a bath or access to toothpaste or clean clothes creates more opposition among the members of the parish than the idea of a politically involved theology. Alternatively, the mixture of races and cultures among those sharing the table of the Lord on a Sunday can somehow prove more controversial for many churches than a radical sermon from James Cone on the Black Christ. There has been a gap in liberation theology and it is, paradoxically, a gap between uncontested ideologies and critical reality.

Sexuality and critical reality

My point is that even conceding that in many cases inclusiveness was (and still is) a high priority in the discourse of militant churches, the liberation theology project was never concerned with inclusivity but only with including *some* of the nobodies of Church and theology, the poor. The underdogs of history (as Gustavo Gutiérrez called them), or the poor (*el pueblo pobre*) required a voice, but not just a voice among many others. The voices for those historically voiceless and silenced by the alliances of power in Church and state in Latin America demanded that the space of traditional voices of authority be vacated. Far from inclusiveness, this was a discourse of privilege, reflecting the precedence of the marginalized and poor in God's plans for the kingdom. In the kingdom of God, the nobodies have the prerogative, as Jesus himself is the historical option of a God who became human by becoming a marginal, vulnerable Jew in a country under an economic, cultural and religious foreign occupation. For the liberationists then this meant that God somehow demanded from Christians, as a prophetic action, that places previously occupied by the powerful and the exploiters needed to become vacant. Inclusiveness becomes a key liberationist concept but only to be seen in the diachronic dimension of the historical *Kairos* (or Hour of God) among the poor. What I am claiming is that the key for an appraisal of the discourse of liberation theology in the last century is to consider the liberationist praxis as related, not to inclusiveness, but to power struggles. Perhaps we can still speak about inclusivity, but only if we acknowledge that the militant churches have never been neutral, but took options (even unconsciously) supporting colonial, theoretical constructions in Latin America such as the ideologies of gender, race and sexuality. Therefore, liberation theology did not set out chairs for poor women, or poor gays – or at least it never did so willingly. The inclusive project affirmed itself by exclusion policies which determined the identity of the poor. The poor who were included were conceived of as male, generally peasant, vaguely indigenous, Christian and heterosexual. In fact, militant churches would not have needed many chairs around the table of the Lord if these criteria had been applied. It describes the identity of only a minority of the poor. The poor in Latin America can not be stereotyped so easily and they include urban poor women, transvestites in poor street neighbourhoods and gays everywhere.

Liberation theology: between myths and mystifications

Theologies work within mythical structures and this gives them power to access and express the religious intuitions of their time. Liberation theology works within a mythical structure originally framed around the prophetic and Exodus themes, and that has been a key to its success. From a postcolonial perspective we are aware of the imperial project that is delineated behind the pages of the book of Exodus[7] but we cannot deny the fact that many generations of oppressed peoples have intuitively identified themselves with the biblical theme of the grand departure from lands of injustice. This is true not only of the slaves; the early feminist theological call from Mary Daly urged women to abandon the patriarchal churches, and the Latin American poor have all identified themselves with the Exodus narrative. Moreover, the Exodus narrative gave them strength and even strategies for the struggle.

We perhaps need to demythologize liberation theology as a naïve theology, but more than that, we need to demystify it.[8] That is, we need to denounce the attempts to harmonize in a hegemonic and authoritarian way the positive and revolutionary elements of difference and dissent in our communities, in order to be able to continue the *caminata* (the walk) of theology. More than trying to affirm liberation theology as a theology based on a premise of equality, we need to understand that no theology can escape the epistemological characteristics of its time, even if it intends to oppose them. The excluded were those

---

7 See, for example, John Collins, *The Bible after Babel: Historical Criticism in a Postmodern Age*, Grand Rapids, Michigan, Eerdmans, 2005.

8 This concept comes from Paul Ricoeur who has been so influential in Latin American biblical hermeneutics. Cf. P. Ricoeur, 'Preface to Bultmann', in Lewis Mudge (ed.), *Essays on Biblical Interpretation*, Philadelphia, Fortress Press, 1980, p. 58.

marginalized from Church and society, the Latin American *Other*, represented by the poor. What they required was grace (freedom/gratuitousness) in contrast to the project of the dictatorial regimes with their logic of exclusion and profit, rather than inclusion and divine grace. Emphasizing this proclamation of grace over against the profit theology of the dictatorial regimes, liberation theologians used contrasting metaphors, such as the 'theology of life against theology of death' or the 'God of Justice against idols'. However, the grace of the liberationists was not based on the absolute gratuitous love of Christ: it shared some of the understanding of the profit theologies from the Cold War. Some years ago, discussing the notorious lack of mentoring between the first wave of liberation theologians and the new generations, the late Guillermo Cook shared with me his conviction that beyond the differences, liberationists had much in common with the military frameworks of the 1970s. Consider, for instance, the contrast between the discourse of inclusion from the aforementioned Father Grande and the rigid hierarchical order of the militant churches. Or again, consider the idea of giving a voice to the voiceless and the exclusion of women in the churches and in theology.

The mythical nucleus of liberation theology was centred on peace and justice, but that is the nucleus of Christianity. The mystification processes started among the liberationists, according to Cook, in the discrimination against women on grounds of a prioritization of tasks. This happened because the liberationist churches obeyed a principle of military strategy, where responsibilities are normally distributed to minimize casualties and to be ready to act at short notice: grace is distributed according to a logic of profit. I have been myself involved in many discussions in the past concerning the prioritization of the struggle in Latin America. Those who considered that the suffering arising from gender and sexual discrimination was of a second order, failed to recognize that they shared the same logic that creates poverty in the first instance.

The fact is that military dictatorships gave way to our Latin American democracies; weak, fragile, dependent democracies but still democracies. Yet liberationists seem to continue to work in military mode, where rigidity and authoritarianism have not given way to difference and disruption. The dualist thinking of the Cold War has seldom been realist thinking, and dualist theologies (including liberationists) hardly reached the definition of *Realpolitik*. However, facts are more ambiguous and subversive than dogmas, which are fixed by definition. Latin American liberation theology, born of an ethos of authoritarianism (social, political and ecclesiastical), has missed the possibilities of theological *poiesis* that comes not from discourses on the idealized poor, but from the reality of the poor as people of different sexual and gender identities.

The point is that in the distribution of the liberationist inclusive spaces, colonial patterns of identity and particularly Christian identity were imposed. The theology that promised an option for the poor also defined, ideologically, a Christian identity based on patriarchal, colonial identities.

Sexuality as ideology

The supposed equality in liberation theology failed in terms of agency, that is, it failed in its practice. Simply, there were no structurally implemented elements for the empowerment required to exercise responsibilities in the Church and in the nation, or to have all the voices of the voiceless heard. If we were to have a broad inclusive table in the twenty-first century we should have to begin by addressing deep-rooted ideologies concerning the *Realpolitik* of the identity of believers in Latin American Christianity and in liberation theology. The poor's identity is configured according to superimposed layers of many races, cultural contexts and sexualities. Liberation theology, whose defining theme has not been just God, but love and loving attitudes which can transform our world, was never grounded in love at the margin of medieval European models of affective relationships, regulated as they were by economic interest. Not surprisingly, our poor have little to do with church patterns of sacralized, patriarchal families: they seldom marry, or live in monogamy, but in patterns of solidarity, characterized by accepting and mutually helping each other in a kind of affective network of extensive family relationships.

Those who call the poor promiscuous ignore the bonding which that promiscuity provides to the realm of the social and in this case, the spiritual. Promiscuity is a less profitable loving relationship pattern, created among the marginalized, with many theological lessons to teach to middle class, heteronormative theologians. In these terms, promiscuity could mean grace, that is, love outside the logic of the law. I myself have somehow learnt more about poverty and sexuality and the subversive power of solidarity and social transformation of the excluded of our societies by reading the Argentinian social psycho-analyst Alfredo Moffat, than by volumes written on Christian base communities. Why? Because liberation theology knows more about dogmas than about people, and more about discourses on love, than about love itself. Only a postcolonial analysis, suspicious of the alliance between European ideologies and Christianity in relation to the construction of people's identities and relationships, can introduce liberationists to new levels of hermeneutical suspicion. After all, liberationists never took seriously the patterns of love and relationship of our own Latin American people.

This brings us to the specific issue of gender and sexuality in liberation theology. These are the two discordant notes in its discourse on freedom and liberation, a discourse which in reversing biblical miracles and wisdom sayings has turned copious wine into water and abundant bread into stones. Liberationists, by a lack of reflection on their discourse on power have systematically denied chairs around the table to the poor, be these women or non-heterosexual people. But even worse than that, they have succeeded in theologically undernourishing a whole generation of Latin American Christians who should have been well prepared to continue interrogating the influence of hegemonic ideologies of a political or gender nature in our continent.

On sexuality, theology and power

Allow me to continue this analysis by stating something that has been a key for my own reflections: every theology is a sexual act.[9] If we were to follow Karl Barth's suggestion of taking both the newspaper and the Bible into the pulpit, then in these times of globalization processes, poverty and exclusion, we should find it difficult to preach on anything except sexuality. And I am not referring here to sexual issues arising from the market society, which uses sexuality as part of a culture of consumption, but rather from the Church. We are continuously confronted, both from the Vatican but also from local parishes, by the Church's obsessive preoccupation with sexuality, or to be more accurate, with its preoccupation with controlling sexuality. This is exhibited in the high priority given to issues concerning the regulation and control of sexuality in abortion, contraceptives, the use of condoms, artificial insemination, sex outside marriage, marriage and divorce. At the same time, paradoxically, issues concerning paedophilia within the ranks of the clergy receive more attention from the media than from the Church itself. There are many documents and encyclicals on marriage and divorce or on abortion, but none on paedophilia. Liberation

---

9 Cf. Marcella Althaus-Reid, *Indecent Theology. Theological Perversions in Sex, Gender and Politics*, London, Routledge, 2000. Also translated into Spanish as *La Teología Indecente*, Barcelona, Bellaterra, 2005.

theologians from the first generation, who knew very well the sexual identity crisis and affective dilemmas of the young men in their seminaries, curiously never reflected on this issue. Neither did they reflect on the fact that in Latin America the whole mission of the Church was driven by a sexual enterprise, the sexual conversion of the Latin American people to patterns of accepted sexual behaviour and relations from medieval Spain.[10] Issues of monogamy, heterosexual marriage and gender codes, treated according to the European prevalent fashion, had such a pre-eminence in the teaching of the Church that, as some distinguished scholars have commented, the Christian mission seemed to depend on sexuality, in particular on the negative portrayal and undermining of the sexual identity of the *Other* (the native). Still functioning as a colonial theology, liberation theology never challenged this imposed order on the poor, and love among the poor. The theology which promised an option for the poor, also defined ideologically a Christian identity for them, based on European patriarchal colonial codes. This was a theology that ignored, for instance, the complex sexual construction of the natives of the Americas, reflected in their love lives and also in their economic communitarian structures. There is a connection between monogamy, monotheism and multinational cartels, just as there is a connection between different Latin American family structures, bisexual deities and the Ayllus (the indigenous economic and affective communities from Peru).

The problem is that, unfortunately, theological discourse in the Church is not a reflexive discourse on sexuality or a truly theological reflection on issues of sexuality: for the most part it is merely an instrument of power. This is why I consider that issues of gender and sexuality are fundamental to the Church. It is not because Christianity depends on who marries whom or when, but because the Church in its discourse on sexuality is sustaining, in reality, a discourse on hegemonic power and control. Some years ago, Leonardo Boff reflected on the fact that the Roman Catholic Church had failed with regard to the liberation project. He perceptively claimed that the Church would never commit class suicide. Specifically in our case, the Church will not commit a sexual or gender suicide. What is at stake is not so much questions about sexual practice, but challenges to the whole underlying pattern of hierarchical thinking and its structures of power.

---

10 Cf. the work done in this area by the Paraguayan theologian Graciela Chamorro, especially her book *Teología Guaraní*, Quito, Abya Yala, 2004.

Sexuality matters

Therefore, if we are talking about the liberation of theology, sexuality matters. It matters in a similar way that the discourse from the socially excluded matters. That occurs in two ways. The first is by challenging ideological formations in the Church and theology, and the second is by restoring the gospel's true message through a praxis of justice among God's people. It is important, after all, that a poor gay sits with his/her community at the Lord's Table, but it is also important that the theological framework that supports alliances, between Church and state or between church representatives and local oligarchies, is denounced and dismantled. It has been my interest to unveil issues of sexual ideology in liberation theology and to declare that no theology, not even liberation theology, can be considered sexually neutral. In my project, which I have called 'Indecent Theology', I have tried to dislocate the entanglement between liberation theology, the option for the poor and issues pertaining to sexual ideology. In the same way that gender is a social construct, subjected to cultural and historical changes, sexuality is not a given. Following Judith Butler in her influential book *Gender Trouble*,[11] sexuality has begun to be recognized as ideologically construed. That is, we have started to differentiate between sex (as biological) and sexuality as a cultural performance. Sex and sexuality, or sex and gender, do not need to match up. Moreover, from an epistemological perspective, it becomes crucial that we interrogate the politics of matching biological data with issues of another nature, such as love and relationality, which are culturally mediated, and not outside understandings of production and profit. Christianity should be based on grace and not on profit. But here is the paradox: on the one hand, the gospel is now used to convert people by subjecting loving relationships to produce and gain, while on the other it is used to condemn relationships such as the LGBT precisely in terms of non-productivity. In reality, we are confronted here by two economies: the economy of the gift (such as *El cariño* in Peru) versus the market economy of profit. Each of these economies has different presuppositions concerning relationships and loving exchanges. Latin American economies are nearer to the grace economy of the gospel than to the Church's actual sexual and economic understanding of community life. What liberation theology, preoccupied with the option for the poor, has forgotten are what Amartya Sen calls the 'constituent

---

11 Judith Butler, *Gender Trouble. Feminism and the Subversion of Identity*, London, Routledge, 1990.

components' of development.[12] That is, the fact that economic development is not an end it itself, but the expansion of the project of human freedom is. Economy should not be thought apart from human rights and that includes the rights of the poor in Latin America to develop their own sexual identity outwith the hegemonic constructions of the Church. These ideological constructions have sacralized heterosexuality to the point of not allowing it to be interrogated.

One of the problems has been that liberation theology confronted structures of hegemonic power without questioning which epistemology grounded such power. Sexuality is about more than who loves whom. This is a way of thinking, relating and producing many significative patterns of exchange among communities. Heterosexuality, in particular, is an ideological form of affective and economic production, which, curiously, has never been the focus of the liberationist ideological suspicion. Moreover, heterosexuality has been sacralized as the only valuable sexual epistemology, when in reality our own Latin American cultures historically exhibit a great diversity on sexual and economic thinking. Anyone who has seriously worked with the poor in Latin America has found the presence of God within the diversity of our communities, which is racial, cultural but also sexual. When middle-class theologians accuse the poor of being promiscuous they fail to see the presence of God in the solidarity of extended families. These families are made by affection if not by law, as the poor build communities around love and compassion rather than by legal ties. In the process of questioning colonial heterosexuality in Latin America, it is not simply that we discover a face of the poor that has been unknown or ignored: it is also a pedagogical process which can teach more about love at the margins and a different face of God when freed from the patterns of thought and practice in medieval Spain. We may even rediscover a different Trinity outside patriarchal relationships, an Ayllu trinity, or a trinity of women loving each other. Why should we countenance the curtailing of the joy of finding novelty, or being surprised by God – especially through the acceptance of the discourse and patterns of sexual ideologies that are not even from our cultures?

Gender, liberation theologies and sexuality

There are only a few of us in Latin America raising questions about the sexual paradigm of liberation theology rather than about gender

---

12 Amartya Sen, *Development as Freedom*, New York, Anchor Books, 2000.

issues.[13] Why is it that sexuality is a more important paradigm than gender for liberation theology? To begin with, gender is an unstable category which presents differences according to times, political economies and cultures. In a way this is what has divided Third World feminist theologies, the realization of the multitude of genders and the different ways of being a woman, which cannot be defined in a universal, essentialized way. Anecdotes abound about occasional women theologians misunderstanding the gendered patterns of other women in different cultures. For example, I remember being criticized for serving the *mate* tea, a traditional herbal drink from Argentina, to a group of family and friends. Women from Britain saw me as fulfilling the traditional role of a woman serving tea. I needed to explain that in my family, in my country, the tradition was that my father had the honour of passing the *mate* tea to the guests. In fact, by taking the initiative, I was reversing the patriarchal custom of my family. Although gender, as a behavioural pattern, needs to be challenged and it is important to keep doing so in our communities, it does not provide us with a sufficient basis for theological reflection. Gender is a surface discourse, while sexuality is deeper. Gender behaviour only fulfils the role of sustaining sexual identities; the fact that men do not use high heels, or women do not shave their faces contributes to a gender sign system which defines who is a man, and who is a woman.[14] Heterosexuality, far from being given by God, depends on these little gestures of legislating how we use clothes or move our hips when walking in the street. In fact, sexual identity depends on gender codes. During the time of the Argentinian dictatorial regime there were laws to enforce gender codes. It was as if sexuality (and indeed the world order) depended on the length of boys' hair or girls using skirts instead of trousers. However, systematic theology is not simply sustained by gender. The discourse on God 'the

---

13 I would like to mention here some names from the new generation of Latin American theologians working on sexuality, such as the Brazilians Mario Ribas, Nancy Cardoso Pereira and Andre Musskopf. Jaci Maraschin has been a pioneer on issues of the body from a class and sexual analysis from the 1970s, and the same can be said of Tomas Hanks and his work in Argentina. Among this new generation I can also mention the Argentinians Iván Petrella (*The Future of Liberation Theology. An Argument and a Manifesto*, London, Ashgate, 2004), Hugo Cordoba Quero in queer liberation theology, and the pastoral theological reflections from Roberto González and Norberto D'Amico from the Metropolitan Community Church in Buenos Aires. For further readings, see my book *Liberation Theology and Sexuality* (London, Ashgate, 2006).

14 For this point, see Judith Butler, *Gender Trouble*. Liberationists should consider the work of Butler together with Marx, Nietzsche and Freud in what Paul Ricoeur called 'the masters of suspicion' for the hermeneutics of suspicion from Juan Luis Segundo.

father' or God as 'he' is not concerned with masculinity, in the sense of what God's gender behaviour (what God does), but with (hetero) sexuality. This is a God who defines Godself as a 'husband' (or a Lord, to be more precise) but specifically, this is a God who procreates with a virgin (or pubescent girl) and has a son. This is the kernel of Christianity, God's sexuality manifested in history in the incarnation of Jesus Christ the Liberator. However, heterosexuality, being a cultural and economic construction, subjected to many changes over the course of history, should not have been sacralized. Ideologies (political, sexual or religious) need to be discussed in order to open the way to liberate theologies and to find a better understanding of God. To use the liberationist words, unveiling ideologies, including sexual ones, helps us to keep rediscovering the face of God among us. Heterosexuality has become an idol in liberation theology. It is time to rediscover the face of God among the *Other* as sexual dissidents, in the midst of other forms of loving relationships and sexual identities. Curiously these dissident relationships may also come to throw light on different forms of economic relationships.

Theology of liberation has said that the Trinity is a society, but it does not need to be an economic relationship of men in solidarity with each other, honest and important as that relationship could be. To introduce a gender change in the Trinity (such as a female Holy Spirit) is not enough, because then the Trinity is infiltrated by identity presuppositions. What is a female Spirit? A mother? A caring, nurturing person? Or an Amazon, a fierce independent woman who loves women? There is more to being a woman than to love a man or be a mother, just as there is more to being God than being the head of a patriarchal tribe. Small wonder that liberation theology became stagnant: all its discussions about God are based on sexual, ideological stereotypes, from which the poor, as a concept, becomes a blanket category which erases sexual differences among them. So much for the principle of theology as a second act, when the Latin American reality is ignored. God has been reduced, has nothing else to say and nothing with which to surprise us anymore. The liberationists' understanding of the Trinity as a society has become what J. Severino Croatto called 'a fixed model,' instead of a reservoir of meaning. Our theology then lacks revelation.[15]

It has been said that feminist liberation theology made a particularly important contribution to feminist theologies in the West. Although

---

15 J. Severino Croatto, 'A Modo de Presentación', in Autores varios, *Mito y Hermenéutica*, Buenos Aires, El Escudo, 1973, p. 28.

the claim has been at times exaggerated,[16] it is also true that Latin American women, conscious of the limitations of the liberationists' paradigms, produced an important contribution to a wider dialogue between race and culture, class and gender. Issues of sexuality have been more recent. The discourse from Latin American women which came from churches and communities may have been a crucial contribution to the praxis of Western feminist theologies but paradoxically, it did not have any impact on liberation theology itself. Theology of liberation is not the homogeneous discourse frequently presented (or misrepresented) by North Atlantic theologians. It is well known that liberation theology has a praxis that needs to be understood with respect to the cultural and historical differences of the continent, which include differences in church perspectives. It may be true that Argentinians, Chileans and Uruguayans have developed somehow a line of theological thinking around human rights, while Central Americans tended to place more emphasis on developing a political-cultural theology. However, Central and South America have been linked by their discourses in solidarity with each other, in spite their different options. The same can be said about individual theologians, who in the past decade have stood in opposition to (or disillusion with) their own churches and also publicly disagreed among themselves. They were united by a sense of solidarity around the option for the poor. However, when we turn to gender and sexuality, apart from a few isolated voices giving occasional statements about theology and gender equality, there has never been any sustained solidarity.[17] None of the great names from the liberationist ranks has ever produced any nuanced, deep theology which could justify a claim that liberation theology has heard the voice of the voiceless when ideologies of gender and sexuality have been the cause of suffering and marginalization of our own people.

---

16 It is important to remember the work of Rosemary Radford Ruether, a pioneer feminist theologian from the USA, whose work has always been characterized by a strong class analysis and social consciousness. Radford Ruether exercised considerable influence among Latin American theologians from the first generation, by introducing issues of gender and race together with issues of poverty and marginalization.

17 For instance, it has not been uncommon to see the odd article on the Virgin Mary written by a Latin American woman theologian in an edited book on liberation theology. Male theologians have also written on the Virgin Mary from their masculine perspectives, without any informed analysis on sexuality and ideology, thus creating more stereotypes and contributing more to the status quo than to revolution in this area. For further readings on this aspect, see Althaus-Reid *Indecent Theology*, especially ch. 2, 'The Indecent Virgin'.

A call to the first generation of liberation theologians

It could be argued that the pioneer theologians were men and that women's issues needed to be developed by women. Yes, they were men, but they wrote about poverty without knowing poverty themselves, at least not the enforced poverty of the slums. They were mostly theologians of European descent and yet they wrote about the lives of the indigenous people in Latin America. They reflected the lives of the coloured and black people of the continent, but they were white. If it were true that only women should undertake reflection on gender and sexuality – according to the simple and empty equalizing formulae applied by many male liberationists – then by the same logic, only the poor should develop a theology with an option for the poor. Unless we have theologians from the slums (not just living there as part of a church project) the liberationist argument of theological representatives contradicts itself.

The point is that the ideological construction of gender and sexuality in Latin American theology is very influential. As liberationists, we have been encouraged to doubt the legitimacy of church hierarchies and government, but never of who is who at the moment of determining sexual identities. In the compact, power structured worlds of Latin American churches, more dependent on old colonial powers for their finances than they would like to be, women and gays are casualties of assaults instigated by many different interests, including economic ones. When issues of gender and sexuality appear, the hermeneutical circle of suspicion disappears.

These are serious, even controversial charges. They arise from my sense of betrayal, betrayal not so much from a group of theologians, as from a church which set out on a *caminata*, a walk of liberation towards political and ideological freedom several decades ago. That risky *caminata* was undertaken in the company of many women and people whose voices continue to be ignored. This point must be made emphatically: the struggle was carried on in the company of women and gays. There were queers among the revolutionaries and also among the members of our militant churches. As Revd Roberto González from the *Iglesia de la Comunidad Metropolitana de Buenos Aires* has said, during the time of the struggle against dictatorial regimes there were other oppressions and concentration camps buried in many of our hearts.[18] As I have already said, the problem is that although

18 Roberto González and Norberto D'Amico, 'Love in Times of Dictatorships: Memoirs of a Gay Minister from Buenos Aires', in Marcella Althaus-Reid (ed.), *Liberation Theology and Sexuality,* London, Ashgate, 2006.

liberationists tried to do theology as a second act, that is, starting not with dogmas but, paraphrasing Marx, with the real actors of theological history, issues of gender and sexuality were always dealt with at the dogmatic (ideological) level. Therefore for instance, the masculinist liberationist gazes upon the Virgin Mary and thereafter supports the submission of Latin American women's identities to colonial (medieval European) Christian patterns. The betrayal undermines affections and relationships and has consequences which go beyond issues of women and equality. It is a betrayal of the project of human freedom which encompasses any economic project of liberation in Latin America and it is a betrayal of the orthopraxis claimed by liberationists. I am calling on liberation theology to become once again an honest theology, that is, a theology that is able to reflect on the lives of the people and the manifestation of God in our communities, beyond the dogma of a sexual ideology such as heterosexuality. Without that we risk continuing to betray the gospel of justice by making of God a prisoner of issues of sexuality and power in the Church and by reducing the project of the kingdom to an ideological apparatus.

To keep unveiling the political and sexual masks and to keep rediscovering the true face of God in Latin America is a daring and risky project which still has not finished. It continues with every Christian person who claims his/her rights to dissent from the imposition of political and (hetero)sexual identities upon our people. For that reason, I call for a jubilee and cancellation of all the external debts of the people of Latin America: the all too obvious debts of the many but also the debts incurred through gender and sexual ideologies, which continue to force people to pay with interest, with their own suffering, for the right to be different from a central hegemonic definition of identity which comes not from God, but actually from colonial structures of power. It is time to honour our name as liberation theologians and liberate people and also God, from the oppression of centuries of injustice and abuse towards those who do not partake of patriarchal, heterosexual ideologies. I call on the first generation of theologians, that courageous generation, 'Will you now honour your old pledge to stand by the poor and those marginalized by ideologies of oppression? Will you now risk your good name by opposing the homophobic, by publicly standing in solidarity against the marginalization of and violence against women and queers?' There is a new generation of theologians doing that already, proud to be queers and proud to the keep the *caminata* of liberation theology going, with all the risks that honesty to God and our theological vocation entail.

6 The Future of Religion: Between Fundamentalism and Modernity

CLAUDE GEFFRÉ, OP

The future of the world is becoming more and more a blank page. Even though one public opinion, ever extending, tries to convince us that the principal threat which we face in the twenty-first century is terrorism, there are a growing number of us who denounce the serious dangers that lie in a mode of globalization that is breeding growing poverty for three-quarters of humanity and destroying the ecological balance of our environment.

Our responsibility as theologians forces us to testify that 'Another World is Possible'. In this context, I would like to raise a question about the future of religions. It refers to the question whether religions can contribute to *humanizing* globalization. I believe that to pronounce ourselves on the future of religion today is the same as asking if religions can face the challenges of modernity or, on the contrary, they can only withdraw into a fundamentalism of identity. Religions have usually seen modernity as a threat. The aim of this paper will be to demonstrate that modernity, understood as critical reason and as democratic reason, is an opening both for the future of religions and world civilization. Before prophesying the end of religion, it would be much better to talk of *religiosity in a different way*.

I will first try to place the religious scenario in a time of globalization. Then I will remind us of the permanent temptation of fundamentalism, which always gives way to an undue sacralization of truth. It is a different way to reflect on the connections between religion and violence. This way we will finally evoke the opportunities within modernity, such as interreligious dialogue and the historical responsibility of religions to make another world possible.

The religious scenario in times of globalization

When trying to redefine the religious scenario in today's world, it is important to distinguish between the plurality of the new religious movements and the plurality of the great historical religions. And in each case, one should verify the impact of globalization in religious pluralism.

Particularly in the West, we are witnessing the proliferation of new religiosities which recruit more and more followers, and which should not be confused with sects as such. Their success lies in the direct connection with the phenomena of globalization. Audiovisual communication tends to blur the frontier between the world of reality and the virtual world: these privilege lived experience against doctrinal or ethical norms; they favour a great relativism in what relates to truth and tend to make the various riches of religion simple objects for consumption. We assist, therefore, in the birth of a religious supermarket which offers consumers multiple products from living religions and even from dead ones (myths, symbols, doctrines, mental techniques, a variety of asceticisms), which are presented as useful for spiritual experience and for curing body and soul.

The dominating feature of these new religious movements is the tendency to *syncretism*. Since they do not take into account the complex religious traditions to which a particular doctrine or practice belongs, the criterion of truth becomes the authenticity of a subjective experience in search of salvation, understood primarily in terms of welfare and maximum fullness. This current attraction toward religiosity in all its stages coincides with the discrediting of modern ideologies and utopia and the lack of a religious culture of our contemporaries, including Christians; it favours a sometimes surprising *do-it-yourself, bricolage*, between beliefs separated from their places of origin. Beliefs float and their frontiers are so fluid that they can coexist or merge without worrying about compatibility. Thus the happy formula created by the British sociologist Grace Davie: 'believing without belonging'.

Finally, it is worth remembering that the success of this plurality of syncretistic tendencies of neo-pagan inspiration, particularly taking place in Europe, coincides with the loss of credibility, if not of Christianity itself, at least of official churches. Faced with the disillusion of modernity under the signs of secularization, a purely technical and instrumental rationality, and a phase lag between an increasingly artificial world and the living world, one can discern a confused aspiration to discover the new, beyond fragmentation, a true enchantment, which is the search for an essential unity between human beings, the universe and God.

Whatever this multiplicity of religiosities may be, if today we speak of religious pluralism, the emphasis is above all on the great historical religions: the great monotheistic religions evidently and also the two great oriental religions, Hinduism and Buddhism, without leaving aside Chinese wisdom such as Taoism and Confucianism. These religions of the East are best known by the public at large and give signs of new vitality. Christianity still remains the first religion with more than 2,000 million followers. Yet Islam already has over 1,000 million followers; and religions such as Hinduism and Buddhism, which are predominant in Asia, have thousands of followers in Europe and North America. Allow me three observations:

Due to globalization, the speed of communications and the great migration flows of population, the *external plurality* of religions has been modified. It is not as easy as it was in the past to distinguish missionary religions with universal pretence and local religions linked necessarily with their ethnic and cultural roots. Most societies have, in fact, become pluri-religious. This is so in a continent such as Europe where, together with the Judaeo-Christian heritage, it is necessary to take into account a European Islam of over 15 million followers, without including Turkey's probable inclusion in the European Union. One has to pay special attention to the growing presence of Buddhism in Western Europe and all of North America. Its religious impact is greater than the number of followers. We witness a kind of role inversion of the previous missionary model. While missionary expansion followed the paths of the colonial conquest from the North to the South, we now have to refer to a new impregnation of religious traditions from the East into the Western world.

Thanks to the ease of exchange within the global village, once again religions recruit their followers in the territory of the other religions. The external plurality of religions is accompanied by an internal plurality within each of them. This religious propaganda can be carried out, softly without aggressive proselytism, due to the fact that many men and women can combine with no conflict, various memberships. I have already referred to believing without belonging; in the same way one can refer to a belonging without believing. As a matter of fact, belonging to an official religion does not prejudge the number of beliefs one accepts. Globalization breeds a growing fragmentation of the great historical religions and the churches. In continents such as Africa and Latin America, it is clear that the very evangelical message is at the origin of new churches, or even Christian sects, which set themselves at a deliberate distance from the Roman Catholic Church and Protestant denominations.

Finally, one cannot evoke the impact of globalization on religious pluralism without referring to the resurgence of fundamentalism or even fanaticism. This may be a reaction against an antisocial and unjust economy. But it is also a protest in the name of identities against a generalized relativism of all religious truth and the moral permissiveness of modern society. One evidently thinks of the terrible drift of Islamism within the Muslim world. But one can find fundamentalist and neo-fundamentalist streaks within Judaism, Catholicism and different Protestant churches in the United States of America.

One feels the temptation to refer to the famous 'clash of civilizations', as if the rich and Christian Western world were on one side, and the Islamic world (with the poor) were on the other. Truly, from a geopolitical perspective, things are more complicated than that. We will see that the three monotheistic religions have earned their reputation for intolerance, which is connected to the notion of truth revealed directly from God. But history teaches us that all religions, including pagan religions, can breed fanaticism. Here lies the whole issue of the relation between the sacred and violence.

The temptation of fundamentalism or the sacralization of truth

When one looks back on the long history of what is religious, one realizes that the balance is profoundly ambiguous. Religions have frequently downplayed the violence of this history. We can do no less than evoke René Girard's theory on the secret collusion between the sacred and violence. The history of religiousness is frequently the history of intolerance, fanaticism, exclusion, of inhuman practices and the abuse of power. But it is necessary to underline the particular connection between the sacralization of truth and the legitimization of violence. In the name of the absolute in a religious truth, what Emmanuel Lévinas calls 'the rough taste of the absolute', one can justify a holy war that slaughters innocent lives. It is the famous anthropological triangle of which the Muslim Mohammad Arkoun speaks: violence–sacredness–truth.

Prejudices to be avoided

We must avoid a first prejudice: believing that truths of a religious nature are more intolerant than atheist ideologies. The recent history of the twentieth century has proved that religions do not hold the monopoly on fanaticism. The worst genocides were provoked by atheist ideologies such as Nazism and Soviet Communism. And we could mention the massive terrorism practised in China and Cambodia.

The other prejudice to be avoided is the one that leads to thinking that religions of revelation, or better said, religions that claim for themselves a revealed truth from a personal God (in other words, the three monotheistic religions), are more intolerant than pagan religions, or diverse polytheisms, or religions with no God, such as Buddhism. History teaches us that all religions can breed fanaticism when they are handled by political power to defend a cause, a race, ethnic groups, social class.

The intolerance of monotheistic religions

It is still true that the three monotheistic religions have earned a reputation for intolerance and this has a direct connection with an absolute truth of which God is guarantee. Each of these religious traditions has a complex history and the causes of intolerance are many.

I must warn that in the case of Judaism, if it has sinned with intolerance, it is due less to the fact that it claimed for itself a truth revealed by God than because it possessed an awareness of being a people chosen over others. And still today, since the creation of the state of Israel, religious authorities of Judaism find it hard to make compatible the tension between justice inherent in the Torah and the right to the use of violence that the whole state attributes to itself in self-defence. If reference is made to the destiny of Christianity, one should never forget the disastrous consequences of the phenomenon of Christendom, which began early in the fourth century and confused spiritual and temporal power. When imperial politics favoured the unity and expansion of the Church, the heads of the Church found it quite natural to use the secular arm against infidels as well as heretics and schismatics. In the case of Islam one should consider the typically fundamentalist manner in which the historical circumstances of the origin of the prophet's religion are used so as to legitimize the use of violence in a totally different context. I refer to the transformation of the *Jihad*, from spiritual struggle with oneself, to armed conflict against the enemies of Islam.

Undoubtedly this had been legitimized in the moment in which Mecca was reconquered, yet was reproduced and used as justification each time Islam faced threats from infidels.

Beyond the particular originality of each form of monotheism, I would now like to discern the specific temptation of monotheistic religions. It is the temptation of *idolatry*, which consists in conferring upon a people, a church, a community, a book, an exclusive uniqueness that belongs only to God. A church father of the fourth century could refer to the displacement of faith towards an 'idolatry of the true God'. While Abraham, the father of all believers in the only God, is a figure marked by hospitality towards strangers who come from afar, this idolatry explains the rivalry and permanent conflict between Abraham's children.

The status of truth in religion

If one wants to reconcile faithfulness to truth and hospitality in relation to others in interreligious dialogue, it is necessary to reflect on the status of truth within religion, particularly in the case of a revealed truth. In the modern era, acts of repentance are insufficient when dealing with the religious intolerance of the past, in conformity with Pope John Paul II's courageous invitation. It is necessary to come face to face with a labour of discernment and ask oneself about the false legitimization of proselytism in the name of the absolute rights of a revealed truth in disdain for the rights of freedom of conscience. It was the merit of Vatican II's *Declaration on Religious Freedom* to have strongly affirmed that 'truth can only be imposed by the strength of its own truth'.

Why is it that the adherence to an absolute truth revealed by God can lead to intolerance, fundamentalism and militant proselytism? Why has that truth been absolutized separate from the rights of other people? It falls into the trap of an obligatory truth under the pretext that it is a divine and salvific truth. All means are good enough to force others to belong to this community, which is presented as the unique source of salvation. Strictly speaking, neither truth nor error, considered in the abstract, has rights. It is always the individual, the conscience, which has rights. In its *Declaration on Religious Freedom*, Vatican II showed that this freedom is based on the dignity of the human being. It is a civil and universal right. In other times, and in various European countries, only Roman Catholics had the right of religious freedom, which included the right of worship, opinion and expression.

From tolerance to dialogue

Towards the end of the nineteenth century, the Roman Catholic Church went from anathema to tolerance when it recognized the legitimacy of a pluralistic civil and lay society founded on a social contract rather than the authority of divine transcendence. But it took an even greater step when, in the middle of the twentieth century, it recognized *religious freedom* as a fundamental right belonging to all human beings, and when it issued positive judgement on non-Christian religions. It then went from condescending tolerance to a true dialogue, which respects and values those who profess different religious truths.

Such a dialogue does not lead to relativism and the renunciation of one's truth if one understands the status of truth in religion. It is necessary to demystify the false evidence of the famous motto: 'Truth is one and error is multiple'. This confuses truths of religion which emerges from testimony with mathematical or scientific truth. Revealed truth which is received gratuitously and freely from God is, of course, unique; but is possessed always in a plural and inadequate manner, in a determined interpretation. This is the drama of all fundamentalisms: to identify the letter of founding texts with the word of God, or in the manner of Muslims, an uncreated book that exists with God.

Scriptural fundamentalism, be it orthodox Islam, or certain kinds of neo-fundamentalist Protestantism, always has its origin in a sacralization of the sacred text and the absence of a hermeneutical reading which takes seriously the historical contingency of the whole work. In this way, truth of religious order does not accept the logic of the principle of contradiction. One can adhere to faith and the truth of one's religious tradition while recognizing that one's truth is neither exclusive nor inclusive of any other religious truth. This, rather than a simple act of toleration of other people's beliefs, is the basis of genuine religious dialogue.

As a Christian theologian I can then initiate dialogue with, for example, representatives of Judaism because I am convinced that Christianity does not eliminate the uncompromising fact that the Jews are the chosen people for God. Equally I can speak with Islam because, if it is true I consider Christ as the fullness of revelation, this does not prevent me from recognizing seeds of truth in the Koranic revelation. I happily return to the profound vision of Franz Rosenzweig, the Jewish thinker, when in his book *Star of Redemption* he wrote that complete truth can only be truth as part of God.[1] The essence of truth is to be shared

---

1 Franz Rosenzweig, *The Star of Redemption*, trans. William Hallo, London, University of Notre Dame Press, 1985.

because the most sacred truth, the most absolute, is always expressed in the contingency of a historical language. This does not lead to relativism, it simply testifies to the inaccessible character of complete truth which coincides with the mystery of God.

The mystery of the one we call God overflows the frontiers and channels of any religious tradition. This is why we have to overcome the belief that we are owners of truth. It is in this spirit that Pierre Claverie, Bishop of Oran, victim of Algerian Islam, can claim that God cannot be owned by any particular faith.[2]

Modernity's openings for the future of religions

In a search for an encounter between religions which – at the same time – escapes the agitations of fundamentalism and the illusion of a tolerance that fears confrontation, we should be aware of the opening offered by modernity. The dialogue between religions is a novelty that coincides with humanity's planetary age and with the awareness that we live in a common home, our planetary village.

This is fortunate for the world community and the religions themselves. For the first time, and thanks to the fantastic progress in science and technology, the destiny of planet Earth and the human species depends on the responsible behaviour of human beings. Faced with this extreme precariousness, the different religious traditions discover that instead of being in their own service, they are responsible for others and the conditions for life itself on Earth. Instead of competing among themselves, religions are invited to conversion. Faced with this religious pluralism, I will bear in mind some principles that should allow us to avoid, once again, fundamentalism and relativism:

1 No religion should exercise hegemony over others in an authoritarian way, as if it had the exclusive monopoly of truth over the Absolute and of what a good life, in the midst of the complexities of individual destinies, should be.
2 And yet, under the pretext of eliminating all sense of superiority, one cannot decree that all religions are the same. Under the appearance of a generous liberalism, we would reach a complete relativism which would be the denial of any value judgement. Above all, we must keep the freedom of judgement to denounce in the name of

---

2 Pierre Claverie, *Le Livre de la Foi: Révélation et Parole de Dieu dans la Tradition Chrétienne*, Paris, Cerf & Conférence épiscopale du nord de l'Afrique, 1996.

universal conscience the way some religions have legitimized and sanctified totally inhuman practices.

3 It is difficult to establish a hierarchy of religions. Despite their limitations, imperfections and even perversions, all religions worthy of the name aim to work for salvation and the healing of humanity in its fullness.

In the light of these principles, I would like to insist on two inseparable factors of modernity that can favour the proper management of dialogue between religions in the service of world community. First, religions must bear in mind the non-religious person as well. Second, laity, properly understood, can be a favourable space for mutual tolerance between the state and religious authorities as well as the coexistence between religions.

Openness of religions to the testimony of universal conscience

Religions cannot be self-satisfied dialoguing only among themselves, they must enter into dialogue with the witnesses of universal conscience. The different religious traditions must learn to listen to the ever clearer message of a *global ethic* which has begun to emerge from the common good of secular ethics and which finds its official expression in the *Declaration of Human Rights*. This is the challenge posed by modernity and which all religions must face.

If modernity is understood as the implantation of critical reason and democratic reason, then all religions must be able to face this reality. It refers to the positive cultural and social modernity that belongs to all civilizations and should not be confused with Western modernity, which gave birth to colonialism and cultural imperialism. Sadly enough, our era testifies not only to the permanence but also to the intensification of different fundamentalisms and even to religious fanaticisms. It would be easy to demonstrate that very often there has been an intention to abort the negotiations initiated with modernity. Recent history shows how, in effect, particularly in the case of Christianity, this modernity, first often seen as a threat for the identity of religions, can later be grasped as an occasion for its transformation and its future. It is not a question of simple opportunism. Religions are invited to prove that they can be more faithful to the better part of themselves and their own genius through the creative reinterpretation of their founding texts, their doctrinal, moral and judicial traditions in light of a certain number of gains which are the object of universal consensus. It is sufficient to note as examples the equality between men and women, the inviolable character of conscience, the value of life here below irrespective of the hope for another life, the right to labour, health and a certain degree of human welfare.

We have to determine clearly the content of what is truly human, the *vere humanum*, as referred to in Vatican II *Gaudium et Spes*. More and more we know what is involved in the truly human. Our era has had the sad privilege of having defined from a judicial point of view what is absolutely intolerable – *crimes against humanity*. I am inclined to affirm that religions, be it in their doctrines or in practices, gravely wound what is truly human, the object of ethical consensus, and must be transformed if they do not want to be condemned to slow decline. It is not a question of flirting with modernity and trailing behind statistics of tradition, rather it is to discern the call which bursts from a human universal conscience.

While recommending the need to emerge from the capsule of inter-religiousness so as to hear the testimony of secular conscience, I do not want to fall into the trap of thinking that the time of religions has passed and space must be made for the 'nearly a religion' of human rights or even for humanist religion. On the contrary, I think that ethical reason needs, more than ever, the moral stimulus of the great religious traditions. And for the future of a world civilization, I trust in the reciprocal exchange of religious morals and secular ethics.

In spite of the screeching disadjustment between the ideal and its practical realizations, one should not despise the ethical vocation of the great world religions. In the prophetic religions the human being created in the image of God has a sacred value, and violating human beings' fundamental rights, is to infringe on God's rights themselves.

But, contrary to what many believe, it would be wrong to think that oriental religions, called mystical, do not care for the dignity of human beings and have no ethical concerns. In Hinduism, for example, the concept of *ahimsa* or non-violence is at the heart of its vision of the world. It invites us to preserve all life forms and not damage the integrity of the Earth. In the case of Buddhism, there is a declaration of one cosmic conception of human beings which does not neglect the responsibility for each person of the universe. One should not forget the famous Buddhist wisdom of 'compassion'. The issue is to cause suffering to no one. Goodness, shared sufferings, joy, serenity, are all basic attitudes that must inspire human behaviour. And in the Chinese traditions such as Taoism and Confucianism, the religious ideal of excellence is wisdom, the search for a correct life and goodness.

In ever more secularized modern society, many seriously question what religious belief can add to the conscience imperatives of all honest people. The golden rule, which is already found in the Hammurabi Code: 'Do not do to others what you do not want them to do to you', is oriented toward the common good. But in the search for a friendlier society, one with greater solidarity, an ethic of human rights and a culture of justice are not enough. It is necessary to use the non-written laws which Antigone invoked. Beyond the equity of distributive justice, there is a *law of superabundance* which must incline the scales of justice in favour of those who have the least. In a world which risks sacrificing the social to the economic, it is necessary to make way for respect toward the foreigner central to the biblical tradition, for mercy as in the Sermon on the Mount, for the Muslim law of hospitality, for Buddhist compassion and the school of emptiness in Chinese Tao.

Secularism as a factor of tolerance between religions

Continuing the exploration of opportunities that modernity has for the future of religion, I would like to mention that secularism in its fullest sense is not only a factor of mutual tolerance between the state and religious authorities, but also of tolerance between religions themselves. In the countries of the European Community, we are searching for a new secularism which is not only non-antireligious but also overcomes passive neutrality or religious indifference. According to Regis Debray's fortunate formula, what is needed is the passage from an *incompetent* secularism to an *intelligent* secularism. It would be desirable to overcome a merely judicial concept of secularism and understand it as a certain *living together* of citizens. This is a demand both for state and religion in any given country. This new secularism could be at the same time guarantee of religious freedom and the best guarantor of democracy against all forms of religious fanaticism. This secularism invites the state to renounce militant secularism. It also invites religious authorities to leave behind the exercise of direct or indirect domination over civil society.

It is the responsibility of the state to respect the rights of all its citizens, including their moral and religious convictions, be they Christian, Jewish, Muslim, Buddhist or non-believers. There is an intimate connection between the principle of secularism and respect for each person's religious freedom. Secularism must normally favour peace, not only civil peace but also peace between religious communities. Religious freedom, as everything that proceeds from the autonomy of conscience, escapes the competence of the state. The state cannot claim a direct or indirect competence over the religious convictions of the people; it cannot appropriate the right to impose or prohibit the profession or public practice of a person's or community's religion. Yet, of course, the state can reserve for itself the right to decide when the freedom of expression of a religious individual or collective conviction runs the risk of altering public order.

The paradox of interreligious dialogue

We have tried to study modernity as an opportunity for the future of religions in the world. I would like to, once again in this last part, insist upon the paradox of interreligious dialogue and the historical responsibility of religions in this time of globalization.

The paradox of interreligious dialogue is to reconcile absolute commitment to its own truth with an attitude of openness, respect and value for the convictions of believers of other religions. It is important to understand that dialogue between religions does not seek a mythical unity between members of various religious as if to construct a common front of all religious men and women against the immense multitude of those who profess no religious belief.

For this reason one should not confuse interreligious dialogue with ecumenical dialogue as practised by Christian churches for the last years. In this case it is a search for the visible unity of Christians beyond the historical disruptions which gave rise to separate churches. The new dialogue between religions which we are witnessing at the beginning of this twenty-first century is not aimed at the illusory unity of members of different religions. This search for some type of world grand-religion would suppose the sacrifice of the religious and cultural richness common to each religious tradition. The dialogue between religions affirms every sense of the exchange of words and mutual listening on equal footing of believers of each religious tradition. The result of this dialogue is an improved understanding of others in their difference, a better understanding of one's own tradition and a reciprocal service for the good of world community.

As has been pointed out, dialogue between religions is not a luxury; it has become an urgent historical need in the face of a globalization whose hidden driving force is the imperialism of the laws of the market. The system which governs our 'global village' is a generator of misery for three-quarters of humanity, without mentioning the terrible degradation of our environment. But another world is possible. This is the common conviction of most of the world's great religions and the aim of the World Conference of Religions for Peace (WCRP), founded in Kyoto back in 1970, which proposes the promotion of justice and peace using the ethical and spiritual resources of each religious tradition. It does not intend to delete the value of our differences; rather it practises discernment to see how our differences can enrich us with the aim of responding in a better way to the world's urgencies.

What will be the future of religions in the world?

Christianity and Islam are the two principal religions in the world today. Both announce an eternal salvation for humanity. Based on biblical and Koranic revelation, both also have an ethical and prophetic dimension which can contribute to give history a more humane face. Neither of them can justify their pretence to universalism if they do not take on the universal causes of human beings today. Islam, in particular, must prove that it can distance itself from the radical Islamism that legitimizes a terrorism more interested in destabilizing the West than in repairing the differences and injustices of the world today.

Faced with serious threats which hover over the future of human species, we know well enough that it is not enough to defend the rights of human beings if at the same time we do not defend the rights of the land.[3] Due to faith in a creator God, the privileged vocation of the three monotheistic religions consists in offering a radical foundation of our faith in the future, in life and in being. The children of Abraham clearly know that God's plan is the success of creation and the achievement of human vocation as administrator of the world entrusted. To do so, however, one must not be blinded by new techniques to dominate the Earth and instead learn to gradually give up lordship over her.

This way, finally, in faithfulness to the best of biblical tradition, the three religions descendent from Abraham must be instances of wisdom. The same way God rested the seventh day, men and women of the third millennium must discover the secret of a *sabbatical wisdom*, which demands worship and astonishment in the face of creation.

---

3 Michel Seres, *The Natural Contract*, Michigan, University of Michigan Press, 1995.

7 Challenges and Possibilities facing Theology Today

DEENABANDHU MANCHALA

I view this task of identifying the possibilities for doing theology as enormous as I recognize the increasing complexity of our world today. One can indulge in offering simplistic solutions to complex problems as well as saying things that do not matter much to the churches – the prime addressees of the theological task, the majority of which also dream of 'Another World', but in quite a different way compared to the movements gathering for the World Social Forum. Therefore, taking into account these limitations as well as the complexity of the world situation, I attempt to approach the theme from my own perspective as an Indian Christian, as one who belongs to a fragmented religious minority in a predominantly multi-religious context, and as a Dalit theologian from the point of view of the socially and economically disempowered sections in India.

Challenges

I would like to reflect on three features of the life-world of the Dalits today in an attempt to identify common challenges as well as possibilities for doing theology together.

The realities of fragmentation and polarization in a pluralistic world

About 250 million Dalits in India and other parts of South Asia are the victims of the caste system – a social order that has its roots and strength in Brahminical Hinduism. Their predicament is the result of centuries of oppression and disempowerment forcing them into intense struggles for survival, identity and power. Segregation, discrimination, humiliation and exploitation are their daily experiences. As those on the bottom step of the social ladder, their history has always been a long story of suffering under the abusive power of those at the top. Even though the intermediary caste communities did benefit by exploiting the vulnerable Dalits, the Dalit struggle has always been primarily a struggle against the vertical social, economic and political powers because of the hierarchical way the caste system organized social distances and relationships. However, the processes of modernization and urbanization have de-ritualized caste to a large extent. Now caste operates on a set of principles that is different from those of ritual hierarchy. Some of the intermediary caste communities have been able to move away from traditional structures of domination. In the new structures of representational political power and market economy, the caste is a political instrument and plays a pivotal role in determining communal identity and power. In other words, what was earlier a monopoly of some is now a battleground for many. Consequently, there is an intense struggle for horizontal power among communities with each striving hard to control or monopolize resources, opportunities and political processes at all levels, both local and larger. The bonds of solidarity and partnership that existed among the low caste communities, who form the majority of the Indian society, are now being threatened in the present scenario that is overwhelmed by struggles for political and economic power on the one hand and for identity and justice on the other. Solidarity and partnership among people and communities are being replaced by competition and rivalry. In these dynamics of power, the Dalits, who continue to suffer manifold disadvantages, tend to get pushed further to and beyond the margins. The faces and names of their aggressors are many and varied and thus their struggles assume new proportions and character. India has always been a pluralistic nation but with the increasing economic polarization, it has come to see fragmentation of the communities and further disempowerment of the disadvantaged, as prominent detrimental results.

Not just India but virtually every human society is touched by this phenomenon of pluralism and is compelled to go through radical changes in the ways it has understood itself and the other. This global reality has also brought with it new possibilities for greater human understanding, interaction and solidarity. We are able to acknowledge and celebrate the rich diversity of cultures, religions, languages, nationalities, etc. However, amidst this diversity of identities, we also recognize intense struggles for identity, wealth, resources and power. There is a kind of new tribalism, making people seek their own identities and interests which not only exclude but also violate the lives of others. People and communities increasingly seem to opt for barricaded lives.

Fear, suspicion, hatred and rejection dominate the language and experience of many people all over the world. Those who have no political or economic power are forced to subject themselves to the interests of the dominant. It is unfortunate that in these power struggles religious identities, more than or along with national, ethnic and linguistic identities, are extensively used in our world today. Sadly, religious language, symbols and leaders are now the instruments of division and conflict instead of being resources for harmony and goodwill. We have seen that there is nothing religious about religious conflicts, whether in Nigeria or Northern Ireland, the Middle East or Indonesia or anywhere else in the world. In all these regions the majority of victims are the innocent and the powerless. With triumphalistic and expansionistic assertions on the one hand and with total indifference to world brokenness on the other, churches by and large seem to opt for forms of witness that do not heal human divisions and fragmentation. On the contrary, they seem to play a major role in provoking and sustaining hatred and suspicion among people and communities. This reality of the fragmentation of the human community and the predicament of the vulnerable and the disadvantaged in a pluralistic but, more importantly, polarized world, are challenges that we cannot afford to ignore.

How do we address the forces of fragmentation and polarization as we celebrate the rich diversity of God's creation? What forms of pluralism do we envision that ensure space for everyone and sustain human solidarity and interdependence?

Globalization of Karma

The Brahminical Hindu society has been able to subjugate millions of Dalits and other low caste communities for centuries not with the help of strong and aggressive political and military mechanisms, but through a colonization of their minds with its doctrine of karma. Karma holds each accountable for his or her own actions. A person's present predicament is of his or her own making. One cannot blame anyone or any force or structure for one's situation of misery or suffering. And no one can change the effects of bad karma because that is the divine order, *dharma*. The only hope of liberation from bad karma is in one's willingness to accept the present predicament as a divine dispensation and adhere to it with a sense of devotion and commitment. Chances are that, in the next birth, one is born into a better situation. By using this doctrine, the dominant sections of the Hindu society subjugated and dehumanized many communities for centuries and through it ensured the sustenance of a social order that gave them unlimited and uninterrupted opportunities. The doctrine of karma is thus the core religious principle that sustains the caste system, and the Dalits are its worst victims. On account of this, many Dalits, together with other disempowered communities in India, continue to live with low self-image, low self-esteem, accepting injustice and deprivation as if they are divinely ordained.

The value orientations of global capitalism also seem similar to the doctrine of karma. Its high priests preach that some are poor and backward because they have not worked hard enough or do not have the ability and assets to produce for the consumption of the market. We are told that the only way the poor can emancipate themselves is by catching up with the system by working hard, by moving out of their homelands, by giving up their traditional livelihood patterns, their communities, even if it results in having to live without any identity as human persons. Thus we often hear about poverty as a problem, but hardly about the scandal of affluence amidst massive poverty. A major moral casualty in these dynamics is the commodification of the human person, an unfortunate product of this process. One's value and worth as a human being is seen in terms of one's utility value, one's ability to produce and to add to economic growth. Those who cannot produce have no place in this regime. Whether by cutbacks or structural adjustments, whether by violence or even natural disasters in any part of the world, the poor and the socially disempowered are the most affected. These are mostly women, children, the aged, the disabled, ethnic and linguistic minorities, racially oppressed groups, the Dalits, the indigenous people, and all others whose dignity as human beings is denied or the denial of which is legitimized by religious or economic structures. Ironically, the orientation of popular Christian teaching and practice seems also to be driven by this individualistic understanding of salvation and one's own pursuit of it. Therefore, overcoming the violence of the powerful and their manipulation of the lives of the vulnerable needs to be seen as a challenge in today's world.

These powers and their value orientations overwhelm our lives today and we are all well aware of their mechanisms. What I want to highlight now is the emerging combination and collaboration among these and other hegemonic powers. In the recent past, we have seen this happening in a very significant way. The world's past and present colonial, economic, military and technological superpowers colluded and pursued their own visions and interpretations of the world by defying the will of the international community and people.

When the powerful and the influential legitimize their illegitimate intentions, the danger is that illegitimacy gradually tends to gain acceptance. The result is the brutalization of society. When political and economic structures are manipulated to serve and safeguard the interests of the greedy and the powerful, values and traditions that have sustained human communities disappear. What is left is a rapidly degenerating world. How do we respond to this challenge? When people and the dynamics of social relationships in an aggressively competitive society are driven merely by survival needs and power interests, ethics disappears and the poor and the powerless are those that suffer the most. I see this as an important challenge for the theological community.

The challenge of human genetic technologies

We have entered a new millennium. Throughout time, but particularly in the last century, the world has been overwhelmed by the potentialities of the human mind. Most of us here have greatly benefited from these developments in many ways. However, these technological revolutions also confront us with questions that seriously challenge our self-perceptions and alter our patterns of human relationships. The need for human interaction and community life has become subjected to one's own economic demands and personal preferences. Furthermore, much has already been said about how modern science and technology, as instruments of economic growth, have also been responsible for enormous damage to the Earth and its resources.

I would now like us to focus our attention on the questions posed by the recent developments in the fields of genetic technologies. Human genetic technologies touch our deepest convictions about the value of human life. For quite some time, these technologies have been telling us that many human traits, whether love or hatred, violence or reconciliation, work or laziness, intellectual sharpness or sluggishness, or even morality, have much to do with genetic formation and can be explained in purely biological terms. In other words, these technologies seem to tell us that some are intellectually and physically strong, some are wealthy and thriving because they have the right genes that could mould them to be so. These also offer possibilities of refashioning oneself according to the standards set by the dominant and the powerful. As a part of this development, genetic engineering adds a new dimension to the capabilities of human beings to modify and change the development of human and other species. We cannot ignore the racist and dehumanizing aspects of eugenics. The Dalits in my country have always been told that they are intellectually morbid, inferior human beings and are thus conditioned to hate themselves, their skin colour, their physical features, their culture and to imitate their oppressors instead. As a result, some Dalits attempt to live with false self-images, deny their identities and behave like their so-called superiors and pursue their own interests by turning a blind eye to those who are left behind. Technologies are not value-free. When the realm of human values and relationships is invaded by technological powers, when new standards are set, what then would be the predicament of the struggles of the Dalits in my country and of all the excluded communities elsewhere in the world for justice and fairness?

Given the result-oriented and utilitarian ethics of the dominant technological culture, these technologies raise several questions. They impact the ecology of values in society and may even redefine the place that sickness and disability have in it. The affirmation of human dignity stands against all forms of the use of human genetic technologies which subject human beings to purely economic interests. Furthermore, if everything is genetic, what then is the role of theology and other human endeavours towards responsible forms of human behaviour and relationships? We, as contextual theologians, need to tackle seriously this context of technological invasion of the realm of human relationships. Unfortunately, religious thinking somehow has always seen these existential challenges, the rapid and complex expansion of human mind, as set outside its realm of concern, preaching and theologizing about a God who belongs to a distant past. Religions have been indifferent, sometimes ambiguous and have even endorsed these powers that thrive by abusing the sanctity of life.

Possibilities

Globalization of solidarity

Indian society during the past two decades has been through a remarkable phase of social mobilization. The oppressed communities, such as the Dalits, backward castes, indigenous peoples, women, artisans, etc., have been getting organized to struggle for justice, fair treatment and opportunities. There are new bonds of solidarity emerging between the Dalit and the Bahujan (backward castes) movements. Their shared experiences of suffering as well as their shared visions seem to bring them together into new partnerships across religious and even linguistic boundaries. Despite the ways the economic and political powers continue with their manipulative politics of division, and despite the horizontal power struggle mentioned before, these people's movements are growing stronger day by day. Recent elections in India have proved that the powers-that-be simply cannot afford to ignore them if they want to remain in power.

During the recent past, the world has also seen some major expressions of international solidarity among common people. Millions of people all over the world organized themselves to protest against the plans of the powerful as they began to invade Iraq. Similarly, the anti-globalization movements have also become numerous and stronger in many parts of the world. The World Social Forum events during the past four years have also been major expressions of this emerging solidarity. These are networks of people which are driven by a spirituality of life rather than neutral theologies and oppressive ideologies. These anti-hegemonic alliances both here and at the local level need to be the locale of doing theology. Swami Agnivesh, a well-known Hindu leader and social activist, says that all major human advances, such as the abolition of slavery, women's and children's rights and environmental awareness, have come from secular, not religious sources.[1] Here is the challenge! Theology, if is aimed at effecting positive changes in the cause of the coming reign of God, has to be an ally of those who are working together for life, for justice and peace and find ways of entering into new collaborations with them.

Centrality of ethics in theology

We have gathered here to do theology with context and experience, the struggles, aspirations, actions and alternatives of the poor as our subject matter. We want to define the contours of a theology for a transformed world. The theme of the next Assembly of WCC in this city next year is 'God, in your Grace, transform the world'. It is a call and a challenge to churches and Christians to reclaim their mandate to transform, to be a ferment of change, to be able to transform swords into ploughshares. As we embark on this creative task of envisioning a theology for another possible world, I would like to draw your attention to three important challenges, which I consider are worth exploring: the first is reclaiming the totality of the Christ event as the site of salvation. We live in a world where the powers insist that violence is necessary for peace and where the religious right corroborates that logic through

---

1 See Swami Agnivesh, 'Social Spirituality'. Available online at http://www.swamiagnivesh.com/social.htm.

the reiteration of the link between violence and salvation. Generally speaking, churches have focused solely on the cross event to present God's salvation in Jesus Christ in an exclusively religious language. This approach has completely left out Jesus' life and message as sites of salvation. If ethical transformation is characteristic of the vision of 'Another World', then we need to recapture the salvation in the totality of the person and work of Jesus Christ. I also see this as necessary for us in India and other multi-religious contexts to be able to present Christ and Christian theology in ways that do not threaten but effect healthy partnerships with people of other faiths and social ideologies. Second is the need to explore alternative meanings and models of power. In a world where many are victims of various forms of power and where manipulative and violent power is glorified, the theological task has to expose these powers and draw on the alternatives that Jesus taught us. Third is a new ecclesiological reflection that thoroughly explores the meaning and purpose of being Church in an increasingly fragmented and polarized world. I would like to mention WCC's work on ecclesiology and ethics, which has highlighted the significance of living with the consciousness of the ethical basis for ecclesial existence. Without that consciousness, churches, especially in multi-religious situations such as India, exist merely as religious communities among many others. Unless our theological formulations confront, challenge and engage the churches, much of what we do here and in the seminaries will remain mere intellectual exercises.

Towards public theology

We recognize that our world is in a deep moral crisis. Its features are many: fear, suspicion and hatred characterize human relationships. Life is blatantly abused and this abuse is justified. The innocent and powerless are constantly and systematically victimized. Life is increasingly guided by the ideologies of the powerful. The values of the wealthy and the powerful dominate all structures and dynamics of relationships. Public life, political governance, international co-operation, solidarity, the values of justice and freedom, etc. are all governed and tainted by these ideologies of the powerful. Our twenty-first century is not guided by political philosophies and social ideologies any more. We also live in a world where there are many signs of hope in the way the disempowered and indignant are mobilizing themselves in defence of life against the abusive and hegemonic powers. The theological community cannot but take sides in defence of life. An agenda of this sort points towards new ways of conceiving the goal and content of the theological task. We have been sharing our stories, experiences and theological entry points. We recognize that these are both specific and varied. These address various questions – political, social, economic, cultural, etc. I think we need to do two things as we dream of our theological task addressing a broader sphere of 'Another World'. Perhaps what we need is a public theology, an exercise towards theological integration that does not limit itself to addressing specific issues and contexts but seeks points of convergence. Our common struggle is against powers and principalities and about the transformation of the world. If our struggle is for the realization of Another World, then our theological task has to address the totality of the predicament and possibilities of life on Earth. Neither traditional Western theologies formulated against the background of a bipolar world nor specific context or perspective-based theologies can adequately respond to the challenges of a unipolar, globalized, technological, pluralistic world. We need to make an attempt to integrate these creative theological endeavours in order to articulate a vision of the world that complements the utopias of many social movements. We need to articulate a new vision of God's *oikoumene* and of the world from the geopolitical perspective of the South, from our shared experiences of suffering and shared visions. Our ultimate vision is to build a global system of human relationships that guarantee justice, dignity, security, development and rights, not only to the rich but even to the most vulnerable child on this Earth.

Before I close, as part of my exposition on challenges and possibilities, I would like to pose a few questions, which I consider that we cannot afford to ignore. It is a fact that many churches in the world today are those that do not belong to the so-called mainline, traditional churches. These are often led by narrow theologies or no theologies. Some are led by the theological interests and options of the charismatic leaders of their communities. I would like us to ask ourselves: Who are the addressees of our theology? How do our theologies influence the way churches in local situations as well as at larger levels effect changes or be or become agents of change? There is also the often acknowledged wide gap between the theological academia and the communities of believers. Theology itself seems to have lost its space in the life of many churches. Moreover, in many contexts in Asia, theology has a very limited space to impact public life or discourse. Therefore, we need to seriously address these questions and explore ways by which the Church goes through a process of transformation and becomes a means through which its faith effects transformation of the world or at least joins those forces of transformation.

8 Trajectories and Perspectives: The European Case

ROSINO GIBELLINI

The question to which I would like to respond runs like this: What is the stance of European theology vis-à-vis liberation theology (taken in all its pluriformity and complexity)? This question offers us the opportunity to articulate an essential perspective on the theology of the twentieth century.

Four theological movements of the twentieth century

Surveying the course taken by theology during the twentieth century, we can point out four movements or four approaches that were employed in 'doing' theology.

The first movement goes under the name of a theology of the word of God, or a theology of Christian revelation. This approach focuses on affirming, with Karl Barth, the transcendent character of the word of God, or, with Hans Urs von Balthasar, the incomparability or the non-comparability of Christian revelation with any philosophy or human wisdom. This approach in twentieth-century theology is concerned with the identity of the Christian faith and with the specificity of theological discourse. During the final decades of the past century and continuing on to the present, these theologies of identity have re-emerged within the context of that complex phenomenon which goes under the name of postmodernity. According to the theologies of identity, the Christian Church should speak its own language and encourage its own praxis in an era marked by the experience of diaspora: theology should follow the lead of the biblical text by practising *intratextuality*. In this context, theology functions as 'the Ecclesial Canon' (Barth's Kirkliche Dogmatik), as 'the Grammar of Faith' (Lindbeck) or even as 'the knowing that opens onto reflecting' (Jüngel).

A second approach combines the focus on identity with a concern about the relevance of Christian discourse for existential, anthropological, cultural and experiential human reality. One may categorize under this heading the existentialist theology of Rudolf Bultmann, the theology of culture of Paul Tillich, the anthropological theology of Karl Rahner, the theology of experience of Schillebeeckx, the ecumenical and interreligious theology of Hans Küng, and the hermeneutical theology of Claude Geffré. Here theology is conceived of as a complex correlation to be worked out between two poles: the pole of revelation and of the tradition which hands it on, and the pole of the present situation in which each human being lives, attains sense and meaning through its projects and receives a superabundance of meaning from the Christian answer. This manner of doing theology has come to be called 'the anthropological turn in theology'. This approach, which is known as 'the hermeneutical turn in theology', is a variant configuration of the anthropological turn. In this context, theology may be defined in the way in which Marie-Dominique Chenu has characterized it: as 'the faith which stands in solidarity with its own time'.[1]

A third approach moves beyond the anthropological and hermeneutical turn into a political turn when proponents – such as (proleptically) Bonhoeffer, and then in particular Johann Baptist Metz, Jürgen Moltmann and Dorothee Sölle – advocate the development of the social and political content of the Christian message. This 'political theology' emerged in the 1960s, underscoring the problem of interrelating theology and practice in Christian discipleship. The faith of Christians has to turn itself into 'praxis in history and society'. Theology takes up the 'option to enter into the field of history' and to understand itself as a 'knowing oriented to doing' which does not simply wonder about the meaning of life and history but which aims to make living in history a practical experience. It sees itself as a way of knowing that leads one to discern public responsibility, a way of knowing that leads to service in the communication of the gospel and of its power to speak prophetically and achieve solidarity in the midst of the conflicts of history. It is a theology which has moved forward by taking on the challenges of its time. In the words of Johann Baptist Metz, 'In the first place, the unresolved conflict with the problems of the Enlightenment, then the catastrophe of the Auschwitz tragedy, and finally, the emergence in the theological world of a non-European world, i.e., the Third World.'[2] Along the same lines, Jürgen Moltmann affirms:

---

1 M.-D. Chenu, *Le Saulchoir. Una Scuola di teologia* (1937), Casale Monferrato, Marietti, 1982, p. 46.

2 B. Metz, *Sul concetto della nuova teologia politica: 1967–1997* (1997), Brescia, Queriniana, 1998, p. 182.

If one takes the church seriously, then on a par with it theology should act a function of the Reign of God in the world. And in this function it should play an integral part in the spheres of the political, cultural, economic and ecological life of society.[3]

In this regard, Jürgen Moltmann asks: 'So, what remains, and what doesn't?' He answers:

What remains, if we want to speak in very general terms, is the recognition of the political dimension of the Christian faith in the cross of Christ and in the Reign of God. What remains is the necessary critique of the idols of political and civil religion. What, in a general way, has been accepted is the preferential option for the poor. What have been developed are the principles of every contextual theology: context, kairos, and community.[4]

A fourth movement in the theology of the twentieth century is to be found in the theologies of liberation, which represent the real 'breakthrough' of the last decades, and which it is the task of this gathering to illustrate, to deepen and to relocate in the new social and cultural contexts of our time.

In synthesis, these movements of European theology can be identified with three key words or phrases: identity, correlation, passion for the kingdom. Perhaps one can say that in these last years we have seen, on the one hand, the ongoing reaffirmation of the search for identity, which is to be clearly distinguished from a fundamentalism characterized by a religious identity that focuses aggressively on exclusion. On the other hand, we note the pressing urgency to understand this identity in constructive relation with other cultures, practices and religions.

If one wished to formulate a concise synthesis of these many trajectories, it might be worded as: theological existence and passion for the kingdom. The phrase 'theological existence' recaptures a well-known expression of Barth and gives expression to the theologies of identity, whereas 'passion for the kingdom' gives expression to the theologies of corelation and the political theologies.

We must also remember that the Catholic theology of the twentieth

---

3 J. Moltmann, *Dio nel progetto del mondo moderno. Contributi per una rilevanza pubblica della teologia* (1997), Brescia, Queriniana, 1999, p. 8.

4 J. Moltmann, 'Political Theology in Germany after Auschwitz', in W. F. Storrar and A. R. Morton (eds), *Public Theology for the 21st Century*, London and New York, Continuum, 2004, p. 41.

century, above all in its European expression, contributed decisively in the preparation of the Second Vatican Council. What theologies were involved in this epoch-making 'turn'? In the analysis proposed by a French historian, this council 'of the church and about the church' actually 'relativized' the Church, in the sense that it deliberately described the Church in terms of its relationship with the Word of God (*Dei Verbum*) from which it emerges and in terms of its witness and mission in the world (*Gaudium et Spes*).

The European theology of the twentieth century is not an innocent theology. Against the background of a dramatic era that happened to be one of the most evangelical centuries in the history of the Christian Church (Congar), 'doing' theology also took the form of betrayal as the 'German theology of war' at the beginning of the century in the fatal year 1914, or, in more recent memory, as the 'theology of the state' worked out in South Africa in defence of Apartheid in Reformed communities of white Europeans that were forcefully denounced in the Kairos document of 1985, which was itself the expression of a prophetic church and a prophetic theology.

It has also shared in the silence of the Christian community and its institutions concerning the Holocaust, when it should have served as its critical conscience there and in other moments of political and cultural significance as well.

But it is a theology that found itself confronted with a awesome task. As the theologian Joseph Moingt has written:

a theology which has come up against a prodigious evolution in mentality and awareness, an overwhelming wave of incredulity which has shaken Christianity to its foundations. It is a theology which has become the interpreter of the experiences and the aspirations of the Christian men and women of our time.[5]

In the Century of Martyrdom, as the twentieth Christian century has been defined, European theology yoked together the 'apologia' with the 'martyria' and this is typified in the names and reflections of individuals such as the Orthodox theologian Pavel Florensky, victim of the Stalin-era gulag, Edith Stein, martyr to anti-Semitism at Auschwitz, and Dietrich Bonhoeffer, martyr in the resistance to the Nazi barbarities at Flossenburg. This last named is uniquely representative of the heart of twentieth-century European theology and has evoked resonances in Christian communities outside Europe. On the walls

---

5 J. Moingt, *Dieu qui vient à l'homme*, Vol. 1, Paris, Cerf, 2002, pp. 17–18.

of prisons in South Korea and South Africa graffiti have been found reading: Remember Bonhoeffer.

European theology and the theology of liberation

How does one go about comparing European theology with the theology of liberation when the latter understands itself on its own terms as reflection that presupposes praxis? Liberation theologians consider themselves consciously responsible for introducing the 'story of the people' into this reflection or, more exactly, 'the story of those whom official historiographers and also Christian and theological writers have dismissed as non-persons and non-histories.' In non-Western cultural and religious contexts these are the ones who put intertextuality into practice (and not just the intratextuality of the theologies of identity).

Within the framework of Catholic theology one notes what might be described in a rather shorthand manner as a shift from Rahner to von Balthasar, that is from the anthropological turn to the retrieval of Christian identity in an age of pluralism. One consequence of this has been the reticence of European theologians regarding the overtures of liberation theology. In fact, to a certain extent they are widely disregarded.

The present situation could also be characterized as one of uncertainty and fear. (At the 2004 congress of the European Society for Catholic Theology, the beginning of the Manifesto of the Communist Party from February 1848 was adapted as follows: 'A Spectre Shakes Up Europe – The Spectre of Fear'). People seem to be looking for a spirituality that tends to privatize the Christian experience and this does not favour the acceptance of the appeals of liberation theology either.

Moreover, one must take into account the situation of Eastern Europe and that of the Russian Orthodox. In the period between 1989 and 1991 these areas experienced a kind of 'liberation', different from that envisioned by liberation theology. A Russian Orthodox theologian recently affirmed during a theological forum in which I myself participated:

We Orthodox had a rather complex relation with liberation theology. Its concession to a so-called 'well-intentioned' Marxism (a definition which circulated in Orthodox circles in the Soviet Union) is absolutely foreign to the spirit of our faith which was subjected to that 'liberation' [i.e. the 'liberation' offered by Soviet Communism].

65

Similar sentiments are expressed by philosophers and theologians of Eastern Europe, particularly by those from Poland.

In general, however, I believe that one can speak of a critical reception of liberation theology within European theology. One need only think of its 'preferential option for the poor', its rejection of the 'structures of sin', its choice of the title 'God of Life' and its introduction and encouragement of new forms of interreligious dialogue. Liberation theology has expanded the conscience and opened the heart of the Christian church.

I conclude, recalling the analysis proposed by the international theological journal *Concilium* at the congress held at the Catholic University of Louvain in 1990 on the theme, prophetic in its formulation, 'At the Thresholds of the Third Millennium'. It was perhaps the first time that European and North Atlantic theology had engaged one another in one of the most prestigious universities of Europe, in a challenging confrontation with the new ecclesial and theological realities which had been emerging in the final decades of the twentieth century. On that occasion the North American Catholic theologian David Tracy addressed the problem which had sprung up repeatedly in the atmosphere of the last years and which was indicative of the direction being taken by Western theology. The title of his presentation was 'On Naming the Present' and it proposed a path that could be taken between two opposite and contradictory positions.[6] For the neo-conservatives and the fundamentalists, modernity is a 'failed experiment' and therefore we must return to the healthy tradition. Even for those who define the present as postmodernity, modernity is still a time to be overcome, not in order to return to tradition but for the demolition of the *status quo* in favour of the *fluxus quo*. Now, if the tradition had a centre, postmodernity is characterized by the 'loss of center', but in this way it offers the possibility of discovering the other, the different, the oppressed, the marginalized. Theology, in a 'time of passages'[7] lives in the tension between modernity and postmodernity. It must embrace the inalienable values of the tradition, it must also embrace the positive advances accomplished by modernity, but, in a spirit of dialogue and solidarity, it must open itself to the other: the outcome could be a new solidarity in the struggle for the true era of justice.

---

6 Cf. D. Tracy, *On Naming the Present. God, Hermeneutics and Church*, Maryknoll, NY, Orbis, 1994.

7 Cf. J. Habermas, *Zeit der Übergänge. Kleine politische Schriften IV*, Frankfurt am Main, Suhrkamp Verlag, 2001.

9 Theology, Spirituality and the Market

JUNG MO SUNG

Our theological reflection on the market will be organized in three parts. In the first, we will deal with two preliminary epistemological questions; in the second, we will analyse the theological and spiritual axes of economy and the market; and in the third, we will propose some questions to further a theological reflection, committed to the construction of another more just and humane world.

Epistemological issues

Before beginning our theological reflection on the market, it is important to point out the conditions of possibility of a theological critique of the contemporary capitalist market that is both socially relevant and theoretically pertinent.

The sacred beyond religion

In the first place it is important to make quite clear that religion, as we know it today, is a sub-system within a social totality, different from the 'secular', it is a creation of the modern world. In the pre-modern world there was no perception of religion as we know it today: the world was not divided between the 'secular' and the 'religious', rather it was divided between the sacred and the profane. All spheres of life, private or public, were organized around this distinction. In this sense we can say that in ancient times there was no relation between religion and economy, rather there was a relation between the sacred or God and the production and distribution of the material goods necessary for life.

It is in the modern capitalist world that the relation between religion and economy emerges. It is here that for the first time in the history of humanity there emerges the notion of a self-regulating market, the economy as an autonomous sphere in relation to the religious values that proceed from the notion of the sacred or God. The relation between religion and market can only emerge as such in the sense that the market is seen as an autonomous social entity, or at least relatively autonomous, in relation to the religious field. The partition of an autonomous social sphere facing the religious field led to the emergence of religion as it is understood today: no longer the foundation and organizer of a social totality, now a relatively autonomous field within the social reality.

When we refer to the autonomy of the market it is important to bear in mind the difference between the market – a social space for the exchange of economic goods – and the market system. The market existed before capitalism, and will exist after capitalism, because it is a need of wide and complex societies. But the capitalist market or the market system is something quite specific within capitalism: the market as the only or principal co-ordinator of the social division of labour, which according to Karl Polanyi, is self-regulating.

A market economy is a system of self-regulating markets; in slightly more technical terms, it is an economy directed by market prices and only market prices. Such a system, capable of organizing the totality of economic life with no outside help or interference, certainly deserves to be called self-regulating.[1]

The absence of external limitations – social or natural – is the logic of the market that allows capitalist economists to talk about capitalism as an economic system which tends to the production and the *unlimited* accumulation of wealth.

Much of the criticism against the market system precisely questions this self-regulating character of the market. Churches and religious groups, for example, criticize the market economy in the name of religious or ethical values found in their traditions, and demand a change of direction in the economy. They want to regulate the economy from a point or place external to economic logic; and in the case of religious critique, a point external to humanity itself. Meanwhile, as the religious perspective of the world – which refers to superior or supernatural forces – is different for other non-religious perspectives of the world and especially the capitalist economy, these critiques can only be understood and accepted by people and groups who belong to the same religious tradition or who share the same religious perspective of the world and of life.

Non-religious people and social groups, or those who do not share

---

1 Karl Polanyi, *Agrande transformacâo: as origens da nossa época*, Rio de Janeiro, Campus, 1980 (original in English, 1944), p. 59.

the same values of a particular religious group, can share this critique inasmuch as the criticism is expressed in the name of certain ethical values which do not demand a religious faith, such as solidarity with the poor. This means that for non-religious people or groups, or people from other religious traditions, to understand and agree with these criticisms, they must be 'translated' to a language common to these groups, a wider language, a non-religious language.

On the whole, as the economy is seen by economic agents and by society as a different and autonomous sub-system in its relation to religion, criticisms based on values, doctrines or religiously based ethics are not accepted as relevant by economic agents and the majority of the population. In this case the separation between religion and economics prevails, as does the separation between Church and state.

We are thus faced with an alternative: we relinquish prophetic criticism in the face of the deep social and human problems created by the capitalist market or we return to the situation before the separation of state and Church, and in the name of a determined faith tradition we voice our criticism and demands against the economy while ignoring its relative autonomy. To give up prophetic criticism would be to deny what is one of the most essential characteristics of the biblical tradition as well as of other religious traditions. To make demands upon the economic field based on values external to it, values founded on a determined religious tradition or a particular interpretation of this tradition, would be to deny the autonomy of the economic field and not recognize the religious and cultural plurality of our time.

To overcome this difficulty and to maintain the specificity of theological reflection, and not fall into the trap of making of theology a second-class economic theory, we must come to see – as we will try to prove in the second part of this chapter – that the modern economy is based upon certain theological presuppositions and a sacrificial notion of the sacred which must be criticized theologically. This means that the separation of religion and economics in the modern world does not signify the confinement of the sacred to the interior of the religious field. In the sense that no society survives without a principle of unquestionable differentiation, without the distinction between sacred and profane, which sustain and allow for the organization and hierarchy of social human life, in the capitalistic society, this distinction has 'overflowed' the religious field and has moved in a special way to the inside of the market.

The theological or prophetic critique of the market thus becomes a critique of the theological presuppositions which sustain the market system and its sacrificial demands in the name of a sacred idolatry.

This is not a simple criticism of the economy based on religious values external to it; instead, it is a critique of the theological presuppositions that are present in the very foundation of the market economy as well as in its spirit.

Religious values and complex society

A point that must be taken into account when we criticize the market economy in the name of values that originate in religious traditions is the fact that the great religions originated and were systematized in pre-modern traditional societies and in economies much less complex than current ones.

The values of solidarity and social justice, for example, have developed with a strong intentional connotation, in other words, the emphasis is placed on the intention of economic and social agents rather than the dynamics of the social and economic structure. An example of this is the messianic expectation of a just king, who with good intentions and power would institute a kingdom of justice and righteousness in favour of the poor and oppressed. This type of expectation or demand for good intentions as a key for social change is understandable, in principle, as part of the 'transparency' of the economic relations of that time. It was easier to understand the reasons behind the poverty of some and the wealth of others.

With the increase of commercial exchange, the monetarization of the economy, the subsequent increase in the complexity of the economy resulted in the creation of a science of economics geared toward understanding new dynamics. The need for this new science not only signified the recognition that economic relations are not transparent, but also the recognition that the economic system had begun to be governed by economic 'laws', by self-organizing tendencies of the economic system,[2] which are no longer subordinated to the intention of economic agents.

Liberation theology saw this from the beginning. The use of socio-analytical mediations stemmed from the recognition that the modern economy could no longer be understood with theological or philosophical reflections alone, even less by an immediate approach, without the mediation of social or economic science. The creation of the concept of

---

2 On the matter of market auto-organization, see Paul Krugman, *The Self-Organizing Economy*, Malden-Oxford, Blackwell, 1996; Jung Mo Sung, *Sujeito e sociddade complexas*, Petropolis, Vozes, 2002; and Sung, 'Teologia da Libertacâo entre o desejo de abundancia e a realidde da escassez' in *Perspectíva Teológica*, Vol. 35, No. 97 (2003), pp. 141–368.

'structural sin' was also a recognition that the fundamental problem of the capitalist economy was not one of (wrong) intentions on the part of economic agents, but rather one in which its own structure generated social problems, suffering and the death of millions of poor people.

Good intentions are no longer enough to solve social problems because the market economy, as a complex sub-system, possesses its own dynamic which is autonomous in relation to the intentions of economic agents that are part of the same sub-system, no matter how powerful they may be inside the sub-system. It is clear that agents who hold strategic places have more power and influence than those who don't. But this does not mean that the powerful have the capacity to impose their will over all the system, because their actions generate intentional and non-intentional effects, reactions from other agents and the system itself. Due to all this, liberation theology from the very beginning assumed that the conversion of people who occupy strategic places within market economy was not enough to overcome the situation of social exclusion and death. What are needed are proposals of solidarity and social justice which take into serious account complex social and economic mechanisms and struggle for deep transformations in the economic, social and political structure.

In brief, we have to criticize the theological presuppositions that sustain and legitimize the sacrificial capitalist market economy and update and make concrete the fundamental values of solidarity and justice elaborated by religious traditions for the complex economic and social reality, taking into account the self-organizing dynamic of the economic sub-system and the separation – dialectical and not metaphysical – between Church and state, between the religious and the economic fields.

Faith and spirituality within the market economy

I believe that theological critique of the market economy and the current globalization process will be socially relevant and theoretically pertinent in so far as they reveal and criticize sacrificial theological presuppositions. These not only legitimize the current capitalistic process of accumulation, which produces deep social and ecological problems, they at the same time fascinate and trap people the world around. An example of this fascination is the Bashundara City Shopping Centre, in Bangladesh, one of the poorest countries in the world. This gigantic and luxurious shopping centre, which cost over 80 million dollars to build and is presented as one of the best of South Asia, is a sign of the fascination that Western consumerism exercises in a poor country with totally different traditions. It is also a sign of the increase in the concentration of wealth and at the same time the increase in the gap between rich and poor. Meanwhile this shopping centre is a matter of pride for the millions of poor people who visit it without being able to buy anything. 'Abdus Samad, a 70 year old illiterate farmer, travelled from far to visit the *shopping centre*. Looking up to the great crystal dome at the entrance is for him proof of how much Bangladesh has improved.'[3]

We must understand what makes a poor farmer believe that the whole country is better off simply because the rich can have fun and consume like Westerners in a luxurious shopping centre, where he himself feels fascinated, even though he cannot acquire anything, except the spectacle of the shopping itself. His fascination is similar to the fascination caused by the contemplation of the great medieval cathedrals.

Faith in the market

As is well known, the ideological principle that moves the current economic globalization process is neo-liberalism. In spite of the variations within neo-liberalism, we can affirm that all its internal trends emerge from a similar epistemological principle: the impossibility of fully grasping or at least satisfactorily understanding all the elements that compose the market system. In the name of such impossibility Hayek constructed all his criticism against Keynesianism and Marxism. The 'fatal arrogance'[4] of socialists and social democrats would be the 'pretence of knowledge' – title of a lecture given by Hayek on the occasion of receiving the Nobel Prize in Economics in 1974, which remits to the myth of Adam and Eve and the notion of 'original sin', which would lead us all to intervene in the market. Since this intervention, by which social aims are pursued, presupposes an impossible knowledge, the inevitable result of all state and social interventions in the market will be yet more economic crises and more social problems. In other words, the main cause of economic crises and poverty in the world today would be the arrogance of sectors of government and society that pretend to know the mysterious and unfathomable market, and in the name of such knowledge, intervene in the economy to realize the desired good of social justice. The 'temptation to do good' – the title

---

3 David Rohde, ' A Lot of Cash in a Very Poor Nation: Welcome to the Mall', *The New York Times*, 19 July 2005.

4 Friedrich A. Hayek, *La fatal arrogancia: los errores del socialismo*, Madrid, Union Editorial, 1990.

of a novel by Peter Drucker,[5] the most important twentieth-century theorist in business administration – would be the principal cause of intervention, and for this reason, of the economic crisis and the preservation of poverty. It is from ideas such as these that neo-liberalism argues that the best way to organize the economy and to overcome poverty is to let the market function freely. State and civil society must restrict their action in the economic field to the defence of the freedom of the market. And in the case of countries with a tradition of state intervention in the economy, they must defend the privatization of all services and state enterprises so that the market can function with freedom.

Here emerges the crucial question: if it really is impossible to know in a satisfactory way all the factors that compose the market system, how can we be so sure that the market will always produce the best economic results and the best way to overcome poverty and extreme social inequalities?

As Paul Krugman affirms, the fact that we recognize that the market functions in a self-organizing way does not mean that self-organization necessarily or presumably is something good. 'Self-organizing is something we see and try to understand, not something we want.'[6] In the measure that our knowledge cannot satisfactorily foresee the results of the self-organizing dynamics of the market – the result of all actions and reactions of every economic agent of the integrating factors – the only way to 'prove' the forever beneficial character of the market is to make of this an issue of faith in the market. Neo-liberals and those ideologically close to them, radicalize their faith in the 'invisible hand' of the market (Adam Smith), which deep down is the application of the theology of divine providence to the market. For this reason Milton Friedman, for example, says that 'underlining the majority of arguments against free market is the lack of faith in the freedom of the market as such'.[7] One of the current principal propagandists of neo-liberal ideas is Thomas Friedman, writer and columnist of the New York Times, who exercises great influence on the Bush administration. This author has popularized the concept, common to all neo-liberals, that the free market is the source of human freedom. John Gray, when reviewing Friedman's most recent book, The World

---

5 Peter Drucker, The Temptation to Do Good, New York, Cambridge, Philadelphia, San Francisco, London, Mexico City, Sâo Pablo, Sydney, Harper and Row Publishers, 1984.

6 Paul Krugman, Self-Organizing Economy, p. 6.

7 Milton Friedman, Capitalismo e libertade, 2nd ed., São Paulo, Novo Cultural (col. Os Economistas), 1985, p. 23.

is Flat, said 'Thomas Friedman is a passionate missionary of the neo-liberal faith'.[8]

Paul Ormerod said that 'protected by the security provided by its great democracies, the economists of the International Monetary Fund and World Bank preach to the Third World, *salvation* comes from the market' and that in economic theory, for a long time now, the ruling *'fundamental belief!'* is that the price of goods, be they bananas or human beings, is determined by the relative levels of offer and demand. For this reason he refers to this as 'conventional economic theology'[9].

Eric Hobsbawm in his book *The Age of Extremes*, also identified the current dominant economic theory as a form of theology: 'capitalist countries have sought radical solutions, many times listening without restriction to the secular theologians of free market, who rejected the policies that had served the economy so faithfully during the Golden Era and which now seem to fail', and 'economy, though subject to the demands of logic and coherence, flourished as a form of theology in the western world, a more influential secular theology'.[10]

Due to space limitations, it is not possible to present further examples of authors for or against capitalism, which show, consciously or unconsciously, this faith in the market as foundation and 'motor' of the expansion of the 'free market' and neo-liberal economic globalization.[11] But I believe it is clear that according to the epistemology assumed by neo-liberals themselves, faith in the market is a fundamental component of neo-liberal discourse.

The cruel mystique and solidarity

When one accepts that there is no way to overcome poverty and social problems other than the market, all discussion on the relation between ethics and economy loses sense. According to this neo-liberal logic,

8 J. Gray, 'The World is Round', *The New Yorker Review of Books,* New York, vol. 52, no. 13. Available online at http://foehrenbergkreis.twoday. net/files/Gray-The-World-is-Round/.

9 Paul Ormerod, *A more da economia,* São Paulo, Compahia das Letras, 1996, pp. 13, 16, 217. Our italics.

10 Eric J. Hobsbawm, *Era do extremos: O breve século XX: 1914–1991,* São Paulo, Compahia das Letras, 1995, pp. 19, 528.

11 For a more systematic view of the presuppositions and theological logic as from the inside of the liberal and neo-liberal economic theory, see: Hugo Assmann and F. Hinkelammert, *A idolatria do Mercado,* Petropolis, Vozes, 1989; H. Assmann, *Desafios e falácias,* São Paulo, Paulinus, 1991; F. Hinkelammert, *As armas ideológicas da morte,* São Paulo, Paulinas, 1985; Jung Mo Sung, *Teologia e Economia: repensando a TL e utopias,* 2nd ed., Petrópolis, Vozes, 1995; Sung, *Sujeito e sociedades complexas,* Petrópolis, Vozes, 2002.

the pursuit of self-interest of the market would be the best and most efficient way to generate the common good; and in this way the contradiction between self-interest and common good would be solved. In more traditional religious language, this would eliminate the difference between love and selfishness. The best way to live the love for one's neighbour, the poor, would be to overcome the temptation to do good and continue being selfish in the market, seeking one's self-interest in a more efficient way. This way, conquering the temptation to do good through economic and social policies turns out to be the main spiritual task in the social field.

Confronted with those who, in the name of more traditional religious ethics and values, find that the above proposal goes against Christian spirituality or other religious traditions, Roberto Campos, one of the principal economists of the military dictatorship in Brazil, said quite explicitly that 'modernization presupposes a *cruel mystique* in the worship of efficiency'.[12] 'Mystique' to overcome the temptation to do good and assume a new form of worship. 'Cruel' because this new worship means the subordination of human life to the numbers of profit, presupposing thus insensitivity or cynicism in the face of the suffering of the less 'competent' and less efficient, the poor. Cynicism is the other side of faith in the market. But according to them, there is no other possible way.

The demand for the sacrifice of human life in the name of the laws of the market or of any other law (civil or religious) is what the biblical tradition calls idolatry. And this is what it is all about: market idolatry. Faith in the market is an idolatrous faith which demands human sacrifices in the name of a human institution that has been elevated to the category of absolute. In this sense the laws of the market are the incarnation of the sacred in today's world.

Idolatry provokes the inversion of good and evil, because evil realized in the name of God ceases to be evil and becomes a necessary sacrifice for salvation and, in this sense, it is good. Behind this disqualification of ethical discourse on the economy lie the idolatry of the market with its inversion of good and evil and the transformation of murders into necessary sacrifices for the general good, or for salvation. This deeper logic of oppression of the market system cannot be understood by economic or social analysis because it is an object that is not part of the methodology of modern science. Here the specific contribution of theological critique is revealed and introduced.

---

12 Roberto Campos, *Além do cotidian*, 2nd ed., Rio de Janeiro, Record, 1985, p. 54.

The spirituality of consumption

The critique of the sacrificial character of market idolatry is not really enough to understand the fascination that capitalism exercises on the world today. It is necessary to go beyond this and see the spirituality that moves the expansion of the market system in all areas of the world.

The current process of economic globalization demands the creation of a bigger and more homogeneous consumerist market. This is the only way global brands and models can be created, massively produced and distributed the world over. This means it is necessary to create models of individuals on a worldwide scale to designate the objects of desire, which will then be desired by people all over the world.[13] For this reason sport idols or artists, such as Ronaldinho, Beckham and others, are paid fortunes to 'educate' the people (consumers) of all nations; the meaning of life is to be like them, to buy what they indicate, and in this way appropriate the desires of consumption of the people of the entire world. Consumerism – symbol of the ultimate meaning of life – is a key element of contemporary economic capitalist globalization.

If in medieval Christianity stained glass windows in cathedrals, with their scenes of biblical passages or the life of saints, were the forms used to educate the people by presenting a model of human life and a lifestyle to be desired, today it is commercials, films, video clips and all the products created by mass media which educate.[14] This education on the meaning of life is not built on the repression of instincts and desires, as in pre-modern societies, but rather on the stimuli to unleash the desire to imitate the pattern of consumptions of the models of desire of today's elite.

If as Juan Luis Segundo says, God's revelation isn't a deposit of correct doctrines, but rather a pedagogical process in which human beings 'learn to learn' to be more human,[15] then we are dealing here with the nucleus of tradition and Christian spirituality: the process of learning to be human. To assume a model of being human which demonstrates the ultimate meaning of life and the effort to follow this model and realize its full sense of life, constitute the principal points of spirituality and the concrete concept of revelation.

---

13 On the issue of models of desire, economy and religion, see for example Jung Mo Sung, *Desejo, Mercado e religião*, Petrópolis, Vozes, 1998.

14 J. M. Sung, *Sementes de esperanca: a fé em um mundo em crise*, Petrópolis, Vozes, 2005, chapters 5 and 6.

15 Juan L. Segundo, *El dogma que libera: fe, revelación y magisterio dogmático*, Santander, Sal Terrae, 1989.

Contra capitalist market

The contemporary capitalist economy has kidnapped the commandment of Christian love – by affirming that, in the market, selfishness is the best way to love one's neighbour – and has also kidnapped spirituality, by assuming control in formulating people's fundamental desires. In this sense we can say that the consumerist culture that pervades our society demonstrates capitalism's victory also in the spiritual field. As Featherstone affirms, capitalistic society is 'far from being a profane material world, symbolically impoverished, in which things, goods, and merchandise are dealt with as mere profit', on the contrary, 'consumerist culture produces a vast and muting spread of signs, images and symbols, and these symbols cannot be conceptualized as something merely profane'.[16]

This 'spirituality of consumption' reveals the daily life of this religion which is capitalism, inasmuch as the idolatrous faith of the market is the fundamental structure of the economy and its legitimization. The spirituality of consumption is the spirituality in which the human being seeks to satisfy its thirst for being more and more human through a process of never-ending consumption.

Whoever falls into this spirituality, rich or poor, sees in the shopping centre a 'temple for consumption' – a concept used many years ago by journalists and which has materialized in the very architecture of shopping centres which remind us of religious temples – a privileged place to live this spirituality with deep intensity. As Bauman says, being inside a shopping centre

> produces a true community of unified believers both in their means, as in their values which can be estimated in the logic of their behaviour . . . for all intents and purposes, the place is pure, as pure as religious places of worship and the imagined (or postulated) community.[17]

The other side of the matter is the denial of the humanity of those who do not consume. The poor, the failed consumers, represent the 'demons' that threaten the identity of consumers partly because consumers see projected in the poor their own fears of becoming failed consumers, but mainly because, if the human dignity of the poor who do not consume is ever recognized, this proves that the race after con-

---

16 Mike Featherstone, *Cultura de consumo e pós-modernismo*, São Paulo, Studio Nobel, 1995, pp. 167–8.
17 Zygmunt Bauman, *Modernidade liquida*, Rio de Janeiro, Jorge Zahar Ed., 2001, pp. 117–18.

sumption is not the way for true humanization. Then the culture of consumerism is itself questioned.

For this reason it is necessary to affirm and reaffirm the poor as non-human or as 'demons' who threaten society and civilization. This is the reason that

> being *poor* is considered a crime, and *impoverishment* is considered a result of predisposition or criminal intent – alcohol abuse, drugs, games of chance, vagrancy, laziness. The poor, far from having the right of care and assistance, deserve hatred and condemnation, as the incarnation of sin itself.[18]

This closes the circuit that explains the fascination for *shopping centres* and other forms of ostentatious consumerism, social insensitivity when faced with poverty or at least, the rejection of economic policies of rent redistribution from the rich to the poor, and faith and spirituality which converge from so many people and civilizations when confronted by free market ideology and its false promises.

Towards 'Another World'

What can Christian theology contribute towards the construction of an alternative world? The first step is to expose market idolatry, its sacrificial demands and its dehumanizing spirituality. A second step is the contribution towards the creation of an alternative vision of human beings and the construction of 'Another World'. Due to space constraints in this chapter I will only introduce some initial reflections.

Theology needs to maintain the identity of theological reflection when looking at today's world and the possibilities emerging over the new horizon. When articulating the local and worldwide struggles to overcome the current model of globalization, the theological community must contribute with its specifically theological reflection on the world and the 'liberation practices' and must not fall into the temptation of becoming a second-class economic or social theory.

Of these contributions, I believe a central piece must be the theology of grace, which shows the intrinsic humanity of human beings, as human above and before belonging to any institution and our classification within any social system. In other words, human beings are beings with dignity before entering the market and becoming

---

18 Zygmunt Bauman, *O mal-estar da pós-modernidades*, Rio de Janeiro, Jorge Zahar Ed., 1998, p. 59.

consumers, even when they are excluded from such a market. It is in 'gratuity' that we are human. This also means that it is through gratuitous relations of solidarity with oppressed people and those excluded from society and the market that we become more human. It is in this recognition of the gratuity of the human dignity of all people and in the experience of gratuitous solidarity with others that we experience the grace of God.

This experience of grace drives us to struggle for a more just society, where all people are recognized in dignity and may live with dignity. Meanwhile we must have a clear understanding that grace is not enough to change society. There is the need that our social, political and spiritual struggles be efficient. A just cause carried out in an inefficient way is a just struggle that will be defeated. The issue is that the efficiency of the struggles born from the experience of grace is an enormous challenge to a committed theology for the construction of Another World.

In this struggle for Another World we must remember that struggle against the market system (capitalism) does not mean a struggle for an economy without a market. Big and complex societies like ours need self-organizing social mechanisms within the economic field; this is the market. The challenge is to imagine the tension between social solidarity and the self-organizing market without falling into either idolatry of the market or its demonization.

Even though our struggles are just and we seek more efficiency in our ways, we know social transformations will be much slower than what we would like and what is necessary to save the lives of many people who live on the fringes of death. In this context, it is necessary to be ready to give the reasons of our hope in the midst of defeat, disillusion or setbacks; hope, not born from illusion, but rather born from the experience of human realization in the struggle against a system that dehumanizes. When our struggles humanize us, we may lose in the political and social field, but we are victorious in the spiritual field. In resistance and struggle against dehumanizing processes we become more human, we learn to live as human beings, and this way we find ourselves, with our sisters and brothers and the Spirit of God which blows among us. Living this spirituality we can reconcile our humanity with our human condition and confess that our faith is not justified in the promise of social and political victory; rather we are justified by faith in one who, being God, emptied his divinity and became a servant in the midst of us.

10 Theology And Liberation: The African Agenda

EMMANUEL MARTEY

Introduction

By the close of the twentieth century, the first publication on the modern African theology movement was over 40 years old. It began with the nationalist reflection on Christianity in the mid-1950s by black Roman Catholic priests studying in Europe who, in the spirit of African nationalism, began addressing and questioning the African condition under colonial oppression.[1] This reflection also led the discussion on *Africanization* as a theological justification of the African revolution and the liberation struggles on the continent. Although the theme of liberation was actively present in African politics, it was completely absent in theological discussions at the time. As Mercy Oduyoye has pointed out, the liberation language of theology, 'scandalized many'; and it was seen not just as a political word, but it was also 'a protest word, even a violent word' associated with 'upsetting existing political order which brings with it chaos and insecurity'; and African Christians, having been educated against all that might bring with it confrontation quickly shied away from it.[2]

From the very outset, Africans did not restrict the hermeneutic endeavour to just the biblical text but included the human condition as well as the African world-view, which were also perceived as *texts*,

---

1 See A. Abble et al., *Des Pretres noirs s'interrogent*, Paris, Les Éditions du Cerf, 1956. It was the publication of this book that was considered the starting point of modern African theology.

2 Mercy Oduyoye, 'Liberation and the Development of Theology in Africa' in Marc Reuver, Friedhelm Solma, Gerrit Huizer (eds), *The Ecumenical Movement Tomorrow*, Kampen/Geneva, Kok Publishing House/WCC, 1993, p. 203. For the presence of the theme of liberation in African political thought and action from the colonial times in the nineteenth century, see J. Ayo Langley (ed.), *Ideologies of Liberation in Black Africa, 1856–1970: Documents on Modern African Political Thought from Colonial Times to the Present*, London, Rex Collins, 1979.

thus allowing a comparative study of the many forms of engagement of the gospel of Jesus Christ with the human situation – a human situation which had been drained of its very essence by slavery, colonialism and racism.

Theological discussions of the Africanization paradigm in these early years had contributed immensely in defining the major theological paradigms in contemporary Africa, including *liberation* and *inculturation*. By the close of the twentieth century, three other paradigms had become serious partners in theological dialogue; albeit, they are still in their infant stages. These include *reconstruction* theology, which calls for a paradigm shift from liberation to social transformation and reconstruction, *Pentecostal-charismatic* theology and *African initiated church* theology, both of which emphasize spiritual liberation.[3]

The liberation hermeneutical paradigm

Liberation as a theological paradigm in Africa is a hermeneutic procedure that seeks to understand the African reality and to interpret this reality in the light of the gospel of Jesus Christ to bring transformation of the oppressive status quo. Since the 1970s, liberation has become Africa's acquisition of a new theological self-understanding and has challenged Africans to discover themselves as human beings with *Imago Dei*. But it has also given Africans the determination to participate in God's redemptive act in history. Liberation has therefore become the African theological choice for anthropological dignity over against anthropological poverty. It is a quest for true humanity.

Liberation theology on the continent of Africa has emerged primarily as a response to white racist oppression and Western capitalist imperialism, which have impoverished the African. But again, liberation is also a response to oppression of Africans by Africans as well as of African women by men. All these different forms of oppression have contributed to depriving the African of human dignity.

---

3 For theological articulation of the reconstruction paradigm, see: J. N. K. Mugambi, *From Liberation to Reconstruction: African Christian Theology After the Cold War*, Nairobi, East African Educational Publishers, 1995; for Pentecostal-charismatic theology and African initiated church theology, see Simon Maimela and Andrio Konig (eds), *Initiation into Theology: The Rich Variety of Theology and Hermeneutics*, Pretoria, JL van Schaik, 1998, chapters 10, 11, 12, 24 and 25. The African *initiated* churches (AICs) have been described variously also as African *instituted* churches, African *independent* churches and African *indigenous* churches.

There are different approaches to liberation in Africa, which have given rise to different theological expressions and movements having different histories, emphases and functions. These varieties of liberation address issues of *race, gender, poverty, culture* and *spirituality*, which serve also as the points of departure for their respective theological systems. While the issue of race finds expression in *black theology* in its South African manifestation, that of gender finds expression in *African women's theology*. Poverty also finds expression in the narrowly defined *African liberation theology*, and, culture in *inculturation theology*. Recently, with the training of theologians from the newer *Pentecostal* and *charismatic* churches, emphasis is being placed on spiritual liberation in their theological writings.

Black theology

Black theology was the first liberation oriented theology to appear on the African scene in the early 1970s. It drew most of its initial insight from North American black theology. The keynote of this theology before black majority rule was liberation, with special reference to racism as manifested in the vicious circle of Apartheid. Therefore, the actual situation that gave rise to liberation in South Africa was Apartheid and the need to demolish it as a sociopolitical system. Black theology took seriously the experience of black people, which was grounded in a history of racial oppression and economic exploitation.

Before Apartheid ended officially in 1994, the development of black theology had already seen two different phases. The first phase began in the early 1970s as a theological expression of the Black Consciousness Movement and therefore initially took over the exclusively race-analyst approach into its reflection. At this time, its task was to conscientize black people to the situation in which they were and the situation in which they ought to be – arousing them to become the vehicles of their own liberation.

The second phase began in the 1980s with conferences organized by the Black Theology Task Force of the Institute for Contextual Theology (ICT). Whereas the publication of the book entitled *Essays on Black Theology*[4] formally inaugurated the first phase, the second phase was

---

4 Mokgethi Motlhabi (ed.), *Essays on Black Theology*, Johannesburg, University Christian Movement, 1972. The South African government soon banned this edition. The British edition, Basil Moore (ed.), *Black Theology: The South African Voice*, London, Hurst, 1973, and the American edition, Basil Moore (ed.), *The Challenge of Black Theology in South Africa*, Atlanta, John Knox Press, 1974, were published.

ushered in by the publication of *The Unquestionable Right to be Free: Black Theology from South Africa*.[5]

Unlike the first phase, the second began to take Marxist analysis of South African society very seriously, which brought a sharp (albeit, false) division between the advocates of race-analyst and class-analyst approaches. Besides, there were others who wanted to hold the two in creative tension as the best way to understand the South African situation. Another important factor present in the second phase was the inclusion of feminist perspectives in black theological reflection.

Since the relevance of Black theology is largely determined by the nature of South African reality, with the change of the political environment, there is bound to be a shift into a new phase. The new post-Apartheid phase ushered in by non-racial democracy is challenging black theologians to consider themes such as reconciliation and black empowerment in theological hermeneutics. There are other themes in which the younger generation of black theologians are very interested; these include human rights, political economy, civil society, democracy, secularism, religious freedom and the engagement of culture in all these themes.[6]

African women's theology

African Women's theology is the theological articulation of women's own experiences of sexism and gender inequity in both Church and society. It is de facto a theology of process born out of experience of pain and of women's vision. As such, it is contextual and analyses religion, culture, socio-economic and political realities of Africa.

African women theologians also focus on their own specific challenges and join other women in the analysis, deconstruction, reconstruction and advocacy that foster the healing of human brokenness and transformation of society. Consequently, women theologians are raising uncomfortable questions that confront the androcentric bias which, for a long time, has informed the predominantly patriarchal religious traditions of the Christian faith.

Forming part of women's theological challenge include: the image of God in African womanhood; who Jesus Christ is for the African woman; the true image of the Church; and the rereading of the Bible.

---

5 Itumeleng J. Mosala and Buti Tlhagale (eds), *The Unquestionable Right to be Free: Black Theology from South Africa*, Maryknoll, NY, Orbis Books, 1986.

6 See Tinyiko Maluleke's 'Epilogue' to Xolile Keteyi's *Inculturation as a Strategy for Liberation*, Pietermarizburg, Cluster Publications, 1998, p. 65.

Others are, African cultural history, religion and the sources of spirituality; elements in the fear of sexuality that result in the repudiation of matriarchy; violence against women; and traditional ritualistic processes and practices that are oppressive to women, such as widowhood rites, polygyny, clitoridectomy, bride-wealth/price, purdah and child-marriage.

African women's theology is unleashing a new dynamic that should vitalize African theological hermeneutics. This is made possible mainly by The Circle of Concerned African Women Theologians (The Circle) which is, perhaps, the most active theological group in Africa today. In this movement even women theologians 'who would not use the language of revolution are also writing with emphasis on "psychic liberation" and "internal transformation"'. Oduyoye explains the rationale behind this approach:

> Liberation on the mentality that keeps women coping with marginalization and repression rather than resisting it has become an area of much reflection. Several have turned to the study of African Traditional Religion and Culture as a source of both empowerment and dehumanization of women. Studying this undergirding factor of life in Africa, is required, if the liberating aspects are to be fully appropriated and the oppressive ones exposed and disposed of.[7]

Inculturation as strategy for liberation

In one way or other, we have all participated in the fruitless inculturation–liberation debate within the context of Ecumenical Association of Third World Theologians (EATWOT). Within the Asian context, for example, I recall the debate between theologians from the Philippines with Carlos Abesamis as their spokesperson and the Sri Lankan theologian Aloysius Pieris at EATWOT's Asian Theological Conference in Wennapuwa in 1979.[8] Again, the tension between African theologians and Latin Americans on the one hand and, on the other hand, between African and black theologians on both sides of the Atlantic are well documented.[9]

---

7 Mercy Oduyoye, 'Liberation and Development of Theology in Africa,' p. 209.

8 For details, see Virginia Fabella (ed.), *Asia's Struggle for Full Humanity*, Maryknoll, NY, Orbis Books, 1980.

9 For details of all these debates, see Kofi Appiah Kubi and Sergio Torres (eds), *African Theology En Route*, Maryknoll, NY, Orbis Books, 1979; Sergio Torres and John Eagleson (eds), *The Challenge of Basic Christian Communi-*

In Africa, as a result of this tension, culture was not seen in a comprehensive way. An artificial gap was created, separating culture from politics and socio-economic relations. Inculturation and liberation became two different and opposing theological paradigms. The former was seen as a mutual interaction or dialogue between culture and the gospel, emphasizing the traditional way of life; and the latter between the gospel and sociopolitical realities, addressing the influence of modernity and the Western way of life.

What most competitors in this debate failed to recognize was that the problems being addressed by both inculturation and liberation were the same *African problem*, with each approaching it from a different perspective. But the path each chose ended up providing only a one-sided solution to this problem. What was lacking at this initial stage was a fruitful dialogue between the two that would foster mutual appreciation of what each was and could offer in service to Africa. Furthermore, both were unable to find common ground from where to agree and proceed to act in harmony to undermine and dismantle the structures of death and decay.

In Africa, therefore, inculturation is not to be seen as one thing and liberation another. That is why today, many Christians in Africa, especially new-generation theologians (even from South Africa), have come to appreciate culture 'for the purposes of conducting a dialogue with Christianity.'[10] The same young theologians are those on whom the influence of liberation has been so great.

The cultural strength of African people cannot be ignored or underestimated. The mistake the early missionaries and colonial administrators made in their contact with Africans was to attempt to obliterate the African cultural identity. The foundation of a people's liberation, according to Amilcar Cabral, is in their inalienable rights to have their own history whose continuity lies in culture. That is why in Africa, liberation is necessarily an act of culture; and the liberation movement in Africa has been seen by theorists and analysts as 'the organized political expression of the struggling people's culture.'[11]

---

ties, Maryknoll, NY, Orbis Books, 1982; Virginia Fabella and Sergio Torres (eds), *Irruption of the Third World: Challenge to Theology*, Maryknoll, NY, Orbis Books, 1983; Emmanuel Martey, 'African Theology and Latin American Liberation Theology: Initial Differences Within the Context of EATWOT', *Trinity Journal of Church and Theology*, Vol. V, Nos 1 & 2, July 1995, pp. 45–63, also his 'An African Examines Trends in Asian Christian Theology', *Trinity Journal of Church and Theology*, Vol. VI, No. 1, January 1996, pp. 24–36.

10 Keteyi, *Inculturation as a Strategy for Liberation*, p. 51.

11 Amilcar Cabral, *Unity and Struggle: Speeches and Writings*, New York, Monthly Review Press, 1979, p. 143.

Africans take both culture and the gospel as active forces of liberation. It is this dual fact of theological understanding in the dialogical process of inculturation that culture and the gospel of Jesus Christ increase the African passion for liberation. Inculturation then becomes empowerment and a strategy for liberation.

Inculturation is liberative in that in the process of dialogue, it recognizes the oppressive and anti-life components in both culture and the Bible, which are then challenged, critiqued and transformed. With such an understanding and a new look of inculturation and liberation, the long debate and division between the two is made inefficacious. With the formulation of inculturation as a strategy for liberation by a new generation of theologians, we have the problem addressed in a non-evasive and creative manner.[12]

In Africa, dialogue between culture and the Christian faith has exposed and is undermining all negative and oppressive elements in culture, especially those that dehumanize women. Besides, it has also led to an inculturated-liberative reading of Scripture that brings to light not just its patriarchal orientation but also its ideological and racist outlook. Such rereading of the Bible, as has been demonstrated by theologians like Teresa Okure, has disclosed the sinful human and sociocultural conditions that have often distorted the constitutive voice of God.[13]

Reconstruction as an act of liberation

Reconstruction as a theological paradigm began gaining currency in the late 1980s and, especially, the early 1990s. At its Fifth General Assembly in Lome (1987), the All Africa Conference of Churches (AACC) favoured theology of reconstruction as a way forward and began advocating for it, especially when it became clear that Apartheid was coming to an end and therefore a new theological paradigm apart from liberation might be necessary.

---

12 The two young theologians from South Africa, Xolile Keteyi and Tinyiko Maluleke are among those who have stressed this point; see Keteyi, *Inculturation as a Strategy for Liberation*, pp. 50–56, 62.

13 See Teresa Okure, 'Bible: Africa' in *Dictionary of Third World Theologies*, Virginia Fabella and R. S. Sugirtharajah (eds), Maryknoll, NY, Orbis Books, 2000, p. 16; also her 'Women in the Bible' in Virginia Fabella and Mercy Amba Oduyoye (eds), *With Passion and Compassion: Third World Women Doing Theology*, Maryknoll, NY, Orbis Books 1988. See also Itumeleng J. Mosals, *Biblical Hermeneutics and Black Theology in South Africa*, Grand Rapids, Michigan, Eerdmans, 1989; and his 'The Use of the Bible in Black Theology' in Mosala and Tlhagale (eds), *The Unquestionable Right to be Free*, pp. 175–99.

The African theologian with whom the theology of reconstruction is largely associated is Jesse Mugambi, who in his address to the Executive Committee of AACC in Nairobi proposed a paradigm shift from the post-Exodus to post-Exile imagery for Africa. He saw *reconstruction* as the resultant theological axiom, thus shifting the emphasis from liberation, as indicated in the title of his book *From Liberation to Reconstruction*.[14] Mugambi is convinced that; 'the twenty-first century should be a century of reconstruction in Africa, building on old foundations which, though strong, may have to be renovated.'[15] He compared the fifteenth- and sixteenth-century secular and ecclesial contexts of Europe with their respective awakenings of the Renaissance and the Reformation and declares:

The 1990s are the beginning of Africa's Renaissance and Reformation. They will commence the process of Africa's reconstruction.[16]

In this shift, the post-exilic text that becomes the centre for 'the new theological paradigm in African Christian theology as a logical development from the Exodus motif' is the book of Nehemiah. Mugambi sees Nehemiah as 'the director of reconstruction project' after the Babylonian exile. In this new paradigm, Jesus' mission is seen to be 'reconstructive rather than destructive' and the Sermon on the Mount regarded as 'the most basic of all reconstructive theological texts in the Synoptic Gospels'.[17]

Mugambi identifies three levels of reconstruction covering all areas of societal life. First, there is the *personal*, which deals with the reconstruction of individual motives and intentions. The second is *ecclesial* reconstruction dealing with all areas of the church's life, including 'management structures, financial policies, pastoral care, human resource development, research, family education, service and witness'. He then sees theology as 'the means by which the church rationalizes its process of ecclesial reconstruction'.[18] The third is *cultural* reconstruction, which has five components of (i) *politics* dealing with the management of social influence; (ii) *economics* dealing in matters of managing resources; (iii) *ethics* dealing with the reconstruction of the

---

14 J. N. K. Mugambi, *From Liberation to Reconstruction: African Christian Theology After the Cold War*, Nairobi, East African Educational Publishers, 1995.

15 Mugambi, *From Liberation*, p. 5, cf. p. 40.

16 Mugambi, *From Liberation*, p. 5, cf. p. 41.

17 Mugambi, *From Liberation*, p. 13.

18 Mugambi, *From Liberation*, 17.

system of values; (iv) *aesthetics* dealing with the sense of proportion and symmetry in all aspects of life; and, (v) *religion*, which provides the world-view synthesizing 'everything that is cherished by individuals as corporate members of the community'.[19] Reconstruction in Africa therefore refers to actions taken in all the different dimensions of societal life and not just in one particular sector of human existence. It is thus a praxis embracing many practices within the social realm.[20]

In the discussion of reconstruction as a theological paradigm on the continent, two important events have taken place within the theological community of the African Church which should be worth mentioning. The first was the 2000 Theological Conference held in Mbagathi, Nairobi, Kenya where for the first time representatives from the Conference of African Theological Institutions (CATI), the All Africa Conference of Churches (AACC), the Ecumenical Association of Third World Theologians (EATWOT), The Circle of Concerned African Women Theologians (The Circle) and the Organization of African Instituted Churches (OAIC) met to clarify their role in the service of the Church and the wider community.

At Mbagathi, the tension between liberation and reconstruction became obvious when black theologians from South Africa, including Takatso Mofokeng and Tinyiko Maluleke, expressed dissatisfaction with Mugambi's attempt to downplay and underestimate the importance of liberation for Africa's social transformation and development. Reconstruction, it is argued, must begin with liberation and all Africans are not yet liberated. For EATWOT members at the meeting, the movement from liberation to reconstruction was not from EATWOT. According to the EATWOT women present, if there was any movement, it was 'from liberation to spirituality' because women's power to bring about change comes from the Holy Spirit. On the theology of reconstruction, one female participant said: 'I am still reading and I cannot relate to it.' On the other hand, there were other participants who also argued that the end of Apartheid should oblige theologians to think of a new paradigm; theology, they contended, 'is above liberation and God is above all'.

The Final Communiqué of this conference brought out the division among members of the African theological community. It declared:

We note that the paradigm of reconstruction has gained wide currency as a model of theological thinking in our contemporary

19 Mugambi, *From Liberation*, pp. 16–17.
20 See Joao B. Libanio, 'Praxis/Orthopraxis' in Fabella and Sugirtharajah (eds), *Dictionary of Third World Theologies*, p. 172.

situation, but for many of us it needs further elaboration and reflection, particularly on the relationship between liberation and reconstruction.[21]

The importance of the Mbagathi meeting was that it put the accent on *both* liberation and reconstruction. Africa needs both emphases for meaningful social transformation and development. Reconstruction is about human development and as such cannot be separated from liberation; for, reconstruction in itself, it was concluded, 'is an act of liberation'.

The second important event regarding Africa's discussion of reconstruction as a theological paradigm took place in 2002 in South Africa during the Conference on Theological Education and Ecumenical Formation, which was part of the interactive process to embark on the Journey of Hope in Africa to make a difference on the continent in the twenty-first century.[22] Unlike the Mbagathi meeting, where there was apparent division between liberation and reconstruction, this conference saw both as complementary and envisioned a journey of hope 'for Africa's *liberative reconstruction* and sustainable development'.[23]

Liberative-reconstruction and Africa's development initiatives

Africa is trapped in poverty. Her poverty stands in stark contrast to the affluence of the developed world. Tears shed by the Church in South Africa five years ago are still the tears being shed by the whole ecclesial community on the continent: one-third of the world's poorest people lived in Africa and although the continent comprises 10 per cent of the world's population, 75 per cent of all people living with HIV/AIDS were in sub-Saharan Africa. It continued,

> One in thirteen African women dies during pregnancy or child-birth, representing nearly half of such deaths worldwide. Nineteen thousand children die in Africa each day as a result of preventable

21 See the 'Final Communiqué' of the CATI/AACC/EATWOT/CIRCLE/ OAIC Conference held at Mbagathi, Nairobi, Kenya, 14–17 August 2000.

22 This conference, which was organized by the World Council of Churches Education and Ecumenical Formation Team (WCC-EEFT), took place 17–22 September 2002 at Kempton Park, Lutheran Conference Centre, Gauteng Province, South Africa.

23 WCC, 'Plan of Action' for the Conference on Theological Education and Ecumenical Formation entitled 'The Journey of Hope in Africa' held 17–22 September 2002 in South Africa, p. 3.

diseases and malnutrition . . . [and] most African nations are ill-equipped to overcome these proplems.[24]

It is such situations prevailing on the continent that compel both ecclesial and theological communities in Africa to share the common vision and pledge of the new generation of African political leaders to combat and eradicate poverty and the culture of death and decay as envisioned in the New Partnership for Africa's Development (NEPAD) plan.[25]

NEPAD is the vision and initiative of African political leaders who have pledged to eradicate poverty; place the continent on a path of sustainable growth and development; participate in global economy and body politic; and liberate Africa from 'the malaise of underdevelopment and exclusion in a globalizing world'.[26]

Presenting itself as a visionary and dynamic initiative seeking to reconstruct and develop the continent, NEPAD condemns the logic of credit and aid binomial that has underlined African development efforts. This is an abnormal situation and there is the need for its reversal. It cautions against the continued marginalization of Africa from the globalizing process; and says this constitutes a serious threat to global stability. NEPAD therefore calls for

> a new relationship of partnership between Africa and the international community, especially the highly industrialized countries, to overcome the development chasm that has widened over centuries of unequal relations.[27]

Furthermore, NEPAD declares that Africans 'will no longer allow themselves to be conditioned by circumstances. We will determine

---

24 South African Churches, *Un-blurring the Vision: An Assessment of the New Partnership for Africa's Development*, Johannesburg, SACC/SABCBC, 2000, p. 9. See also the Final Declaration of Committee on HIV/AIDS of the 26th United Nations General Assembly Special Session, 27 June 2001; *Africa Recovery*, vol. 16 no. 1, April 2002; see also www.un.org for the United Nations Development Programmes etc.

25 For a comprehensive African Church's response to the New Partnership for Africa's Development (NEPAD) initiative, see *Un-blurring the Vision*; and for the whole African theological community's response, see the 'Plan of Action' for the Conference on Theological Education and Ecumenical Formation on The Journey of Hope in Africa, 2002.

26 Department of Foreign Affairs – Republic of South Africa, *Part I: Constitutive Act of the African Union (AU), Part 2: New Partnership for Africa's Development (NEPAD)*, p. 17, henceforth referred to as the NEPAD Document.

27 NEPAD Document, paragraph 8, p. 8.

our own destiny and call on the rest of the world to complement our efforts.'[28]

The importance of NEPAD is contained in the fact that it is the only comprehensive, long-range plan for Africa's development that has received support from both African political leaders and developed countries. Besides, it is the only continental development plan that, despite its weaknesses, has been hailed by both the ecclesial and theological communities in Africa. Others, like the Lagos Plan of Action and the Lome Conventions did not enjoy such ecclesial and theological support. For instance, questions as to how NEPAD could help fulfil Christ's promise of meaningful and abundant life for all African people; or what kind of theological principles should be emphasized in assessing NEPAD's development initiatives and others have been asked and discussed.

The commitment of the theological community of the African Church was demonstrably established when at the 2002 Conference in South Africa, bishops, patriarchs and other Church leaders committed themselves and pledged to disseminate the NEPAD vision and information to the grassroots. The 'Plan of Action' of this Conference declared:

> It is the Christian church's mission in fulfilling Christ's promise of meaningful and abundant life for all of Africa's people that compels us to engage critically with NEPAD in a spirit of mutual responsibility and commitment to Africa's reconstruction and development.[29]

Although the NEPAD document itself hardly uses the term 'reconstruction', theological responses from both ecclesial and theological communities in Africa emphasize liberative-reconstruction as a theological principle in assessing the initiative. For example, according to the South African churches, 'NEPAD contains several important elements that could be further developed into effective mechanisms for Africa's reconstruction and development.'[30]

For all its promises and capabilities to transform Africa into a continent of peace and prosperity, NEPAD has not escaped criticisms. The most systematic and constructive criticism has come from the South African Council of Churches, which accused NEPAD of having 'a blurred vision' when it focused on globalization, privatization and its

---

28 NEPAD Document, par. 7, p. 8.
29 WCC, 'Plan of Action', p. 3.
30 *Un-blurring the Vision*, p. 25, cf. pp. 7, 10, 26, 27, 29.

failure to engage the people of Africa to solve Africa's problems.[31] The Council further explained,

> . . . NEPAD's vision is blurred when it attempts to identify new resources for Africa's reconstruction. It fails to see beyond the self-serving economic prescriptions proffered by an industrialized world that has grown rich off the plunder of Africa . . . The political will generated by NEPAD must be focused into a truly participatory transformation of Africa through direct, immediate, and decisive action to overcome the causes of Africa's deepening impoverishment.[32]

By fixing its eyes on increased global integration, NEPAD indeed has a blurred vision and must be helped to restore its vision. For those of us coming from the underside of history, globalization has become a notorious term. It is a concept that has come to be associated with paternalism and domination. To some it is only a smokescreen and a cover up for a dominant culture to absorb and dominate the rest of the world. To others, it is the latest stage of capitalist imperialism. NEPAD cannot also pretend to be unaware of the severe negative impact that privatization of basic and social services has on poor people in Africa. Again, failure to focus 'on Africa's people first . . . can result in an increasingly divided Africa at the continental and national levels'.[33]

The way NEPAD has presented itself as a visionary and dynamic initiative seeking to reconstruct and develop the continent challenges all African theological communities. We also must try to find the strengths and weaknesses of this plan and help un-blur its vision to promote authentic liberative-reconstruction that will bring meaningful social transformation and development of Africa.

Conclusion

In Africa, as Oduyoye has observed, we have come to see paradigms of liberation and transformation, 'not only in the experiences of God recorded in the Bible but also in our African history, religion and struggle to be whole'. Africa's participation in 'the liberation of theology, the theology of liberation and in liberative theology, liberates and

---

31 *Un-blurring the Vision*, pp. 7f.
32 *Un-blurring the Vision*, p. 10.
33 *Un-blurring the Vision*, p. 8

empowers us'.[34] And it is this liberation and empowerment coming from the Trinitarian God of love, grace and hope that has given us the spirit of resilience not only to survive all kinds of dehumanizing and death-dealing forces but also to join all those who seek to transform all forces of death and decay to bring humankind life in its fullness.

34 Oduyoye, 'Liberation and the Development of Theology in Africa', p. 209.

11 Theologies in the USA

DWIGHT HOPKINS

At the beginning of the twenty-first century, we can point to, at least, four theological models in the United States of North America: neo-conservative theology, liberal theology, the religion of US monopoly capitalism and prophetic theology.

Neoconservative theology

Neoconservative theology is the main form of theology in the USA today. Its basic theological anthropology is the following: the purpose of an American citizen is to fight for the global supremacy of US dominance. The God of neoconservative theology is the *open face of aggressive US empire*. Or to put it in different words: God has called the USA to make the rest of the world into the image of the United States. The rise of neoconservative theological anthropology has been aided by the fact that the Union of Soviet Socialist Republics no longer exists. Neoconservatives believe that the United States represents God and the USSR represents Satan. Because the USSR no longer exists, it means that Satan has been defeated by God's kingdom, which is the 'American way of life'. Neoconservatives believe that it was their Cold War policy against the USSR that caused its decline. And since their policy was correct, it is their right now to spread their type of theological anthropology globally. This is what is taking place throughout the world. Without the USSR and without cohesive networks of resistance in the Second and Third worlds or domestically within the USA itself, neoconservatives argue that just as God made the USA in God's image, then the USA is going to make the rest of the world in its own image.

Domestically within the United States, the neoconservative theological anthropology has two major human values. First is the value that states that the USA as a country is *number one in the world*. It is number one because neoconservatives claim that no other country can rival the sheer power and strength of the USA. This feeling of 'number one' reveals itself in the military occupation of countries in the Third World. It is also shown in the religious fever displayed at international sports events like the Olympic competitions. To be number one is to have a feeling of absolute supremacy. If any country or non-Americans challenge or disagree with this neoconservative theology, then they will be totally destroyed.

A second value in the theological anthropology of the neoconservatives is their belief that not only is the USA number one, but it is also the *best country in the world*. If it is the best country globally, then the rest of the world is both secondary and inferior. These two values combine to produce a unique American arrogance in American spirituality. These spiritual values assume that the USA is always right; that the USA never has to admit a mistake; that when an American wants something done, it should be done immediately; and that the only real rules and ethics are those defined by the USA. Neoconservatives can also be generous and show concern for the poor. But if the poor want to determine their own humanity or if another country has a disagreement with the USA, then the neoconservative spiritual generosity is withdrawn or it is turned into a spirituality of vengeance.

Finally, neoconservative theological anthropology argues that each US citizen should make it on their own without help from the government. They also state that those who have wealth are the best examples of how to work hard and make it on their own. These images of a human being have two implications. The government is moving away from providing safety nets for the majority of its citizens. Instead the government is calling for more and more privatization of social services. Second, neoconservatives are carrying out a major restructuring of the US economy and social policies where wealth is being radically redistributed upward. Workers are losing benefits. The taxes of ordinary people are being used to give to corporations. The class divide between working people and the wealthy is increasing. Again, the ideal theological anthropology is the small group of wealthy in the USA who should be granted increased wealth. Because they are the ideal of what a person should be, their success somehow will trickle down to the majority of US citizens.

Nor is this re-shifting of US society just on the economic level. It is, in addition, a restructuring on the social level. The gains of people of colour (or minority communities), women's rights, lesbian and gay citizens, unions, the environment, regulations against corporate monopolies, freedom of speech (and other bourgeois rights) and more are all under attack in an open and aggressive manner.

Neoconservative theology is a justification for a form of Christianity that does not allow for any type of public discussion that disagrees with it. In this example, Christianity is one official party line. The party line becomes public through the neoconservatives who control various aspects of government and the media. In fact, when someone does disagree with them, neoconservatives attack others as being Christian 'heretics', or falsely subordinating Christianity to 'secularism', or not being 'patriotic' because to disagree with neoconservatism is to disagree with the definition of what it means to be an American citizen. Thus, it is to disagree with the special calling that God has given to the USA.

Liberal theology

The second major theology in the USA is liberalism. It too has a theological anthropology linked to a conception of God. Its God consists of a return to the foundations of the bourgeois revolution of North America in the eighteenth century. In a word, its God is *bourgeois rights*. Here the purpose of an American citizen (that is, what does it mean to be called by the God of bourgeois rights) is to fight against those attacks on individual freedoms: such as individual free speech, assembly, separation of Church and state, freedom to worship (as long as it does not affect the public realm), freedom to debate different ideas in the public, the right to work, women's rights, the rights of minority citizens of different colours, the right to vote, the right to privately own wealth and property, responsibility of the wealthy to those who are suffering, the importance of using reason when there are differences of opinion and the view that government should represent all the people. We can restate a liberal theological anthropology in the following way: the God of bourgeois rights has called all human beings to come together around a common table and be fair to one another. And part of being fair is to be sensitive to those who are at the bottom of society.

Like the neoconservative theology, liberal theological anthropology believes that the image of US citizens should be the global model for how people should relate to one another. Liberal theology, furthermore, agrees that the Cold War was necessary and the decline of the USSR is evidence that the global model for human beings is the USA because it is the only superpower throughout the world. The difference between neoconservative theology and liberal theology is around the nature of God and what this God has called human beings to do. What liberal theology wants to spread around the world are bourgeois rights as defined by the United States: individual rights, freedom of religion, the importance of public debates based on who can use reason to persuade others, the right to vote for two bourgeois parties, free trade, US culture, the right to private ownership of wealth and property, etc. The decline of the USSR and the rise of one superpower has not meant that liberal theology now calls for the USA to pull back from the global scene. Nor does liberal theology support different countries in their efforts to pursue their own way forward. Liberal theology is for advancing the God of bourgeois rights, best revealed in the US way of life. This God is the US style of democracy.

Domestically within the United States, liberal theology has a theological anthropology that is inherently a contradiction. On the one hand, humans are called by a higher goal to pursue bourgeois rights, which means maintaining individual freedoms for all Americans regardless of their class, racial or gender status. This aspect emphasizes the 'rights' part of bourgeois rights. Here we find liberal theology arguing for racial and ethnic minorities, women, labour unions, the environment, etc. On the other hand, humans are called to affirm the bourgeois structures that the USA is founded on. This means that liberals affirm the right to private ownership and accumulation and monopolization of wealth and property. Here we find the emphasis on the 'bourgeois' part. The ideal theological anthropology for liberal theology is a person who can balance this contradiction so that everyone enjoys a fair and just way of life. Despite the best intentions of liberal theology, it fails to see that the God of bourgeois rights includes an antagonistic contradiction. Bourgeois rights, first of all, maintain a preferential option for the bourgeoisie – those who own the most property and capital in the USA. Because the majority of people cannot attain the ideal status of becoming a bourgeois person (which means they would enjoy the full rights of liberal theology's God), liberal theology usually supports only reforms for the marginalized, and never questions the God of bourgeois rights itself.

A major spiritual value of liberal theology is that every American (regardless if one is an oppressor or oppressed) has the *right to their own views*. But the God of bourgeois rights has already sided with the bourgeois sectors of US society. It is not a level playing field for all US citizens when it comes to who has the resources to make their views known in the public realm. A second spiritual value is *fairness*. But again we see the contradiction between 'bourgeois' and 'rights' come to the surface. At first it sounds good that all US citizens are called by the God of bourgeois rights to be fair. Yet, all citizens can enjoy the fairness of their rights as long as these citizens do not threaten bourgeois privileges and the government that supports those privileges. The values of free expression and fairness are not objective; they are ultimately in favour of bourgeois sectors of society.

Because a liberal theological anthropology contains a deep contradiction internal to what it means to be a human, liberal theology cannot take a firm stand on fundamental fights. Because it too often takes different positions on the same issue and because of the strong, unified force of neoconservative theology, liberal theology cannot mount a successful defeat of neoconservative theology's drive to restructure the entire economy and social arrangements in the USA.

The religion of US monopoly capitalism

Both neoconservative and liberal theologies operate within a larger religious context that liberals and neoconservatives both support. Specifically, I argue that US monopoly capitalism itself is a religion. The God of this religion is the *concentration of monopoly finance capitalist wealth*. God, in this sense, is not merely a belief in the accumulation of capital for private possession by owners operating inside one country; that stage is a lower one in the development of capitalism. On the contrary, the God of monopoly finance capitalist wealth embodies the ultimate concern where there is a fierce belief in the intense concentration, in a few hands, of finance capitalism on the world stage. It is an extreme expression of the private ownership and control of capital in various forms of wealth spurred on by the rapid movement of finance and capital on a global scale. Monopoly wealth is a power in its own right that makes its adherents bow down to it and pursue any means necessary to obtain it. All who believe in it are possessed by it; it is the final goal above all else.

Like all religions, the religion of US monopoly capitalism advances a theological anthropology. (Theological anthropology defines and regulates what it means to be a human being in a religious system.) What does a God require of human beings in order for them to be human? Such a human being is one who has the most concentrated financial wealth accumulation on a global scale. Ideally, since religions have an inclination for utopia, a small group would control the world's capital. Here capital includes both the majority of the human population – real people – and the environment – the Earth's natural and human-made resources. In the future utopia on Earth, all social relations among human beings will be defined by the God of concentrated wealth. In other words, to be a human being is to fit on an unequal scale of wealth ownership. Wealth redistribution goes upward into the possession of a small group of citizens.

In contrast, theological anthropology for the majority of the world suggests another reality of what it means to be human in the religion of US monopoly capitalism. Prior to the arrival of this religion, especially in Third World indigenous communities, human beings were valued for who they were as members of the human race created by some divine power. Now this global religion rebaptizes them into a new man and woman, where the measure of worth becomes what one consumes. The US global religion forges new tastes and sensibilities throughout the world while it attempts to manufacture one transcendent culture – the culture of market consumption. A true human being becomes one who actually possesses commodities or one whose goal in life is to do so. Despite the fact that the vast majority of Third World peoples live in poverty, the religion of US monopoly capitalism attempts to transform them into adherents of the faith by inducing in them a desire to perceive themselves as owning the products from the developed capitalist world. This fact touches the core issue of the new religion, which wants people not only to purchase products but to reconceive of themselves as people. To change into something new, various groups must, besides redirecting their purchasing habits, re-feel who they are in the present and re-envision their possibilities for the future. Communities are baptized into a lifestyle to fulfil the desire for commodities and to follow further the commodification of desires.

Globalization pursues relentlessly this refashioning of the new man and woman throughout the globe. It seeks a homogenized monoculture of the market to bring about the transformation of people who are valued in themselves to people who are determined by their dependency on commodities. A world culture producing one definition of what it means to be a human being is predicated on serving the market.

The spreading of different values is closely linked to theological anthropology. As one redefines oneself, by accepting the new religion's re-creation of the human person, one internalizes values appropriate to the new man or woman. The point of the religion of US monopoly capitalism is to craft new values to accompany the new person. First is the value of individualism. If monopoly finance capitalist wealth is to succeed as the new God throughout the Earth, it has to erase the idea, particularly in Third World indigenous cultures, that the individual is linked to, defined by, accountable to and responsible for his or her family and extended family. A sense of communalism and sacrifice of individual gain for the sake of a larger community stands in stark contradiction to the new religion of US monopoly capitalism.

Once an individual converts to the new religion and reorients his or her self-worth and feeling of worthiness to a mode of individual gain, regardless of the well-being of those around him or her, this person has successfully undergone the rite of confirmation into the new religion and has accepted faith in the new God as a personal lord and saviour. The value of individualism (e.g. individual gain by any means necessary) is central to the God of monopoly finance capitalism.

Individualism opens up the additional value of accumulation of things for the individual's primary benefit. In other words, gaining and amassing personal possession as a means of acquiring more personal possessions flows from a focus on the self for the self. This acquisitive desire manifests itself in diverse ways. It downplays sharing. It weakens the art of negotiation and compromise. It blinds a vision of mutuality. And it fosters a utilitarian way of being in the world where people, places, and things become tools for and stepping-stones toward increased personal profit.

Prophetic theology

This is the final model of theologies in the USA. In the absence of sustained, massive movements on the part of ordinary people, prophetic theology is hard to observe. Yet there are pockets of prophetic theology on the local level. Prophetic theology conceives of God as liberation toward the practice of freedom. Therefore theological anthropology understands itself to be called by God to work in liberation struggles in order to produce freedom, especially for the poor, working people, the brokenhearted and the marginalized. Prophetic theology works for a holistic liberation and freedom – where the wounded spirituality of the individual is transformed at the same time that demonic social structures are radically altered.

And prophetic theology organizes on several levels simultaneously and not sequentially. It is concerned about the liberation of and practice of freedom of working people, races and ethnic groups, women, lesbians and gays, and the environment. Because the eventual practice of freedom means each individual person having a healed spirit while participating in new social structures defined as a common wealth, then prophetic theology struggles for spiritual and material freedom.

In the academic arena, we see prophetic theology being taught by US minorities of the Ecumenical Association of Third World Theologians (EATWOT), white feminists and a very small group of professors developing a white theology of liberation.

On the Church level, a small progressive group of churches are prac-tising a prophetic theological anthropology – they preach a holistic gospel of individual spiritual change and structural change. Prophetic theology, as a larger movement, is manifested in the Samuel DeWitt Proctor Conference. This conference is a national network of the most progressive wing of the African American churches. Each year it brings together pastors, lay leaders, seminary students and professors, men and women, to discuss the theology and practice of justice, freedom, ethics and politics relative to personal liberation and domestic and international issues. It defines personal salvation as a process linked to the well-being of community. Furthermore, these black religious gatherings are very concerned about the survival and self-determina-tion of Third World countries. In fact, the Proctor Conference was initiated and sustained by the leadership of prophetic African Ameri-can pastors across the USA. Various congregations within this national network have ministries dealing with working people, the poor, racial and ethnic communities, the environment, and women. Some have ventured out to heal the brokenhearted among black gay and lesbian Christians. Moreover, they are actively making connections with liberation theologians worldwide. Though small, it is with prophetic theology, especially where it continues to root itself among working people, where a better world is possible.

Although the one world superpower has advanced its demonic dimensions of globalization, empire is both most dangerous and most vulnerable when it allows no dissent. When the dragon removes even the pretence of bourgeois rights and international co-operation, it is approaching the end of its rule. For, if it could rule its own people and the rest of the globe with a smile, then it would be at its strongest point. Only when it is wounded and losing its grip on exploited peoples and oppressed nations will it resort to open, brute intimidation both abroad and at home. But human history and God's role in human history have shown that ultimately it is the peoples' struggles that yield a new social configuration where the human person becomes the defining criterion of healthy social relations and a spirituality of compassion and global friendship. Now is the opportune time to intensify the work toward justice and build even stronger international bonds among prophetic theologies of all kinds. Even in the midst of storm clouds in the mid-night hour, we know that joy will come in the morning. The Lord will make a way out of no way.

12 Notes on God and Gender

ELSA TÁMEZ

Starting point

We begin with two historical confirmations: the murder of women and the feminization of poverty. We all know that women are being murdered in a systematic way. The data is horrific. In Guatemala, a country of one million inhabitants, over 400 women were murdered by their husbands, concubines, lovers or partners. In Ciudad Juarez, young dead bodies appear in useless empty plots. A third of women in Latin America are physically attacked, as happens in other countries, rich and poor. We also know, due to official statistics, that poverty has a woman's face; there is a feminization of poverty.

These crucial issues against women must be the starting point for thinking about God and gender in a conference motivated by the hope that 'Another World' is possible.

For women, beginning from these very grave issues does not imply asking what theology has to say about them, or what the Church is doing to avoid feminicides. It implies rather asking the question of in what way the Church is an accomplice to these murders and to what degree Christian theology legitimizes these murders. It also implies asking why there is no efficiency in liberating theological discourse to bring this evil to an end. Theologically, it is not a question of reflecting on the silences of God in the face of the suffering of women; rather the question should be what God, what images do we have of God in the society in which we live and to what point do these images contribute to feminicides?

In this sense the methodological contribution of liberation theologies is crucial to rethinking the issue of God and gender as second act of a discriminatory and murderous experience against women.

The feminist theologies insist that society, educational institutions, the Church, the Bible and theology are patriarchal. This means that the masculine is placed in the centre as the 'principle for organizing society, culture and religion'. The problem is not only that this principle is masculine, but that it is absolutely hierarchical.

The fundamental problem here is that 'male is assumed as a superior entity and woman as inferior'. This phrase, repeated till exhaustion, becomes trite and causes no impact; men will once again say 'not more of this again, there is nothing new in the discourse of women'. And yet, this simple belief, considered to be true, assumed both consciously and subconsciously, breathed in all fields, is the cause of murders and of the permissiveness granted to all society with its institutions, its epistemology, its religion and theology.

To create a truly liberating theological discourse we must be honest with reality, which is the starting point, this means to say, the murder of women and the feminization of poverty result from society, Church and patriarchal theology. How can we then have any authority to speak against feminicide if our theology and churches are patriarchal? What degree of efficiency do we achieve if God is presented with patriarchal language which excludes women or subjects them to obedience?

God and gender

For liberation theologies, reality as a starting point is central to being able to speak or think about God. If we begin talking of God and gender, independently of reality, we can fall into a discussion which has no crucial incidence in the search for a theology for a world that will not kill nor exclude women.

We need a theology that does not serve as the base or the foundation for feminicide or exclusion. Is this theology possible? It is not within the framework inherited from the Judaeo-Christian tradition, or within traditional liberation theology. In the same way that it is not believed that 'Another World' is possible within the current parameters of economic globalization, it is not believed that a theology that is not transformed from its roots will be possible for a world in which women are not murdered.

We can ask ourselves: Does it make any sense to discuss the gender of God? Probably for male theologians it is irrelevant, yet for women it is fundamental. It encloses a profound complexity which demands being dealt with due to the described reality; which is feminicide and feminization of poverty.

One of the contradictions of Christian theology is that it affirms the transcendence of God as divinity with no gender, but in its concrete manifestation it takes on the features of a masculine God. It is said that all, men and women, are created in the image of God, but in the incarnation the divine manifestation is interpreted as masculine; and from a tangential reality – Jesus is Jewish and male – a dogma is created by which women cannot be ordained. If for centuries the Church has been governed by men and the majority of theologians have been male, and we live in a patriarchal society, obviously the dominant images of God, the discursive structures, the imaginary on God, is masculine and patriarchal. The good news is that women theologians, who have been incorporated into theological activity over the last few decades, perceive this and question it.

Theology manifests itself in human language, and language has the cultural marks of whoever expresses it. This way, the images of God so often reflect the experiences of those who evoke them. If the predominant image of God is male and father, it is because society grounds itself and turns round this patriarchal axis. God as father, judge, chief, king of kings, lord of lords subconsciously reinforces the power and control which men have in patriarchal society.

When reading feminist theology from Africa, Asia, Latin America and the First World, one finds there is a constant rejection of the concept or image of God as all-powerful, omnipresent, eternal, perfect, immutable. That is the classical – Western – way in which God is perceived in catechisms. Women see and feel in such a scheme the foundation of power and divine control over human beings, of some over others, of men over women, of humanity over nature, of rich over poor, of whites over blacks and indigenous peoples.

Since liberation theology has the poor as reference points it has advanced in finding sensitive dimensions in God, such as compassion and mercy with those who suffer, yet we have remained within patriarchal categories or images. Already at the beginning of the 1990s, the Brazilian theologian Ivonne Gebara expressed her concern about the patriarchal theological epistemology within which liberation theology was constructed. As she criticizes simplistic formulations of liberation, Gebara asks whether we will destroy others to rescue the poor in the name of the God of the poor? And in a self-critical mode, Gebara discovers that what women do in liberation theology is feminist patriarchal liberation theology. For Ivonne, women theologians continue to consume patriarchal religion and are servants to patriarchal ecclesiastical projects. I believe she is right.

It is for this reason that feminist theologians propose to deconstruct so as to reconstruct. Some are more radical than others. Repeatedly bodies are thought of, sensitive and sensual, as hermeneutical categories of divine manifestation. A balance is sought for between 'the totally' other masculine with 'the totally close' feminine. God will have to get hands muddied in the mud of creation and not create a world with gloves launching the spirit from the infinite. According to Sally McFague, thinking of God as Mother implies giving birth to humanity and the universe, and as such to see humanity and Earth as the sacred body of God. To think of the world as body of God helps to reinvent the way we interrelate with God and nature. With these sorts of images it is intended to combat the concept of universal transcendence which ostensibly includes all, but in the imaginary symbolism the subject is abstract masculine. To talk of God and humanity without gender, race or ethnicity can hide an unconscious perception of a God and subjects who are male, white and well off.

The problem of feminine images

The contribution of feminist theologies in creating feminine images of God has been a good one, like a kiss to the heart which needs the tender hands of a sensitive and loving God.

Above all because the Judaeo-Christian God, unlike gods from other religions, does not have a spouse. It is like addressing God as Mother and Father, trying to remove the patriarchal tinge which only sees God as father. Though I did hear Rosemary Ruether mention that an important question to be asked when faced with this image of God as Mother is whether this maternal image is on the same plane of equality as that of a paternal God. As we mentioned at the beginning, the fundamental problem that provides leeway for murder, lack of respect for otherness, is considering one – Father – as superior to the other – Mother. Clement of Alexandria created fabulous feminine images of God but did not leave behind his patriarchal vision of the Church. He sees Christ as milk from the Father for the faithful, which implies that Christ represents God's breasts and that God is Mother because God has breasts.

Creating feminine images of God is an important step in the gender balance; it may contribute to diminishing violence against women, to making us more humanly sensitive, but it is no guarantee of a gender relationship based on equality. Feminist theology proposes to go one step further, based on everyday experience, and reinvent images that challenge patriarchal reality and contribute to its transformation; and this is only possible outside the classical patriarchal categories of rigid dichotomies. To see God on a plane of relationship with everything, as seen by ecofeminist theology, is an interesting proposal worth considering.

To conclude, let us return to the starting point: feminicide and the feminization of poverty. I believe that for a theology to be liberating it must consider this reality of women; and in doing so, it will undoubtedly have to be ready to be reconstructed from its roots; in other words, it will have to de-patriarchalize and de-Westernize. The challenge posed by reality is immense, as is the courage to take the step to reposition theology radically as both liberating and inclusive, leaving behind the complicity of our theological discourses.

13 God, Ethnic-Cultural Traditions and Globalization

JAMES MASSEY

Introductory remarks

I would like to begin this chapter by raising a few questions. First, who are these ethnic communities, whose cultural traditions we are concerned with here? Second, what does globalization mean in relation to a specific context and how does it affect the ethnic-cultural traditions in that context? Third, what has God to do with these various ethnic-cultural traditions and the process of globalization? I do not intend to answer these questions literally, but they will be at the back of my mind during the discussion of this paper. Also in the discussion, my specific point of reference will be the Indian context and more specifically a particular community, namely 'Dalit', the community to which I myself belong. Dalits presently number more than 240 million worldwide, out of which about 200 million live in India alone. Their numbers alone would make the case of the Dalits important. But the other reason I choose to refer them is because they represent one of the most oppressed communities of the world and their case can help us to draw our attention to other oppressed communities of the world. For the sake of convenience the discussion of this paper has been divided into three parts:

- Ethnic-cultural traditions
- Globalization in a specific context
- God and 'Another World'

Now, before moving to the actual discussion, a word about the term 'Dalit' for the sake of those who may not be familiar with this term. 'Dalit' is derived from the Sanskrit root *dal*, which means burst, split, broken or torn asunder, downtrodden, scattered, crushed and destroyed. Here our Old Testament scholars may be surprised to know that an intriguing connection has also been drawn between the Sanskrit root *dal* and the Hebrew root *dal(l)*, whose meaning is to hang down, to be languid, weakened, low and feeble. Because Sanskrit and Hebrew belong to two different linguistic families – the Indo-Germanic and the Semitic – some scholars would describe the linguistic connection between the two roots as mere coincidence. But I must add here, a reading of some of the 50 or so passages in which the Hebrew root *dal* appears in the biblical literature can shed fascinating light on the situation of Dalits in India today.[1] With these introductory remarks, now I move to the actual discussion of my paper as proposed already.

Ethnic-cultural traditions

A number of definitions for the expression 'ethnic' as well as for 'culture' are available. We are not going to deal here with different definitions either of 'ethnic' or of 'culture'. Concerning the term 'ethnic', we only have to say that in general this term 'is no longer confined to groups identified by race or descent, now it includes identification by any (or a combination of) cultural markers thus, we have racial, linguistic, religious, caste, tribal ethnicities'.[2] It is mostly in this sense that the expression 'ethnic' is used in India.

But there is also another group of thinkers, who lay emphasis on the situational (contextual) nature of the ethnic identity group. They also put emphasis on the multidimensional aspects of ethnic identity.[3] The specific ethnic community with which we are concerned in the Indian context, namely 'Dalits', falls closer to this understanding of an ethnic group. Because the Dalits today draw their distinct identity not from any of the traditional factors or basis, but from a unique form of discrimination, which they receive at the hands of so-called high caste groups of India.[4] Maybe to understand this point further a brief note on the context of the Dalits needs to be added here.

---

1 James Massey, *Down Trodden – The Struggle of India's Dalits for Identity, Solidarity and Liberation*, Geneva, Risk Book Series, WCC Publications, 1997, pp. 1–11.

2 Mukherji, Partha Nath, 'Nationalism, Nation-building and the State in India', in Manoranjan Mohanty, Partha Nath Mukherji and Olle Tornquist (eds), *People's Rights: Social Movements and the State in the Third World*, New Delhi, Sage Publications, 1998, p. 104.

3 Ishtiaqu Ahmed, 'The Nature and Structure of Ethnic Conflict and Separatism in South Asia', in Mohanty et al., *People's Rights*, p. 153.

4 Oliver Mendelsohn and Marika Vicziany, 'The Untouchables', in Oliver Mendelsohn and Upendra Baxi (eds), *The Rights of Subordinated Peoples*, Delhi, Oxford University Press, 1944, pp. 66–7.

The context of the Dalits involves four major historical layers of colonization: Aryans, the Muslims, the British and the dominant powers in independent India.[5] Each of these layers has added to and deepened the problem of Dalitness. But actually the present caste-based Indian social order, which has its origin during the period of Aryan colonization, is directly responsible for this problem. The story of this social order had its historical roots in one of the earliest conflicts, which took place between the first settlers of ancient India and the latecomers. The second group described themselves as *Arya* (noble) and the first group they called *Dasa* (slave). The detailed story of these two hostile groups is found in the ancient written source the Rig Veda (around 1500 BC). It is in the Rig Veda that we find the first reference to the social order with which we are concerned here. According to the Rig Veda, each part of human society was formed out of the body of the creator god, *Brahma*. Therefore it has a divine origin. A verse from a hymn of the Rig Veda, which deals with this part of the story of this order, reads as follows: 'The *Brahman* (priests) was his mouth, both of his arms were the *Rajanya* (*Kshatriya*, warriors). His thighs became the *Vaishya* (traders), from his feet the *Sudra* (serving caste) was produced' (Rig Veda 10.90.12).

The point to be noted here is that this social order described in the Rig Veda was only confined to the *Arya*, and not to the first dwellers of India. Also, after going through the text of the Rig Veda, it becomes very clear that the first dwellers of India were those who, today, make up the 'Dalits' and the *Adivasi* (indigenous people). One result of the conflict described in the Rig Veda was that, at a later stage, the opponents of the Dalits were able to divide them into a number of groups by assigning them the lowliest jobs. Today the Dalits are divided into more than 850 sub-groups. The Dalits are not only horizontally divided, but have also been vertically divided by their opponents, based upon the purity or cleanliness of their prescribed (forced) occupations.

The oppression of the Dalits was not limited only to the extent of their physical suffering. They suffered much more socially, culturally and religiously; and this was primarily responsible for pushing them into their present state – a state 'with no identity', or 'no people' or 'no nation'. This is the reason that scholars who have been interested to make them the object of their study, though they are willing to place them 'at the bottom of Indian society', nevertheless confront the problem in treating them as a separate class. They find that although all of them belong to the bottom of the Indian society, they do not represent

---

5 See Massey, *Down Trodden*, pp. 12–28.

any single ethnic identity; they do not possess a common physical form or cultural identity, they do not speak one language, and they do not even have one religion or worship style and have variety of social life. This makes it all the more difficult to consider them as a single group or class. The only commonality that they do have is a unique form of discrimination that they receive at the hands of high caste people, and this forms the basis for their 'distinct grouping within India'. Therefore it is this situational factor that gives the Dalits a unique ethnic identity.

With regard to the cultural traditions of the Dalits, we have only to add here that during the long history of oppression and different layers of colonization, the Dalits have lost almost everything that they could have claimed as their own. This includes their cultural traditions. It is only recently that they have come to know, through their reconstructed history, that they possibly have a rich cultural heritage, which included well-built cities, a relatively mature culture with a high standard of art and craftsmanship and also a developed system of pictorial writings.[6] But the story of the Dalit's vanished rich cultural traditions only tells us, if any ethnic community is not careful, what can happen to its members through any form of colonization. This story also compels us to look very seriously at the whole challenge, with which we are faced today, of a neo-colonization brought about by globalization. This point brings us to the next part of our discussion related to the globalization process in a specific context.

Globalization in a specific context

We shall examine globalization in a specific context, namely, that of India, where for more than 3,500 years the society has been controlled by a minority of the country, including various so-called caste groups to which later on other communities were also added. Among these, the most powerful, enjoying all the human rights, were/are Brahmins, because others had various reduced rights according to their caste. For example, Brahmins had the right to education as well as to teach others, *Kshatriya* had the right to education, but not to teach. The third caste, *Vaishya*, had a only very limited need-based right to education. The fourth caste, *Sudra*, did not have any right to education, but they were still recognized as human beings. In the case of Dalits, who were considered as outcastes, they had no human rights as their own,

---

6 See James Massey, *Roots – Concise History of Dalits,* New Delhi, Centre for Dalit Studies, 2004, pp. 10–17.

because they were non-human for the so-called caste people. Therefore it is the minority, which today form 18 per cent (among these only 5 per cent Brahmins) of India's population, who really enjoy the various rights according to their grade. So India as a country has been controlled by a minority, which also includes control over all the economic and human resources.

Throughout history the caste-based minority of India has supported politically the 'rightist' ideology, which always opposed the existence of a secular state. The upholders of a secular state or centrist ideology believe in the middle path of a partly state-controlled planned economy, social justice for all, nationalism based on secular values and recognition of the composite culture. But the minority that most of the time ruled India believed in one religion-based culture or nationalism and a system of free enterprise and market economy. Both the social and economic thinking of the latter group run almost parallel to the basic ideas of globalization, particularly when we talk about it as privatization and liberalization of international trade and investment. If we look very carefully, we find the meaning of this kind of globalization process matches well with the ideological meaning of both the cultural nationalism and a free enterprise cum market economy of India's rightist group. Both groups, one at world level and the other at national level, are making efforts to create 'a world' based upon either their mono-economic understanding or their mono-religious basis.

Globalization is understood today primarily as the free movement of goods, services, people and information across national boundaries. This definition of globalization may look simple as well as harmless. But to understand the meaning and to fix a specific perspective particularly from the perspective of Dalits, we need to look into the meaning and implication of globalization more critically. First, we will all agree with the view that 'globalization is now a fact, not an option. The communication revolution has turned the world into a global "village" where everyone knows what is going on and what is available.'[7] The supporters of this process claim:

> The process of globalization is a central source of change in the world today. It can lead to widely shared inclusive prosperity or highly uneven development from which a significant number of countries and people are excluded. To benefit fully from it, to turn it into an opportunity, India has to adapt its policies.[8]

7 India Development Report 1999–2000, New Delhi, Oxford University Press, 1999, p. 27.
8 India Development Report 1999–2000, p.28.

Now what are the policies behind the globalization? *Human Development Report 1997* summarized the answer to this question by pointing out:

A dominant economic theme of the 1990s globalization encapsulates both a description and a prescription. The description is the widening and deepening of international flows of trade, finance and information . . . The prescription is to liberalize national and global markets in the belief that free flows of trade, finance and information will produce the best outcome for growth and human welfare.

At the same place this report adds:

The principles of free global markets are nevertheless applied selectively. If this were not so, the global market for unskilled labour would be as free as the market for industrial country exports or capital . . . Lacking power, poor countries and poor people too often find their interests neglected and undermined.[9]

Globalization also has its winners and losers. The winners include output, people with assets, profits, people with high skills, educated, professional, managerial and technical people, capital, creditors, those independent of public services, large firms, the strong, risk takers, global markets, sellers of technically sophisticated products, global culture, global elite, and firms with market access and branding. The losers include employment, people without assets, wages, people with low skills, uneducated workers, labour, debtors, those dependent on public services, small firms, the weak, human security, local communities, sellers of primary and standard manufactured products, local culture, global poor, and firms without market access and no branding.[10] Now in the case of the Dalits of India, without any doubt we can say that as things stand today they are among the losers of globalization.

It is interesting to note that all the human development reports, which offered the analysis of the impacts of globalization, agreed that not only are the interests of the poor countries and the poor in general neglected, but the benefits of this process have mainly gone to the more dynamic and powerful countries of the North and South. These reports also agree with the fact that liberalization, privatization and tighter intellectual property rights are shaping the path for the

9 Human Development Report 1997, New York, UNDP, pp. 82, 97.
10 Human Development in South Asia 2001, New Delhi, Oxford University Press, p. 15.

new technologies, determine how they are used, but then all this is controlled by powerful corporations and in the process: 'Poor people and poor countries risk being pushed to the margin in this proprietary regime controlling the world's knowledge.'[11] Besides this, the global gap between haves and have-nots, between know and know-nots is widening for the following reasons: (a) in private research agendas money talks louder than need; (b) tightened intellectual property rights keep developing countries out of the knowledge sector; (c) patent laws do not recognize traditional knowledge and systems of ownership; and (d) the rush and push commercial interests protect profits, not people, despite the risks in the new technologies.[12] All this actually means that the right to knowledge or education is limited to a small minority as part of the strategy. Here we must also add that when we talk about education in relation to globalization, it means universal quality basic education both at the secondary and the higher level of education. There is also a definite need of commitment to social reforms on the part of government, without which globalization will not succeed either in transforming the local society or the economy in any situation. In the case of India, we lack both quality education, which is presently available to a very small percentage (between 3 and 5 per cent),[13] and real commitment to any social reforms on the part of successive governments. So, communities like the Dalits are always excluded from any benefits of any form of development including what is being claimed to be the benefits of globalization.

Since we are restricting our discussion here to a specific Dalit perspective on globalization, it is pertinent that we focus also our attention on the history of globalization. Though the history of the present form of globalization goes back to the colonialist era of the seventeenth to nineteenth centuries, its real history began after World War Two. Then global rules to manage trade in the world economy were established. For this purpose, three world institutions were founded: the International Monetary Fund (IMF), the World Bank (WB) and the General Agreement on Tariffs and Trade (GATT)/World Trade Organization (WTO). By the last decade of the twentieth century, the present form of globalization had come into existence, going beyond the territories of nation-states by the process of economic exchanges, political homogenization, technological advances and cultural influences. Presently globalization in the form of human power is, in truth,

---

11 Human Development Report 1999, Oxford, UNDP, 1999, p. 6.
12 Human Development Report 1999, p. 57.
13 James Massey, *Alternative Approaches to Education for All*, Delhi, CCCC Study Document 1, 1999, p.10.

without any control, because it does not recognize any boundaries, whether political, national or even natural. However, for Dalits, the history of their colonization cum globalization goes back more than 3,500 years. As pointed out earlier, in the case of India both the promoters and the beneficiaries of globalization are the traditional groups belonging to the so-called upper castes and, likewise, the victims of this process are those who were also the victims of caste-based Indian social order. Dalits have been the most victimized group among these groups.

Besides becoming victims of globalization along with the poor in general, the Dalits are also becoming losers on other special counts. The Constitution of India, recognizing the need to improve the conditions of the Dalits, has offered them reservations of jobs in the public sector (articles 16, 320, 353). Article 46 of the Indian Constitution offers special provision to promote the educational and economic interests of the Dalits and it also offers them protection from social injustice and all forms of exploitation. But, with the coming of globalization, these rights are being taken away through the process of privatization. Accepting the recommendation of the Structural Adjustmental Programme (SAP) since the early 1990s, India has opened its market and consequently started privatizing all the public sector units gradually. Under the previous rightist-group ruled government, this process accelerated, and with this the privileges enjoyed by the Dalits under the Constitution, especially with regard to the jobs in the public sector, were directly affected. The upholders of the caste system have already declared them outside the purview of human society, but now as the large majority of the Dalits do not have the possibility of getting quality basic education, which could have made them the beneficiaries of globalization, they automatically lose the right to become citizens of the new world order, which is being proposed to be established by the promoters of the World Economic Forum (WEF). It is in this context that the World Social Forum (WSF) becomes relevant for them, because the WSF's declaration in 2001 and adoption of the same in 2004 that 'Another World is Possible' has given them and other oppressed communities of the world the much needed hope for the recovery of their rights in future.[14] This point brings to us to the discussion of the next section of this paper on God and 'Another World'.

---

14 James Massey, 'The Dalits at the World Social Forum 2004: An Analysis', in T. K. John (ed.), *Broken Among the Victims – Dalit Presence at the World Social Forum 2004*, New Delhi, Centre for Dalit/Subaltern Studies, 2004, p. 105.

God and 'Another World'

In our introduction to this paper, we raised three questions and in our discussion of the last two sections of the paper, we have discussed our first two questions: who are these ethnic communities, whose cultural traditions we are concerned with? And, what does globalization mean in relation to a specific context and how it affects the ethnic-cultural traditions in that context? The case of the Dalits of India, who today have lost everything, including all their cultural traditions, was referred to in detail. That story also revealed to us the nature of one of the most important challenges with which we are faced today, that of neo-colonization through the process of globalization. From the discussion of the section on 'globalization in a specific context', we learned the Dalits of India have experienced a number of historical layers of colonization, which have deepened the problem of their Dalitness. Today, with the coming of globalization in the Indian context, they have started losing the small ray of hope, which they had seen in post-independence India. But thanks to some efforts of the various Dalit communities along with other oppressed communities of the world, they have created a possibility of hope for change. This point became very clear in January 2004 in Mumbai when every day during the Fourth WSF more than 100,000 members of various oppressed communities came, out of which nearly 60 per cent were Dalits. Partly it was the central theme of WSF – 'Another World is Possible' – which brought them there. But what was the role of God in this whole affair of the WSF? Will God be interested in the possibility of 'Another World'? Here an observation made by Professor T. K. John on Mumbai WSF 2004 may be worth noting:

It is significant theologically too that the World Social Forum . . . is the second major contribution of the Latin American Christian community to the wide world community. The first was Liberation Theology . . . Both . . . are born of the experience and perception of the situation of poverty and dehumanisation on the one hand, and that of oppression and injustice on the other and these had given birth to radical examination of the social situation. The human consciousness had been growing like a flaming torch exposing the sophisticated barbarities being committed against the deprived of the world. The same torch has been shedding light on the plight of the victims as well as on the callous midway walkers too. In other words, the Spirit of God is exposing the deviancy in human collective behaviour. The author of creation is gathering His people towards the unique task of restoring sanity to the disoriented world; the appeal is to rectitude of behaviour that benefits the human nature and a call to restore the social order.[15]

The message of this observation is very clear, and it makes two important points with regard to the role of the Spirit of God. First, she is exposing the deviancy in human collective behaviour, which is created by the process of globalization; and, second, as she did in the first act of creation, the Spirit of God is once again gathering God's people that they may work in 'restoring sanity to the disoriented world'.

It is true what Professor T. K. John has observed about the work of the Spirit of God, which means God is working among us. But we need to note that God is not only working among us, he is also working in a very special way along with the oppressed of the world, who are excluded from society defined by the dominants. This has been his design of working throughout the history of human society. We find this very clearly from his recorded acts in the Bible. Two examples, the Tower of Babel (Genesis 11.1–9) and the experience of the first group of believers at the day of Pentecost (Acts 2.1–13), very clearly show that God has not only created the diversities which included the various ethnic-cultural traditions, but he also continues to uphold and honour these.

God's direct interventions in human history have again been the very clear proof of his interest in the situations with which we are concerned in this World Forum on Theology and Liberation. We will refer here to two examples of God's interventions to make our point clear. First, when an ethnic group, namely Israel, was faced with a threat to their very human identity from the hands of the imperialist powers, the Pharaohs of Egypt, God, after seeing Israel's sufferings and oppression, intervened and 'came down to deliver them from the Egyptian' (Exodus 3.7, 8). God through his action became a part of their struggle. This action shows God taking the side of the oppressed against the oppressors. This act of God was not so much a religious action, it was actually a political act with economic and social dimensions.

The second major intervention of God in human history was his becoming human being in Jesus Christ (John 1.14–18). In the act of incarnation, God did not become just as any human being, but one who gave up his otherworldly identity completely for the sake of human beings and became poorest of the poor (Isaiah 7.14, Luke 2.7) – in a real sense, according to the Indian context, a Dalit. Again the

---

15 T. K. John (ed.), *Broken Among the Victims*, pp. 144–5.

purpose and mission of this intervention has been spelled out in Luke 4.18, 19. Here we very clearly see him on the side of the poor, captives, blind and oppressed. The final agenda is declared in verse 19 with the proclamation of 'the year of the Lord's favour', which meant that the time has come when God will save his people. This announcement, I believe, was the beginning of God's reign on this Earth. God's incarnation in Jesus Christ was for the restoration of the original plan, which was inaugurated by Jesus on the day of the beginning of his ministry in Nazareth and through his action on that day, the foundation for 'Another Possible World' was laid down. But the completion of the construction of that world is still awaited. Because God is waiting for his people to complete that job, which he began through Jesus Christ in Nazareth almost 2,000 years ago.

Concluding remarks

I would like to conclude the discussion here by quoting an observation, which I made at the end of my reflection on Mumbai WSF 2004:

> WSF movement definitely can help in establishing global solidarity of the oppressed and of the poor of the world including the Dalits of India. Because this global solidarity of the oppressed communities of the world is only a possible way to enter into an alternative process, which will enable them to establish a new world, where all will live with equal and full human dignity.[16]

God is with the WSF movement in this endeavour, because he is indeed for 'Another Possible World'.

---

16 Massey, 'The Dalits at the World Social Forum 2004', p. 115.

14 Social Context, Language and Images of God

WANDA DEIFELT

God talk, or theology, is the result of experience. Feminist theology has made it very clear that we can only talk about God as the result of experience, in its relation to the human condition and its finiteness, its aspirations and hopes, all of which provide sense to human existence. Christian theology, in particular, has traditionally had a multiple programme: it refers to the gospel of Jesus Christ and the faith that responds to this gospel. This is achieved by study and interpretation of Scripture, working within and for the Church, and in tune with world events. Theology re-reads the history and tradition of the Church and sustains doctrines and formulations based on the truth of the gospel it is called to proclaim.

The twentieth century produced new challenges and possibilities to this God talk, which on the whole differ quite clearly from the traditional description provided above. The challenge, mainly from liberation, feminist, womanist, mujerista, black, dalit, minjung and aboriginal theologies, can be summed up in the questioning of the universal pattern of revelation implicit in the talk about God that Christianity produced. In other words, these theologies affirm that we know Christianity from a necessarily limited perspective or point of view, which emerged in Europe during the first centuries, copied from a hegemonic cultural model.[1] This perspective became normative, not only to grasp and evaluate the experience of divine revelation within Christianity, but also to evaluate the totality of the manifestation of

---

1 The critique expressed by feminist and liberation theologies affirms that Christian word and practice, particularly after Constantine, represent a distancing from the primitive Christian movement. When Christianity becomes the religion of the empire, it is clear that ecclesiastical power is related to hegemonic practices. In this sense the critique sums up the worldwide Graeco-Roman culture (with its dualisms and hierarchies), and which also includes the persecution of dissident religious expressions (accused of heresy).

God. Liberation theologies affirm that divine revelation goes beyond the limitations of our understanding, challenging us to find a new language to refer to the divine so as to experience its message of love and justice coherently.

[handwritten margin note: But is this a paradox in itself?]

Language about God

As our God talk can only take place within the limitations of our own language and is impregnated by our culture, no theology can grasp the totality of divine revelation; in this sense there have been theologians who propose not to talk of theology but rather of theo-anthropology, in the sense that talking about God can only happen within human language.[2] Theological discourse must reflect on the world and the concrete existence of the faithful, relating the divine to the concrete reality of people. As such, theology is not only doctrine about God, but also the discourse of the relation of God with humanity, and of humanity with God. God is one of the many names used to talk about the divine.[3] As in all discourses there is diversity in the talk about God. An abstract discourse on the divine is not possible without it being related to human existence. Theology, influenced by the Platonic ideal, has understood this as a failure. Contextual liberation theologies, on the other hand, understand social context and experience as the place of revelation, welcoming these factors.

[handwritten margin note: What has influenced our perception about God?]

To recognize the fact that context and reality influence the development of language about God is not something new. The ancient prophetic tradition revealed how time and time again God was called upon to justify or sanctify the status quo. Prophets, both men and women, had the special mission to denounce injustice and announce *Shalom*, being understood as a new dimension of peace, much more intense than simply the absence of war. *Shalom* is the establishment of the fullness of life. It is the restoration of relationship between God and humanity, between human beings and between humanity and the whole of creation. This restoration appears in the Hebrew tradition as

---

2 K. Barth, 'Evangelical theology in the 19th century', in *The Humanity of God*, Richmond, VA, John Knox Press, 1960, p. 11. Curiously the concern for theo-anthropology does not originate in the Third World, but rather in Europe. This text of Karl Barth, from the end of his career, represents a good summing up of the changes which took place in the theological language of the nineteenth and early twentieth centuries. It represents a true revision of his early postulates on the infinite distance between God and humanity, though remains critical of a theo-anthropology.

3 P. Tillich, *Dynamics of Faith*. New York, Harper, 1957, p. 54.

Tikkun Olam, in which all injustices in this world are overcome; there is home, food and dignity for all people. This reality is understood as God's will for all humanity.

The Jewish tradition does not refer to limitations, rather it accentuates the dangers of theological language that coincides with and supports all systems of oppression and corruption.[4] Because of this, pronouncing God's name in vain is an act of disobedience to God's commandment. The prophetic tradition denounces the use of God's name to manipulate, oppress and reduce the divine to human interests – to the point that God's name cannot be pronounced. When affirming God's presence in our midst, and mediated by our experiences, it is also necessary to recognize God's difference.

Sallie McFague, in her seminal work, demonstrated that God can only be described in metaphorical language. Human language will never be able to describe divinity in its totality, because no human experience can encapsulate it. Our perceptions are always partial and so is our language. 'A metaphorical theology accentuates personal and relational categories in its language about God, but it does not do this in the way these categories have traditionally been interpreted.'[5] To use metaphorical language is to recognize that our way to describe God is simultaneously true and not true.

The limitations of human language

To talk about God, human language must recognize its limitations and possibilities. It is impossible to ignore our limitations and pretend we are able to understand and proclaim the totality of the message on the divine. This human arrogance, when associated with power and authority, can be translated as sin. This reduces speech about God to one cosmovision, to the exclusion of all others, in the name of an absolute. It is sinful to universalize one's own experience, making it the norm. It is the sin of reducing the infinite to the finite. Womanist, mujerista or feminist theologians, and also liberation theologians, have for a long time denounced the dangers of this universalization, because it reinforces a normative and limited speech, perpetuating asymmetrical power relations. To reduce the divine to a metaphor, to an only name, is idolatry. A racist, sexist, classist and homophobic language

[handwritten margin note: Do we ignore our limitations when we place people within or without the church? We claim to judge as God judges?]

---

4 Milton Shwantes, *Amós: meditaçôes e estudios,* Sâo Leopoldo, Sinodal, 1987.
5 Sally McFague, *Metaphorical Theology,* Philadelphia, Fortress Press, 1982, p. 21.

reproduces a world order in which racist, sexist, classist and homophobic ideologies are divinely sanctioned. Divinity is not only reduced to a particular vision of the world; even more dangerously, this particular vision is considered the only divine manifestation. It accentuates the one and denies the others.

The role that both context and culture play in the creation and upholding of metaphors is evident. We will analyse the development of one metaphor in particular: God as father. Used by Jesus, this is a legitimate biblical metaphor. The problem is not the metaphor, the problem is its absolutization.[6] Mary Daly has denounced the abuse of this patriarchal metaphor which even led to idolatry. She says that if God is father, then father is God.[7] Language maintains the power of *pater*, it does not question the interconnection between the power structures that sustain this, and even worse, it establishes hierarchical structures as divinely ordered. The perversion is so great that it would seem that God has established pacts with sexist, racist, classist and homophobic values. Because of this, to be suspicious of language is also a way to be suspicious of the reality that gives birth to language. Language reveals ideologies and practices.

The use of the father metaphor to refer to God is a concrete example.[8] Jesus refers to God as *Father* 170 times in the New Testament. In Hebrew Scripture, God is referred to as father only 15 times. The number of times this metaphor appears in each gospel is a clear evidence of the influence of social context and how this metaphor was gradually imposed. God is only referred to as father 4 times in the oldest Gospel, Mark. In Luke, 15 times and in Matthew, 42 times. In the most recent Gospel, John, it appears 109 times. What is at stake is not the legitimacy of the metaphor as one of many forms of talking about God. What is questionable, in the first place, is its absolutization; in second place, the suspicion that the metaphor is used to perpetuate paternalism. We have reached a point in which it causes quite an uproar to use any feminine metaphor to refer to God. God can be

---

6 The use of the metaphor *Father*, like all metaphors, contains a partial dimension. It is urgent that this metaphor be deconstructed and reconstructed with gender analysis in a way that demonstrates aspects of divine paternity closer to those of modern countries. In other words, the language of the divine insists on describing God as all-powerful, distant, authoritarian, judge, with no consideration of the paternal dimension as expressed by Jesus when using *Abba*, loving, caring, close father.

7 Mary Daly, *Beyond God the Father*, Boston, Beacon Press, 1973.

8 Information on God as father in Joachim Jeremias, *The Prayers of Jesus*, Naperville, Alec R. Allerson, 1967, p. 29.

addressed as rock, but it is offensive to call God mother. When any metaphor becomes absolute, it is idolatry.[9]

The transition from an ecclesiastical model in which small groups met in homes (including women's homes) to a model closer to Graeco-Roman culture reveals how one metaphor adapted easier than others. The *Abba* (father) of Jesus is synonymous with a close, kind and loving divinity. While the *Pater* (father) of Graeco-Roman culture is absolute lord, with power over life and death of wife (wives), children and slaves. When in the first centuries the Jesus movement adopted a Greek mind frame and a Roman administrative way of living, the almighty father language became normative. This is why to suspect language is also to suspect the reality it generates. Transforming language is a constitutive step in the transformation of reality.

The one-dimensional accent on language, the view of language as an absolute truth, and the sinful arrogance by which experience or a particular practice can encapsulate and transmit the totality of the divine has led many religions – and particularly Christianity – to develop practices that deny the basis of their original message and their particular ethos. In the Christian religion the plurality of religious and spiritual manifestations present in primitive Christianity (described by Paul in 1 Corinthians 12, when using the image of the human body) gave way to a centralized and patronizing religious system. When a movement becomes an institution it can lose its prophetic power, adopting forms of organization and language that serve the interests of the powers of this world. It forgets and denies the prophetic voice and praxis with which it began.

Language not only reflects practice, it also defines it. A language of demonization has been used to define diabolical individuals or groups which do not conform to the proposed hierarchical model. To accuse the other person of being evil or of introducing evil into the world (without recognizing one's own participation in the perpetuation of demonic practices and systems) is itself evil. The Brazilian theologian Ivone Gebara has already drawn our attention to this.[10] Religious lan-

---

9 This same principle is also related to feminine metaphors. Feminist theologians do not propose to substitute the term *Mother* for the expression *Father* in prayers, because this would again turn the metaphor into an absolute. When this happens metaphor loses its symbolic nature. The purpose is to diversify and find metaphors that celebrate plurality.

10 The writings of Ivone Gebara are a fundamental step towards the demystification of the questions of evil and to demonstrate how within the Christian understanding of sin there is a sexist, classist and racist construction. She presents five versions of the construction of evil: the feminine as the evil of not having, of not being able to, of not knowing, of not being worth anything, and

guage that thrives on such absolutes does not understand the complexities of human existence nor the beauty or grace of living. This language does not recognize life as a gift. Language about God can only speak metaphorically or poetically. One can only talk humbly and provisionally.

The possibilities of human language

When the limitations of language have been verified, it is possible to head towards a new approach: the possibilities of human language. Based on the theology of creation, this approach affirms that as creatures made in the image and likeness of God we participate in divine creativity. The many names of God found in Jewish and Christian Scripture inform us that God has many characteristics: wisdom, justice, peace, word, woman in labour pains, midwife, rock, fire, way, spirit, love . . . among others. The divine has many names because human beings experience divinity in different ways. It is part of human creativity and freedom to name God based on the experience with the divine. This is what Hagar, the Egyptian slave, does in Genesis 16.13 when she calls God *El Roi* (the God that sees). Divinity always escapes from new stereotypes and refuses to be reduced to a unique metaphor (Hosea 11.9 'because I am God and not man' *ish,* male). The divinity affirms the dynamic of the name 'I am who I am' (Exodus 3.14).

To speak of divine revelation is a paradox. The limitations of the language about God reaffirm its possibility. To affirm the possibilities of God talk is at the same time to recognize its limitations. The divine is experienced in our lives' daily experiences, in the everyday. Yet the divine upsets familiarity, it displaces and surprises us with possibilities we cannot even imagine because we find ourselves in a sinful situation. Bent over ourselves, human beings can barely see our own navels. We can only perceive our situation because of grace. We recognize our dependency; that we need each other, and we dare to dream beyond the horizons of our possibilities. This allows God to be God and allows us to be human. The human answer to the divine affirmation 'I am who I am' recognizes that 'you are who you are'. God is totally familiar and at the same time totally other, strange, a stranger.

Recognizing the human interdependence, of human beings with creation and the divine with humanity, is also to recognize that the divine

---

stigma due to the colour of one's skin. The conjunction of these elements reduces the feminine to a non-being.

does not exist as an absolute outside of creation. We exist because the divine exists. Yet the divine exists because we exist. We can only refer to this divinity because we have entered a relationship of mutuality and interdependency. Following the Exodus metaphor – and we include here our need to live in community – we could say: 'I am who you are/I am *because* you are'. Language on the divine needs mediation. This mediation takes place through existence, experience, context and culture. The creator is known through creation and its creatures. The divine can only live in us and inhabit among us using forms we can understand and to which we can relate. The language we understand is the image of caring, of justice, of welfare, of promoting peace, affirming dignity and love. To say 'I am who you are' implies a commitment, the recognition that we are interconnected, an affirmation of 'otherness' that is not outside me, rather, it is part of me.

Language about God is spoken in many dialects. Christianity, in particular, has not always celebrated the richness of these dialects. On the contrary, it has perceived them as threats and attempts to delegitimize purity of doctrine. Sadly enough it has become common practice within dominant Christianity to adapt the divine revelation of 'I am who I am' to the prototype 'you are who I am'. In this colonial practice there is a complete inversion of the model that celebrates diversity and accepts dialects. This model accentuates homogeneity and leads to conformity and passivity. The model of uniformity affirms that it is necessary to institute hierarchies so as to supervise the purity of doctrine. In the name of truth, hierarchy ceases to see multiple manifestations of the divine, the surprising ways God intervenes in history and reveals God's love for humanity. Ironically, it becomes idolatry.

The relation between social context, language and image of God takes place in a creative tension. It uses metaphorical language that struggles with the need to speak of the divine and its incapacity to do so. It goes through the experience of now, but not yet. I can speak of God in a language that is familiar, relational and culturally located. But I try to overcome the limitations of my own experience and language precisely in the encounter with others. This otherness is the divine otherness, while at the same time it is the otherness celebrated in the encounter with other human beings and with our environment. Liberation theology argued that we could only talk about God from an experience of divine solidarity with humankind, of the God who is revealed in the language of simple people. Feminist theology adds that it is only possible to talk about God, as Jesus did, through the use of parables: 'parables as metaphors and the life of Jesus as a metaphor of God, provide the characteristics of theology; it is an open theology, tentative, indirect, in tension, iconoclastic and transforming'.[11]

The language of bodies

In Latin America and in feminist theology the human body has become a parable to refer to God. The parable not only provides meaning about God, it also provides meaning about who we are. The parable *is* and at the same time *isn't* what it says. It provides the prophetic and contextual, it reveals possibilities and limitations, it is and it isn't. 'Bodyness' is one of these ways to refer to the divinity.[12] It is not a question of echoing the narcissist and hedonistic obsession put forward by the media, where human bodies become commodities for the sale of merchandise. It does not try to reproduce patterns or aesthetic values that render worship to the body simply because it fits into particular shapes.

The three narratives presented below will help us understand the concrete and everyday understanding of body and are an example of the notion of 'bodyness' upheld by feminist theology. The story shows how the human body determines perception, how it mediates knowledge and language, and how it is the context (locus) of revelation. Naturally the body as a parable of language about God is limited by the perception of the particular context. It is not an absolute language, rather a language convinced of that divine presence which imbues everyday life and human experience. It affirms the divine presence even in those situations where life itself is denied.

Leonildo, a farmer of one of the MST (Landless Movement) settlements in Viamao, RS, stands on the side of organic rice plantations and says: 'all that is here was planted by us.' His voice reveals the joy of producing food with his own hands, using the resources the community has, in the land they conquered. On the way to the field he shares the joy of the small achievements the community has reached. The long days in camps on the side of the road, in barracks only covered

---

11 McFague, *Metaphysical Theology*, p. 19.

12 The question of 'bodyness' – understood as the human body and its network of relations – forms part of the Latin American scenario. An ideal example on how to deal collectively with the issue is the book prepared by the Gender Research Nucleus of the Ecumenical Institute of Postgraduate Studies of the Escuela Superior de Teología de Sao Leopoldo, RS, Brazil. Marga Ströher, Wanda Deifelt and André Musskopf (eds), *A flor da pele: ensaios sobre género e corporeidade*, Sao Leopoldo, Sinodal/CEBI, 2004.

in black plastic, these are all of the past. Yet he is still in solidarity with the millions of men, women and children who have not yet got the land to harvest and suffer the violence of hunger, social exclusion and armed conflict. Part of the rice harvested is destined to feed the families who still live in camps by the side of the roads.

The struggle for land in Brazil is an example of the vulnerability of simple people. The conflicts for land have cost thousands of lives.[13] The lives of women, children and men who work the land – subject to constant harassment, in danger of being murdered by hired gunmen and at the mercy of child labour – these are the parables of feminist theology. It is not the idealized body, rather the concrete body, mistreated by hunger, overwork and the struggle for dignity. It is also the body that celebrates small victories. This body is the parable to refer to divine revelation. God is in the midst of us. The body is the gift, in the same way that the land is also a collection of gifts. The body is fragile, it lacks care and attention. To affirm that God is in the midst of us is to celebrate incarnation. The divine becomes human, becomes body, to announce hope and resurrection. The divine chooses vulnerability. God becomes a vulnerable child to live among us. Vulnerable bodies become the verb of divine manifestation.

When Daniela talks about her job in the field of popular education, as part of a quilombo community, her eyes glow. She is Afro-descendant and has created a deep relationship with this community in the interior of Sao Lourenco do Sul, RS. The quilombolist were runaway slaves (in the time of slavery) and formed free communities. The community lives practically in isolation, searching to rescue history, music, dance and spirituality and has become a passion for Daniela. To teach the young to dance capoeira is to rescue her own culture, her dignity and worth. To assume her identity as a black woman, with pride in the colour of her skin, is to de-legitimize centuries of racist ideology. For Daniela this is a joy no one will be able to take away from her, which must be celebrated in community.

The body as a parable is not restricted to the individual body. There is the collective, the community, the sense of belonging that floods human relations. The quilombo community is a parable of this social

---

13 In Brazil, in the state of Pará (alongside the Amazon) alone, over 1,700 farmers were killed in the last 20 years in conflicts about land. Landowners and lumber owners hired gunmen to kill the leaders. Among the victims was Sister Dorothy Stang, a 73-year-old missionary working in Anapu, PA.

body. Its history, rich in challenge, resistance and conquest, suffered from discrimination and social marginalization. But Daniela's story at the same time shows the limits of the parable: the social body needs the critique of deconstruction as well. In the same way the community is found in geographical isolation, it also suffers from the sociocultural and religious isolation of its environment. Its experience of struggle will not be valued by the larger community until it values itself. Daniela's experience of finding in this community a cultural reference speaks of this interconnection and dynamism.[14] The social body of the quilombo community is, in this sense a parable which refers to the divine experience.

In the recycling factory in Lixo in Gravatai, RS, Nilda tells us that before having a place in which garbage could be separated, she sought materials in the rubbish dump (known as *basurero* = *garbage place*). The garbage truck would unload in this place, and she, together with other people, would hunt among the garbage. The search for survival – to find paper, plastic, glass, metal, anything that could be sold – this forced her to fight with rats and flies over rights to the garbage. The National Movement of Searchers helped her eke out a subsistence, but with dignity. 'I used to live in the midst of garbage and I felt the reject of society. Now I have a job working here with other women. This has given us a new sense of hope.'

The degradation of the body, reduced to objects, denies the sacredness of life and creation. That a human being feels it is garbage in society demonstrates the urgency with which we need to affirm human dignity for vulnerable bodies. This also leads to profound questioning on the way Christianity has treated the human body. The idealization of certain bodies has led to the rejection of others. But this has not ended in resignation. There are signs of hope, precisely among those who have been cast out to the margins of a globalized consumerist society. The body as a parable also has an ethical dimension, the commitment to proclaim life abundant.

---

14 More information on this initiative can be found in the commemorative book for the 25 years of the Support Centre for the Small Farmers. Suzanne Buchwits, *O tempo compartilhado: 25 anos do CAPA*, Porto Alegre, Centro de Apoio ao Pequeño Agricultor, 2003.

The body as a parable of divinity

These stories of Nilda, Daniela and Leonilda are an integral part of the Latin American reality. Their experience reveals an understanding of God that mixes both the holy and the profane. Its language is profoundly theological in spite of not using technical jargon. It clearly reveals a society that does not protect the vulnerable, but rather discriminates, stigmatizes to the point of death. The capacity for resistance and solidarity, however, also reveals the presence of the divine. The decision to live overcomes all obstacles and provides hope for life in fullness. For this reason, the concrete everyday living of these bodies illuminates theological reflection.

The work of feminist theologians such as Rosemary Ruether helps us understand that creation is a manifestation of divinity.[15] Ecofeminism accentuates the interconnection of the parts with the whole and the interdependency this generates. The divine is known to us as creator, a God whose power and dynamism is manifest in a continuous creation and re-creation. Theological reflection and concern for the welfare of creation – which includes humanity as an intrinsic part – are not exclusive to Judaic or Christian religions. Actually it is a reality more present in other religions and spiritualities than in Christianity.[16] In these the concrete dynamic of creation is perceived: there is a careful balance between life and death, being born and dying, the cycles of life itself.

In this sense Christianity needs to recognize the catastrophic role it plays in our culture and society, as it feeds a dualism between nature and culture, the material and spiritual world, individual and community, body and soul. The language of the divine has led to an erroneous understanding of creation. These dichotomies not only reinforce hierarchies, but are also a hindrance to an integral vision. The wisdom of farmers – who know that if we do not care for the land, the next generation will not survive – does not have any place whatsoever in a globalized neo-liberal economy which only has eyes for individuals, their immediate interests and profit for the few who live in abundance.

The ecological conscience of interdependency also relates to other human beings. If creation is the body of God, the social body is where

---

15 Rosemary Radford Ruether, *Gaia and God: an Ecofeminist theology of Earth Healing*, New York, HarperSanFrancisco, 1992.

16 This is a reality in ancestral religions still practised by original people of Latin America. A major concern for the welfare and care of the land is just an example.

we live this love in the concrete acts of justice and reconciliation. God has created man and woman and did so in the image of God. This has established a relationship which is not always considered. To affirm that human beings are created in the image of God means that all other human beings should be treated with the same reverence the encounter with divinity deserves. Our encounters with other human beings are far from this. We not only don't treat others with the same respect and dignity as we treat the divine, we tend to use indifference, lack of respect and, very often, humiliation. We treat other bodies as garbage. There are concrete implications for this theo-anthropology. One of them is clearly the way we treat other human beings. The vulnerable body of other people is clearly an image of God.

The divine gift of life is extended to the totality of creation and not only a segment, namely, human beings. The divine is revealed in creation and creation needs caring. As human beings we are responsible caretakers of our place of living, our *oikos*. All of creation gives testimony of the justice and love of God. As creatures we live according to our creator, in thanksgiving and gratefulness for the gift of life. By grace we receive the invitation to live our faith fully in the present times. Christianity, however, has worried excessively about salvation beyond death. It has prioritized salvation of the soul. The bodily language brings us to the here and now and demands from us that we take special care of the present. To use the body as a metaphor, a parable, to talk about God, requires that theology be concerned not only about the salvation of the soul, but also the welfare of the body.

This ethical implication is a demand that life abundant is not only for those who benefit from the current style in which our culture and society are organized (or disorganized), in other words, for those who exercise power and authority in the current patriarchal structure (or kyriarchal, to use Elisabeth Schüssler Fiorenza's expression). This demands that rights and responsibilities be vindicated, so that all human beings can live with dignity. The criterion for this vindication is the care for the integrity and welfare of each other. Our relationship with other human beings is, in the last resort, an encounter with the image of God. The concrete, material and bodily existence of one another is a language used by God to communicate with us.

Our Western culture is not one of hospitality. It enhances the individual who survives for him or herself, who is successful at the expense of others, and who creates a legal system that privileges one over the rest. When language about God speaks of mercy, compassion, grace and the divine embrace, we remember the divine solidarity of creator with creation. We should suppose that this language would have an impact on the way we see ourselves and how we act in this world. We are travellers on the way and we will not survive if we do not take others into account, trusting them and celebrating ourselves as God's concrete bodies. To be created in God's image means we participate in this divine creativity, in which we can, with the help of God, contribute to the blooming of small signs of hope and life.

The human body as a parable of the divine leads us to affirm a theology of creation in which God creates us in God's image and gives us dignity. The centre of Christian tradition leads us, as well, to recover a theology of the incarnation, in which the good news that God opts for the vulnerability of bodies is announced. The social and communal dimension, the interdependency of bodies, is both gift and challenge. This collective body which forms us has to be subject to examination and questioning when it diminishes possibilities and inhibits creativity. The body is a language used by God to communicate. It is a vehicle and place of revelation. The body is a parable to talk about God.

15 Indian Theologies: Retrospect and Prospects, A Sociopolitical Perspective

FELIX WILFRED

A map of the city in the hand gives some people supreme self-confidence. The city, for them, is literally in their hands, as the American soldiers probably felt when they swept into the heart of Baghdad on 9 April 2003. On the map, one is able to identify the arterial roads, tourist spots, various monuments, army headquarters and, what's more, hiding places of weapons of mass destruction (WMD). What else does one need than a city map and a 'road map' to have the euphoric feeling of everything being under control? How delusive such a feeling could be is now a matter of history!

It would be sheer arrogance if theology were to claim overtly or covertly to have a map of God, or God's map for our world and humanity. There is another way of knowing a city; it is the way of exploration by the side streets, passing by petty shops and bazaars, and it is best done by many detours from the centre and arterial roads. A person taking the side streets and narrow lanes – probably not found in the city map – encounters the abysmal poverty of the slums and pavements; she learns of cultures and ways of daily life, gains an understanding of people's moods and motivations by conversing with them and listening to them. We have another picture of the same city with other sources of knowledge, and ultimately a different kind of experience.

The path of Indian theologies will resemble, certainly, not the knowledge of map-people who would like everything to be fitted into a theological cartography. Creative Indian theologies have been, in general, weary of any theology in terms of systems. They have developed theological insights and orientations by experiencing and exploring the unknown paths and lanes to encounter the unfathomable mystery of God and some of the deepest human experiences which open a window to the same mystery. There is then a fragmentary sense to all kinds of Indian theologies. This fragmentary situation is also the creative moment of Indian theologies as they try to cope with ever new and overwhelming situations calling for fresh responses.

I speak of Indian theologies in the plural. How else could we speak? The puzzling complexity resulting from a wide variety of social, political, cultural and religious situations calls for different kinds of theological reflections, even though the various Indian theologies have a 'family resemblance' among them. Individually and cumulatively, these various theologies of India have contributed significantly and have evoked much interest in other parts of the world. Of course, there are people for whom Indian theology is an enfant terrible. They are very apprehensive about it, and do not cease to malign it. But what has Indian theology done for such divergent responses? Maybe a retrospective view will help clarify to ourselves where we stand.[1]

Part 1: Retrospect

National concerns in the formation of an Indian theology

If we leave behind the last 25 years and go down a little further on the lane of history to the first decades of the twentieth century, we will note that the major preoccupation at that time was to form an Indian theology which would distinguish itself from the received mainline Western theology brought by missionaries. Efforts were made to adopt Indian concepts and categories in the place of Western ones. A more thoroughgoing approach was initiated by the Protestant thinkers known as the 'Rethinking Christianity in India' group, consisting of Vengala Chakkarai, Chenchiah and A. J. Appasamy and others.[2] At first sight it may appear that this latter movement was aiming at a theology which would be pursued through Indian thought patterns and categories. An analysis of the background of this movement will show that there was much more to it. The theological orientation associated with this movement was an expression of patriotism at a time when

---

1 The retrospect is made from a sociopolitical point of view, and does not enter into the religio-cultural aspect which requires a treatment all by itself. For a more comprehensive analysis covering the region of South Asia highlighting the contribution of Aloysius Pieris, see Felix Wilfred, 'An Interpretative Overview of South Asian Theology in the Twentieth Century', in David Ford (ed.), *Modern Theologians*, Oxford, Blackwell (3rd edition shortly to appear).

2 The movement derives its name from a book published under the same title just before the International Missionary World Council's Conference in Tambaram (1938).

*the missionary theology continued to pursue its way blissfully igno-
rant of the sociopolitical developments in the country, and particularly the struggle for independence, which was gaining momentum.
Rethinking Christianity in India needs to be viewed as a theological
response to the then prevailing social and political situation.*

The pursuit of such a theology functioned also as a critique within
the churches regarding the management, administration, personnel,
finances, etc., controlled by foreign missionaries. On the whole, this
theological movement helped Christianity to get rooted in the soil and
to interact with the wider sociopolitical movements. As a result, we
could note a progressive change that was taking place in the Christian
communities regarding nationalism and nationalist concerns. As a
broad general background to this movement of theology, we could
refer to Indigenous church movements which emerged in some parts
of the country.

The same line of thought continued in the post-independence period
under the watchword of 'Nation Building', which called for reflections
in the line of theology of development, and further on it gave place to
a theology of liberation in India. The Indian Theological Association
devoted one of its important annual meetings precisely to this question.[3]

For quite a long time Indian theology was thought of as singular and
the various issues were integrated into this one theology. When the
issues of inculturation and dialogue were broached and expanded, the
question was what should be the major characteristic of Indian theology – liberation orientation or ashram orientation. There was a period
of theological tension regarding the amount of attention to be given to
each one of them.

Transition to a plurality of theologies

The founding of the Indian Theological Association (ITA) coincides in
a way with the transition to a plurality of theologies. Of course, in the
earlier years of its existence, the tension inherited between liberational
and ashramite orientation continued to influence its deliberations.
Slowly but surely, the coming together of theologians in the forum
year by year led to the recognition of a plurality of situations, and

---

3 For the proceedings of the meeting, see Paul Puthenangady (ed.), *Towards
an Indian Theology of Liberation*, Bangalore, NBCLC, 1986.

hence the actual need of a theological pluralism within India.[4] The plurality is founded, among other things, on the difference in the social location, or the difference in the nature of issue one is dealing with. In this sense, the emergence of tribal, feminist and Dalit theologies are due to a deeper social and political consciousness. Without going into this plurality of theologies in any detail, let me make a few comments on some of them.[5]

Dalit theology and its achievements

I would consider Dalit theology as the greatest achievement of Indian theology, seen especially from the sociopolitical angle. It has made a significant impact on the way theology is to be pursued in India and has also attained international attention. While in many other areas of theology, the gulf between statements and reality is larger, as far as Dalit theology is concerned, we could confidently state that the gap is not that wide. In the first place, Dalit theology has shaken the traditional way of pursuing theology by drawing our attention to the experience of the most oppressed and marginalized groups in the Indian society. *Immediacy, concreteness and a certain urgency* characterizing Dalit theology have spared it from futile theoretical discussions and theological narcissism.

The realism of Dalit theology derives from its direct contact with the Earth and the experience of hard physical labour and sweat. The *experience of negativity* by the Dalits has created an atmosphere more conducive to the projection of alternatives than to compliance with the system or following of the trodden path. For example, the depth of suffering (material deprivation, psychological wounds, dependency and social humiliation) as a positive reality has triggered the Dalit imagination for new theological trajectories mirroring their experience more closely. Further, the nature of Dalit experience is such that it has also led to radicalism in thought. It is counter-cultural in spirit.[6] The millennia of suffering and oppression have created in the

---

4 The Indian Theological Association has done a very useful service to scholars, by bringing out a volume containing all its statements during its 25-year existence. See Jacob Parappally (ed.), *Theologizing in Context. Statements of Indian Theological Association*, Bangalore, Dharmaram Publications, 2002.

5 For some of the major issues in Indian theologizing, see Felix Wilfred, *On the Banks of Ganges. Doing Contextual Theology*, Delhi, ISPCK, 2002.

6 For a very useful volume giving a comprehensive picture of Dalit theology discussing a wide range of issues, see James Massey (ed.), *Indigenous People:*

Dalit people an anti-establishment and anti-hegemonic urge, which can be seen reflected in their theology. The radicalism of Dalit theology can be seen also in the way it unmasks the traditional social constructs of purity and pollution, high and low, and its restlessness regarding the ideological justifications, be it in the society or within the Christian communities.

It is the merit of Dalit theology and subaltern theological orientation to have challenged the development of Indian theology along the traditional Sanskritic and Brahminical lines and the exclusive use of so-called classical texts.

Dalit theology has its seminal roots in the autochthonous tradition of the Dalits. The first thing we should remember about this autochthonous tradition is that it is a living tradition surviving from ancient times, though dependent and powerless. It appears in the form of myths, proverbs, songs, festivals and rituals. They tell the story of Dalit origin and their enslavement under religious symbolism. Protests and the search for justice and equality are often explicitly expressed in songs, rituals and festivals.[7]

As a result, Indian theology was brought to the realization of the plurality of sociopolitical and cultural experiences in the country. Within the Christian communities themselves, Dalit theology has led, at least, to a greater awareness of the issue. The 'success'– if that term can be used in our context – of Dalit theology is due in great part to its co-operation with *Dalit movements*, from which it has derived a lot of inspiration, tools of analysis, and it has on its part also animated the Dalit movements, particularly among the Christian communities. There has also been a very concrete hermeneutics on the part of Dalit theology, and biblical studies are beginning to emerge which offer a lot of fresh and innovative insights. I would like to highlight the doctoral dissertation done by my student, Maria Arul Raja, a Dalit himself, on the passion narrative of Mark interpreted through the experiences of Dalit suffering.[8]

Dalits. Dalit Issues in Today's Theological Debate, Delhi, ISPCK, 1998; Arvind Nirmal, *A Reader in Dalit Theology,* Madras, Gurukul Lutheran College and Research Institute, n.d; V. Devasahayam (ed.), *Frontiers of Dalit Theology*, Madras, Gurukul Theological College and Research Institute, 1997. See also Samuel Rayan, 'The Challenge of the Dalit Issue: Some Theological Perspectives', in V. Devasahayam (ed.), *Dalits and Women. Quest for Humanity*, Lutheran Theological College and Institute, Madras, 1992, pp. 117–37.

7 A. M. Abraham Ayrookuzhiel, 'Dalit Theology: A Movement of Counter-Culture', in Massey (ed.), *Indigenous People: Dalits*, p. 260.

8 A. Maria Arul Raja, *Dalit Encounter with their Sufferings: An Emancipatory Interpretation of Mark 15:1–47 from a Dalit Perspective* (an unpublished

Yet another important contribution has come about through the Dalit movement and Dalit theology. It is the affirmation of the earthliness of human life and the fulfilment of material needs of life as constitutive of salvation, and salvation itself as total well-being.[9] Dalit theology is also functioning as an important check on theology, guarding it from taking recourse to abstract and abstruse discourses.

Indian mission theology

Another achievement of Indian theology in the past few decades has been a fresh and context-related understanding of Christian mission. The missiologists in particular deserve special mention for their contribution, which found support among other theologians and biblical scholars.[10] The new understanding of mission has effected a significant shift from the times and attitudes which placed the Christians on the pedestal of preachers to the country. Missiological thought in India has helped us to listen to the different voices in the country and read various signs of times and places. It has created a theological orientation and mental attitude, that has put us in a positive encounter with our neighbours.[11] In the Christian communities themselves the new missiological thought has so percolated that it is becoming more and more difficult to find Christians who would still believe that the main task of Christians is to preach, convert and baptize non-Christians. The role Indian missiological thought has played is very timely. For, in a communally charged atmosphere, persistence with the traditional theology of mission would have caused a lot of serious damage in terms of relationship with fellow-citizens of the country. Conversion has been one of the most controversial issues, with serious societal and political implications. Indian mission theology has approached the

---

doctoral dissertation written under the guidance of Felix Wilfred and presented at the University of Madras), Chennai, 2000.

9 Cf. Felix Wilfred, 'What is Wrong with Rice-Christians? Well-being as Salvation. A Subaltern Perspective', in *Third Millennium* 4 (2001), pp. 6–18.

10 Cf. George Soares-Prabhu, 'Two Mission Commands: An Interpretation of Matthew 28.16–20 in the Light of a Buddhist Text' in *Biblical Interpretation* 2 (1994), pp. 264–82. For his other important contributions in the understanding of mission, see *Biblical Themes for a Contextual Theology Today* (Collected Writings of George M. Soares-Prabhu vol. I, edited by Isaac Padinajarekuttu), Pune, Jnana-Deepa Vidyapeeth, 1999, pp. 3–47; M. Amaladoss, *Making All Things New. Mission in Dialogue*, Anand, Gujarat Sahitya Prakash, 1990.

11 Cf. Jacob Kavunkal and F. Kranghkuma (eds), *Bible and Mission in India Today*, Bombay, St Paul's, 1993; Joseph Mattam and Sebastian Kim (eds), *Dimensions of Mission in India*, Bombay, St Paul's, 1995.

question in a very refreshing way, true to the biblical tradition, but at the same time sensitive to the sociopolitical context.[12] The Christian community, thanks to the new theology of mission, has been prevented from the danger of fundamentalist and semi-fundamentalist thought and approach.

The theology of mission has widened its scope particularly through a fresh biblical hermeneutics. Biblical scholars like Soares-Prabhu, Pathrapankal and Lucien Legrand have contributed to the development of a broader biblical perspective on the theology of mission. Indian theology has been able to develop the understanding of mission and salvation in such a way as to make us realize how sociopolitical involvement is a 'constitutive part' of our Christian existence. In particular the concept of salvation has been interpreted in relation to the struggles in the sociopolitical arena.

I would especially like to refer to the many grassroots movements with which some of the Indian theologians were associated, and which helped also support a shift from a theology of development to an Indian theology of liberation. However, what were discussed at the initial stage in terms of salvation and human development helped to give a then much-needed earthly dimension. In this way, the dichotomy which characterized the traditional approach between salvation and earthly commitment has been overcome to a great extent. In evolving these perspectives, it should be admitted that Indian theology availed itself of the insights developed by liberation theology worldwide, especially in Latin America.

Secular connections

Yet another important achievement in Indian theology has been its openness towards the leftist and secular forces in the country. This is not something to be taken for granted. This openness is very significant against the background of outright opposition to Marxism and socialist thought on the ground that they are atheistically inspired. The inherited theology was one which taught to view these movements and ideologies as opposed to Christian faith. It is significant that from such a position there has come about a radical transformation in theological thought. Some of the concrete struggles waged against injustice

---

12 A most recent work, excellently researched, goes into the details of the debates on conversion: Sebastian C. H. Kim, *In Search of Identity. Debates on Religious Conversion in India*, Oxford, Oxford University Press, 2003.

and exploitation in collaboration with leftist movements have further strengthened the theological orientation.

The dialogue and collaboration with leftist and secular movements has helped theology also to respond to the *communal problem* plaguing the Indian society. As is well-known, the secular and leftist movements have been a strong force against the communal divide of the society. The dialogue of Indian theology with secular forces has been the contribution of many theologians – both among Roman Catholics and Protestants. In particular we may recall here the contributions of M. M. Thomas, Sebastian Kappen, Samuel Rayan and others.[13]

Tribal contribution

As for tribal theology, a critical distancing from traditional theology and moving towards a theology that will incorporate the tribal culture was a welcome change. Instead of reproducing a theology that is foreign to their life and world of experience, it has contributed to making the tribals feel a little at home in Christianity. The anthropological and cultural studies which have found a way into tribal theologizing have helped its growth. Biblical themes like *'promise [sic] land, Pentecost, exodus* and the *alien'*[14] have served as key concepts in interpreting some of the tribal experiences.

The tribal theologizing has unfolded before us extremely rich resources whose significance goes far beyond the tribal areas. The strong sense of community and practice of solidarity at a time of aggressive individualism, the sense of wholeness and harmony with nature at a time of serious ecological crisis are some of the important insights which the tribal peoples can contribute to theologizing. The tribal situation leads us to reflect about the indissociable relationship between ecology and social justice. In the light of all this we could say that a more appropriate question would be, what is the contribution of the tribals to theology, rather than how we could pursue tribal theology.

However, there are many thorny questions and issues which need to be responded to. One such crucial issue is that of *identity crisis*. It is a focal point which explains the situation of Indian tribals, and the

---

13 For detailed treatment of the thought of some of these authors, see Felix Wilfred and M. M. Thomas, *Theologiegeschichte der Dritten Welt. Indien*, München, Chr. Kaiser, 1992; see also Felix Wilfred, *Beyond Settled Foundations. The Journey of Indian Theology*, Madras, Department of Christian Studies, University of Madras, 1993.

14 K. Thanzauva, *Theology of Community. Tribal Theology in the Making*, Mizo Theological Conference, Aizawal, Mizoram, 1997.

experiences and struggles they are undergoing. Tribal societies are in transition in the midst of many political convulsions, and in some parts in situations of armed struggles. There is a serious cultural crisis caused by the whirlwind of modernity and globalization that tries to blow them off their feet. Many tribals are pushed into *a situation of anomie*, torn and pulled in all directions. Tribals feel that they are exploited on their own soil and are alienated from their natural habitat. Attention to the sociopolitical developments, and a critical approach to the society and a more dynamic understanding of culture are important issues to which tribal theology has to respond.

Budding feminist theology

Indian feminist theology is struggling to emerge and it has to face quite a lot of problems. The call to the experience of women as starting point of feminist theology is beginning to create some ripples, though there is a long way to go. The emerging feminist theology, unfortunately, has not been able to make a dent, as the Dalit theology has done, for example. This is not to discredit the laudable work of a few committed and pioneering Indian women doing feminist theology in an environment in general hostile to their initiatives, but to underline the complexity of the gender issue. What is happening within Indian feminist theology only reflects what is happening in the wider society, in which the caste issue has been much more in the centre of debate than the gender issue. Feminist theology would find even greater difficulties. The predominance of clericalism tends to suppress the critical questions women raise both within the Church and outside.[15]

In spite of all this, I would like to highlight some of the advances feminist theology has achieved in the past few years.[16] First and foremost it has created greater awareness especially in the Christian com-

---

15 Cf. Margaret Shanti, 'Women Towards a New Ecclesiogenesis', in Margaret Shanti and Corona Mary (eds), *We Dare to Speak*, Tiruchirapalli, Word Publications, 1994, pp. 36–61.

16 Though there does not seem to be any single work giving a comprehensive and up-to-date survey of Indian feminist theology, its general orientation could be inferred from some of the contributions: Prasanna Kumari, *A Reader in Feminist Theology*, Madras, Gurukul Publication, 1993; Ursula King, *Feminist Theology from the Third World: A Reader*, London, SPCK, 1994; Gabriele Dietrich, 'On Doing Feminist Theology in South Asia', in *Kristujyoti* 6 (1990), pp. 26–55; Dietrich, 'South Asian Feminist Theory and its Significance for Feminist Theology', in *Concilium* 30 (1996), pp. 101–15; Stella Faria, Anna V. Alexander and Jessi Tellis Nayak (eds), *The Emerging Christian Woman. Church and Society Perspective*, Bangalore, WINA, 1984.

munities and institutions, about the oppression suffered by women, their struggle for survival and the urgent need to respond to their plight. This has been done, among other things, by attempts to re-read and interpret the Christian Scriptures. Women from a tribal background have particularly given attention to the interpretation of their experiences in the light of a critical reading of the Christian Scriptures.[17] In the process, Indian feminist theologians have also sharpened their critical sense and have unmasked those symbols and institutions, attitudes and ideologies that have served to legitimize their subordination. Their critique assumes a cultural and religious critique of women's subordination. Knowing the importance of symbols, feminist theologians have sought to draw from the Indian universe those symbols, images and myths that contribute to the cause of women's liberation.[18]

Feminist theology has also created consciousness about *inclusive language*. Another development is the linkages that feminist theology have established with grassroots feminist movements, which augurs well for the future. Finally, feminist theologians are getting organized through various *associations and fora* to articulate and reflect theological issues. Thus we have such bodies as Women Theologians Forum, Indian Women in Theology (IWIT), an ecumenical forum, and Ecclesial Women of Asia (IWA). A sign of the changing situation within the Christian communities is, for example, the entry of women as lecturers and professors – even full-time – into seminaries and other institutes of clerical formation.

Part 2: Pointers to the Future

Some basic issues

After having taken stock of the achievements of Indian theology, which are quite remarkable for the brevity of the period in which all this has come about, we need to turn our attention to the future. From a socio-political perspective there are certain questions and issues to which the various emerging Indian theologies should respond. The responses will

---

17 For a study by Naga feminist theologians from North-East India, see the recent work by Limatula Longkumer and Talijungla Longkumer (eds), *Side By Side. Naga Women Doing Theology in Search of Justice and Partnership*, Jorhat, CCA-EGY and NWTF, 2004.

18 Pieris has made a very significant contribution to feminist theology in the first part of his work *Fire and Water. Basic Issues in Asian Buddhism and Christianity*, New York, Orbis Books, 1996.

mould their future shape. It appears to me that there are *four clusters of issues* which need to be addressed.

First, we are faced with a situation of globalization and new economic policies that are causing serious violence to the life of the poor and jeopardizing their survival. There is a growing amnesia of the poor, even as social and political consciousness is fast disappearing. Second, there is the situation of a strong right-wing and militant political orientation in the country. It is spreading far and wide and penetrating deeply in every segment of life, deploying certain religio-cultural symbols. The current political situation raises, among other things, crucial issues like the mode of governance, democracy, minority rights and so on. Third, there is the question of affirmation of various suppressed and alienated identities which are trying to give voice and expression to their selves, discovering in the process their own histories, cultural, literary and religious sources, symbols, etc. Diversity and pluralism have become central issues. Finally, there are the challenges connected with creating communities in a situation of deep division and contradiction at all levels. Amidst contradictory trends and forces, what does it mean to be a people, a nation, and above all what does it mean to be truly communities of love, truth, freedom and justice? The question implies the interrelationship among different religious traditions. The various Indian theologies will encounter in different configurations the working of these forces at the local level, and they need to be addressed.

We need to consolidate the gains of Indian theologizing, and move further on in our theological journey by responding to these and other clusters of issues. For this purpose some fundamental questions need to be addressed. Here I shall highlight five such issues.

Christianity from survival to proactive existence

The nature of our theology will depend upon our perception of Christianity in India at large. It appears to me that the reforms that have taken place in the mainline churches would give the impression that they try to answer implicitly the question: *How could Christianity survive in India in the changed times and conditions?* The face of Christianity in the country required a transformation. Many attempts were made in the churches in this regard. In the Roman Catholic Church a central concept that has characterized its life and praxis has been the concept of *inculturation*. I take this as the key concept responsible for the changes in various areas of life in the Church. The Protestant churches have been using more the concept of *contextualization*.

My proposal is that we reconsider the concept of inculturation and the exaggerated importance it has come to acquire, distracting us from tackling some vital issues. Such a reconsideration is important for the future of Christianity in India, and consequently for a change in the present theological pursuit. Inculturation basically is a process meant to keep Christianity meaningful in the Third World in the postcolonial period, after the cultural alienation that took place during the period of missionary expansion. It is interesting to note that the concept of *culture* has been very much employed when speaking of non-Western peoples, whereas the concept that is mostly used for the experiences in the West has been *society*. In this regard, it may be pointed out here that for a long time India was not studied from a *sociological perspective* but from an *anthropological perspective*. What we call today sociology started as anthropology in India.

The underlying presupposition in this approach of reserving culture to the study of peoples in the South is that the societies in these geographical regions are static. The predominance of the cultural concept came to indicate that the peoples of the developing world are objects of study from a cultural perspective, leaving aside the social dynamism.

It is interesting to note that, for reasons totally other than those underlying the Western interest in the concept of culture (and therefore tying up this concept with the new shape of Christianity in the South), the right-wing militant Hindutva elements focused on culture as defining the Indian nation. Consequently the concept of inculturation adopted from the West helped the Christian community in India to show that Christianity is not alien, and that it has an indigenous cultural face.[19] Unfortunately, here again the question of culture has played the role of diverting attention from more substantial issues.

Let me now come back to the question with which I started. The question of survival of Christianity in the cultural context can and has made Christianity more inward looking, and has placed it in a centripetal movement. Inculturation would appear to be part of this general mood. But the issue of culture should not be isolated, rather it should be placed within the dynamics of the society. Therefore, the real question for the future of Christianity is: *What proactive role can Christianity play in a society that is undergoing fast changes with new forces and factors at work?*[20] With this question and starting point, we are in a position to respond to the issues raised by Dalit movements,

---

19 Cf. Roger Heduland (ed.), *Christianity is Indian. The Emergence of an Indigenous Community*, Delhi, ISPCK, 2000.

20 Cf. Felix Wilfred, *Asian Dreams and Christian Hope*, Delhi, ISPCK, 2003 (2nd edition).

tribal aspirations, feminist movements and those of the many marginalized groups. A Christianity that is proactive to the dynamics of the *society* with its political, historical and economic components will be one that will also evolve continuously and ever more into an *Indian* Christianity. It is in responding to the dynamics of the society that the self-shaping also takes place. Radical openness and other-centredness is the basis for one's self-definition and fulfilment, as in the case of individual identity-formation. This is also the case with Christianity as a collective body.

The future of theology will be directed to this proactive role of Christianity, which will also be a process of finding its own identity in the concrete. And this cannot be done with the Western inculturation agenda. In short, the future of Indian theology will be determined on the basis of how it interacts and serves the transformation of Indian society. Such a theology will become politically very sensitive and conscious of the contradictions marking the society.

The dialectics of integration and prophecy

The future course of theology will also depend upon how Christianity in India gets rooted in the soil, and at the same time remains prophetic. I surmise that this will be a continuous source of tension and dialectics. Insertion in the sociopolitical dynamics of the country, which also includes its culture, could easily lead Christianity into accommodation to the status quo or compliance with the powers that be. Nationalist churches in the past succumbed to the temptation of going along with the ruling classes and the prevailing state of affairs. Integration into the society needs to be accompanied by prophecy.

On the other hand, we just cannot think of a Christianity in our times which simply makes prophetic denunciation from a moral high ground. As the experience during the times of missionary expansion shows, Christianity is vulnerable to being viewed and branded as alien to our societies. Still worse, Christianity risks not being taken seriously because of its failure to insert itself within the societal dynamics. Christianity is most effective when it is able to both integrate itself and at the same time function as a prophetic voice. In other words, how to be rooted, and yet be prophetic; and how to be prophetic and yet be rooted. This is what I mean by dialectics of integration and prophecy. I would consider this as the most intricate question Indian Christianity, and Asian Christianity at large, is facing.

The addressees of Indian theology

The future of Indian theology will also depend upon the question: to whom is it addressed? As it is, Indian theology is addressed to the Christian community, and even here, as is well-known, it is very much restricted to a small clientele of the clerical group, since theology forms an important part in the preparation of religious personnel and ministers. This kind of theology could easily become a *ghetto theology*, which is harmful to the universal implications of our faith. We want theology in India to be *catholic* theology – catholic understood in its original etymological sense. The addressee of theology will be *all* the people of the country, cutting across religious and ideological barriers, and it is this which will make theology integrally *Indian*. This catholicity will be then the mark of Indian theology. This cannot take place as long as theology is restricted to the Christian community, much less to the clerical group.

The reflections we made above challenge us to view the whole of society as the addressee of theology. Let me immediately sound a note of caution. This is not meant as any triumphalistic, integralist and Christian chauvinistic statement, as though Christianity wants to impose its theology on the society. Rather, it is meant to challenge Christianity, so that what is found in the Christian Scriptures and traditions are so interpreted that their universal import emerges concretely in relation to the situation of the society. As is clear, the proposal is not meant to dilute the Christian faith and message. What is envisaged is that the universalistic character of the Christian message becomes actual inasmuch as it enters into interaction with all those questions and issues affecting the people in the larger society.

This wider addressee of theology, while making the theological enterprise very enriching, also makes it a very challenging one. Having to address all the people means new responsibility. Theology needs to be transparent, and therefore every part of it, and every interpretation, needs to be checked as to what extent it contributes to the society. It is also a check to find whether there are aspects of theology that foster fundamentalism or semi-fundamentalism which could be detrimental to the society. More importantly, theology has the responsibility to rethink every aspect of Christian belief in relation to the concrete sociopolitical experiences we are going through and bring out the universal character of every one of those beliefs.

This thoroughgoing approach will bring to light the most significant and universal aspects of the Christian faith, without triumphalism, but in service of truth and the transformation of society. Interaction with the society will also lead to the realization of the so-called 'hierarchy of truths'. Not all that Christians believe will have the same value when re-thought from the interactive perspective. A non-triumphalistic and interactive approach to Christian mystery and belief will find partners who will help to bring out theological richness from the Scriptures and the heritage of Christian tradition.[21] The call for a theology that will be addressed to all has as its fundamental presupposition that faith, love and hope are inherent in any authentic human experience – whether religious or secular. And a theology that is built on this presupposition and addressed to all will not go unheeded or go without response.

By having the larger society as the addressee, theology will also fulfil its social responsibility and public accountability, because every belief, idea and praxis performed in the public realm has its repercussions in the society. Either it helps the society to transform itself, or it creates disorientation. Therefore, theology will be conscious of its public accountability.

The addressees of theology will cut across religious and ideological barriers. But that does not mean that we are going to have one single theological development. Here too there will be delimitations based not on confessional difference, but on the basis of the collective geographical region, group, issue, etc. And this will pave the way for a plurality of Indian theologies.

Theology is answerable

Much of the professional theology, because of the present-day setting in which it is done, has taken seriously its responsibility to the Church. And this commitment is to be appreciated. But there is a question less asked and not sufficiently answered: How about the responsibility of theology to the larger Indian society? What about its responsibility towards other religious tradition, other experiences? There are many areas in which Indian theologies are answerable. Does the present content of theological teaching and learning contribute to the creation of communal harmony and understanding?

Theology is answerable to the poor. If Jesus proclaims that the poor are blessed, and the kingdom of God is promised to them, it is important that we scrutinize every form of theology to see whether this central piece of the gospel is translated into theological practice. The purity of theology and its orthodoxy needs to be measured not

---

21 On what that could mean when we speak of Jesus Christ, cf. Felix Wilfred, 'Jesus-Interpretation in Asia', in *Vaiharai* (2002), Vol. 7, No. 4, pp. 3–19.

only with reference to theology's responsibility towards the Church community, but as well with its responsibility towards the society and the poor. An orthodox and authentic form of Indian theology emerges when it shows itself to be responsible to the society around, and especially to the plight of the poorest of the poor. In this way, the concept of 'purity' does not become something connected with the elites (about which Dalit theology is very conscious) and their concerns, but becomes truly a matter of sincerity and fidelity to truth in all its manifold expressions and demands.

Pluralism as the defence of the poor – a theological agenda

A fifth important dimension of the future of Indian theology will be the extent to which it is able to affirm pluralism in praxis and theory. In this contribution I am concerned about pluralism from a socio-political perspective, and not so much from a religio-cultural perspective, which merits a treatment all by itself. Pluralism, I think, ultimately is a question of *justice*. Justice demands that we respect the other (individual and collective) in his/her/their 'otherness' – which also includes religion. This is the foundation for any theory and praxis of justice. Denial of pluralism kills justice before destroying unity. It is by affirming their difference that the poor have a chance to reclaim their very selves. Pluralism is a defence of the poor and hope of the poor in a homogenizing world.

We need to stress this when we are speaking of pluralism. For often pluralism is reduced to the question of truth and relativity. That would be a reduction to an epistemological issue of what is, in fact, an issue of daily life. To opt for pluralism in our Indian society is to opt for the poor, for, amidst the many homogenizing tendencies and the practice of various forms of hegemonies, the liberation of the people at the margins of the society rests on how we are able to uphold the ideal of pluralism. If so, the consequences of pluralism for theology and theological education in India, and Asia at large, are as great as those of the option for the poor in the biblical understanding. In everyday life we witness that the opposition to pluralism coincides with the agenda of the powerful – socially, politically, culturally and religiously. The ideal of pluralism as understood and lived in India, then, should become a matter of *the defence of the poor*. In this sense, pluralism is part and parcel of the liberation agenda. Whereas, the upper castes and classes tend to do away with diversity as a threat, the future of the marginal people depends very much on achieving their right to be different with all its consequences. Unity is certainly an important value. But we cannot forget that it could become a cloak to cover the vested interests of the upper castes and classes. True unity is the result of dialogue, negotiation, mutuality, and not a matter of fitting everything into a ready-made system.

Part 3: Some Methodological Trajectories

Given the radical pluralism characterizing human existence and the sociopolitical and religio-cultural conditions, theologies will be plural and they will call for a plurality of methods. What follows are some tentative reflections and suggestions for one of the possible theological methodologies. I thought that it is high time that we stop repeating the need for a different methodology, and enter into tentative attempts to delineate methodologies, even at the risk of being incomplete.

On the other hand, what I have been trying to say in Part 2 would be incomplete if I do not also add some thoughts on the method. In fact, the question of method is a sequel to the five issues we took up for reflection in Part 2. If theology, for example, is addressed to all the people, we will certainly need a corresponding change in methodological orientation. The methodologies of today cannot be the same as when metaphysical categories dominated theology. At the global level we could notice a shift in methodology when theology moved from metaphysical categories to more historical ones. Today, the need of the hour is contextual categories – deriving both from sociopolitical experiences and from the religio-cultural realm.

An epistemological premise

The question of methodology is a common issue the various disciplines of humanities and sciences face. Theology could comfort itself with the thought that the methodological flux is not peculiar to it; it has become a common problem of disciplines. The parting of ways among the practitioners of the same science is characterized by the difference in methodology. In particular, I would like to point out that theology has had in the past strong metaphysical moorings, at least since the Middle Ages. This is especially true of Roman Catholic tradition. No wonder then, that the dissolution of metaphysics is today seen as coinciding with the 'dissolution' of Christianity in the West – be it through the interpretation of secularization or through the advent of postmodernity. Be that as it may, the point I wish to underline is that theology may take a dangerous and fundamentalist turn if it wants to still be confined to the metaphysical realm. In other words, there should be an 'epistemological vigilance' over the realm of theology. The truths of its assertions need to be sensitive to the epistemological question and the process of acquiring, critically developing and organizing knowledge. If so, theology will be able to share with other sciences similar epistemological concerns.

Crucial to the question for all sciences in grappling with methodology is the epistemological issue of objectivity. The question of *objectivity* has been common to all forms of knowledge, and the question is posed much more sharply with regard to the humanities. Theology also shares with other organized forms of knowledge the traditional question of the validity of its knowledge, which is commonly supposed to be to the extent that it is objective. Today we realize that this classical picture is changing as the self-perception of the disciplines are undergoing a profound mutation.[22] The developments in epistemology and sociology of knowledge have also contributed to a change in this situation. Part of the ongoing change is the progressive recognition of a role of the subject (individual and collective) which, however, varies. The consideration of subjective and objective in any discipline is something specific to every discipline. There is no common understanding of objective and subjective which could be generalized and applied equally to all the disciplines. In natural sciences the choices of themes for study, the individuals and institutions which do or support research, etc. would be the subjective conditioning in the production and dissemination of knowledge. Naturally, the role of the subject in humanities and social sciences is even greater.

We need to go a step further and view the attempt to see the problems involved in the representation of reality as one of a dialectics between the subjective and the objective. Every form of knowledge bears the stamp of this dialectics, and it is important to be conscious of it when we consider theology and theological discourse. We need to particularly highlight that the subjective is not something which we need to guard ourselves against, as it may tamper with objectivity. Rather, very often the subjective is very much necessary as a means to

---

22 As for the social sciences, a good overview of the question with points under debate could be found in: Immanuel Wallerstein (ed.), *Open the Social Sciences. Report of the Gulbenkian Commission on the Restructuring of the Social Sciences*, Delhi, Vistaar Publications, 1996; cf. also Richard Whitley, *The Intellectual and Social Organization of the Sciences*, Oxford, Oxford University Press, 2000 (2nd edition).

a more complete understanding and approximation to truth. As the psychologist Eric Fromm noted way back in 1950, 'objectivity does not mean detachment; it means respect; that is the ability not to distort and to falsify things, persons and oneself'.[23]

The emotional content as an expression of the subjective need not be an element in theology, which takes us away from truth; rather the emotionally charged thought can lead us closer to truth. How else are we to understand the important truths the Dalits, the tribals and women, for example, are telling us? Similarly, the collective agency of the subject (whether Dalits, tribals, women or a particular group of people experiencing the same form of suffering and oppression, etc.) is indispensable in the process of theologizing and reaching theological knowledge. Time and space are inherent in any self-constitution of the individual and collective self, and consequently in any form of relationship and creation of knowledge. To use a terminology from social sciences we may say that time and space are *variables* inherent in the subject and not merely external circumstances under which knowledge is produced and constituted. Consequently any theological theme treated in two different sociopolitical *contexts* (time and space) of the subject will not be the same.

The components of a possible method

Having made the epistemological premise, let me now propose a possible theological method in its various components. Today, a good theological pursuit will be one in which there will be three important methodological components: (a) empirical data, (b) critical interpretation, and (c) liberative process of knowledge. Let me briefly present these three components.

Empirical data

Theology needs to become more and more empirical. This should not be interpreted in a positivistic sense with its assumptions, for example: truth is only when it is shown experimentally through hard facts (as once the natural sciences were thought to be), something that subsequently became also the methodological bedrock for anything to be

---

23 Eric Fromm, *Man for Himself*, London, Routledge, 1950, p. 105. In the same work the author notes that 'objective' is not identical with 'absolute', p. 16.

scientific.[24] I am distancing myself from such an assumption; nor do I intend to enter into the long-debated question of whether theology is a science. These discussions flourished when the focus of discussion was centred on relationship between reason and faith. Further, the proposal of the study of empirical data is different from what was known as positivist theology, meaning thereby the attempt to cull out passages and texts from Scripture and tradition with reference to any particular theme.

What I mean by *empirical* theology is the theological investigation and pursuit that begins from sociopolitical facts and data. This is something very important because in this way every single issue we are treating will have *a concrete social location*. In India, the Dalits and the tribals have taught us about the earthliness of our existence, and the importance of paying attention to concrete realities related to survival. We just cannot build a theological castle without taking into account the facts and figures about poverty, oppression and the experience of negations undergone by the various segments of people. A vague description or rhetoric on the same cannot furnish an adequate and reasonable basis for the beginning of theology.

If theology is being done in a particular community or group, the empirical data will be the ones pertaining to them and their condition, which however needs to be studied and recorded in detail. If I were to join others in theologizing, my approach would be one of participant observation.

This first stage of methodology involves, while dealing with any theological treatise or theme, asking, what is the empirical data corresponding to that treatise or issue. The data need to be collected and studied in depth and thoroughly. This is also part and parcel of the theological process. It is a fact that most often theological discourses make too general and sweeping statements about empirical realities in order to be able to ascend quickly to an a-historical plane. And if there

---

24 In this regard, it should be pointed out that, in the history of Christianity, the opportunity for theology to develop itself in close collaboration with empirical sciences was lost when the line of orientation followed by Grosseteste, Roger Bacon, William of Occam, Duns Scotus and others (represented in the Oxford approach of the fourteenth century) lost the intellectual battle to an abstract kind of theology least sensitive to empirical realities. In this connection, Norman F. Cantor, in his scholarly study on plague, notes how development in experimental sciences was prevented, for example, through the prohibition of vivisection by adducing abstract theological motives. See Norman F. Cantor, *In the Wake of the Plague. The Black Death and the World It Made*, New York, Perennial, 2002, pp. 112ff.

is effort to relate to these realities, theological discourses often content themselves with making impressionistic and anecdotal statements.

Critical interpretation

The collection of empirical data will be followed by critical interpretation. This could happen in three stages. These three stages could be also viewed as three different streams of interpretation which meet and merge:

Interpretation through the help of critical sciences

Depending on the theological question or the issue, different disciplines need to be drawn into the picture. In so doing, the tools and methods specific to that particular discipline need to be followed. Often, the help of more than one science may be required to interpret the data. I want to underline that enlisting the collaboration of sciences is part and parcel of the *theologizing process itself.* We could look at the process analytically from two angles:

In relation to sciences: Since the production, organization and distribution of various knowledge fields are themselves very much linked to external factors and motivations, it is important to be *critical* as well in employing the sciences for the interpretation of data. Often an uncritical approach goes with sciences becoming supporters of the status quo. Since within the same discipline there could be very different orientations, we need to choose the kind of orientation that is geared to change and transformation. That would tally with one of the basic presuppositions of any genuine theology, namely that all theology is directed towards change – personal, collective, societal, etc. The theological enterprise needs to guard itself against the danger of sciences becoming new absolutes, a temptation to which theology itself has been exposed.

In relation to theology: Theology itself needs to be counterchecked by social sciences and humanities, lest there be triumphalism – something which is not just a matter of the past, but also characterizes attitudes today. One need only study the views of an influential thinker like John Milbank in regard to theology, which for him is so overarching that it cannot only do away with other sciences, but even replace them.[25] But, in fact, consciousness of the socio-economic conditions

---

25 See the excellent thesis presented by a Filipino at the University of Leuven, Belgium: Daniel Franklin Pilario, *Back to the Rough Grounds of Praxis. Exploring Theological Method with Bourdieu*. Beyond Liberation Theology

in which theological discourses are produced calls for a critique of the ideological and idolatrous elements, and the very language of these discourses themselves.

Interpretation through the help of the Bible and Christian traditions

Religious scriptures have a unique place since they are the *pramana* or documents of faith. The process of knowledge does not end with the operation of reason, which, in any case, cannot give us the truth but only function as a regulatory and ordering principle. The Scripture acquires a character of certitude for believers because the knowledge of faith it gives is self-validating and not requiring further validation, which if pursued could lead to infinite regression. All this is true of Christian approach as much as Hindu approach.

The function of reason is not to judge the truth of the Vedic statements, but to determine their true import, free from inconsistencies and in conformity with established facts. They are not to be accepted dogmatically, but through intelligent interpretation compatible with perceptual and inferential knowledge. *Sruti* awaits rational analysis to yield its true import. [26]

Thus, in interpreting the Christian Scriptures, all the tools that have been developed to study and understand the Bible, its background and its universal message will be employed. Similarly, the Christian traditions will also be explored to study how a particular issue or theme has been treated in different contexts of history. I need not go into these issues in detail.

My presupposition here is that the Bible and Christian traditions are meant to serve life and its flourishing in all its expressions. Also presupposed is that these resources are oriented to effect change and transformation at all levels. Particularly with reference to tradition, it should be pointed out that, regrettably, many of the theological themes are in practice identified with the tracing of its history. No wonder then that we are witnessing how, for example, the kind of theology that sticks to traditional formulations is more and more being sidelined as irrelevant even within the Church, not to speak of the general public. That is why the interpretation of tradition needs to be directed towards the enlightenment of data collected and interpreted at the first stage.

---

and Radical Orthodoxy, Leuven, 2002. Pilario subjects to critical scrutiny the position of Milbank representing radical orthodoxy on the one hand, and questions Clodovis Boff's theory of praxis, on the other.

26 Cf. Sivanandam Panneerselvam, 'A Hindu Response to the Pope's Encyclical Letter "Fides et Ratio"', in *Concilium* 2003/4, pp. 79–89, p. 85.

Not all informations from the past may have relevance, or may serve to illumine the question at hand. Therefore, there will take place a judicious selection from the traditions. This need not trouble us, since tradition itself is not a unified seamless garment (which we often tend to believe it to be) but is made up of different streams originating from widely different social and cultural contexts and backgrounds. Further, since theology has to have constant reference to the empirical data and its analysis, it will be helpful in studying the particular traditions also to note how particular beliefs and doctrines have affected society and with what consequences. In other words, the social effects of Christian doctrines are important to relate them to the particular theological question or issue we may be dealing with today in our contexts. For example, it would appear that some of the heresies in early Christianity were more expressions of nationalism and identity-affirmation than matters of orthodoxy and heterodoxy.

Interpretation through religio-cultural resources

This third stage or layer of interpretation will take into account the religio-cultural resources of a people or group. Since the empirical data are derived from a field with a particular religio-cultural environment, these resources will be able to throw more light on the particular theme or issue. For example, Dalit, tribal or feminist theology will go into the critical analysis of the resources regarding their genesis and their social effects.

In studying these resources, it is important also to *classify* the sources in different ways. Some of them may be deriving from the so-called classical, and others from sources of the marginalized peoples and groups. The analysis will go into the sources in relation to particular forms of society, ideas and institutions they helped to sustain or the changes and transformations they were able to effect. These resources may also furnish the concrete modality or self-expression of theology. For example, the '*Tribals sing their theology*', which is an indication of the deep affinity of the musical resources to theology.

Speaking of cultural resources, I think it is very important today to take into account developments in the literary field. In India we have an immense wealth of literary production in our different languages. Unfortunately, theology remains aloof from these literary productions reflecting various facets of life. Our data and experiences could be illumined and interpreted through the literary works in rich and variegated Indian languages.

Intertextual interpretation

More specifically in interpreting Christian Scriptures and tradition, we could do more than draw from other religio-cultural resources. We need to enter into some kind of intertextual interpretation The practice of interpreting one text that originated in a particular sociocultural context in relation to another text from another context, can throw much light in our attempt to understand both of them in a very refreshing and creative way. Intertextuality is not a matter of stating the fact that what is found in the text of one tradition is *also* found in another tradition. Nor is it simply *using* one text for interpreting another text. Intertextuality, as Aloysius Pieris has rightly pointed out, is a matter of a *symbiotic encounter*, and the result is something very creative. As Pieris notes,

> Cross-scriptural exegesis of the symbiotic type is quite an innovative exercise in inter-religious dialogue. For here a seminal teaching in the scriptures of one religion, sown and buried in the text, when exposed to the warm light that comes from the teachings of another religion's Sacred Writ, sprouts forth and grows into a fruitful source of new insights. In this 'symbiotic' approach, no room is left for diluting or distorting the basic teachings of either religion; and no effort made to indulge in easy equations or odious comparisons.[27]

Further, sacred texts are not simply carriers of meaning or reservoirs of semantic potential. There is an intimate connection between the sacred texts and religious identity, inasmuch as the sacred texts are those before which the founding and interpretation of the self (individual and collective) takes place. In regard to sacred texts, it is not a matter of interpreting them, but also a question of being interpreted. This also opens up new possibilities and avenues for the self and for the community.[28]

Hence an encounter at that level between the Scriptures of two religious groups has the power to draw to each other much more effectively than other means. We see how Pandita Ramabai,[29] who constantly

---

27 Cf. Aloysius Pieris, in Philip Wickeri (ed.), *Scripture, Community, and Mission* (Essays in honour of D. Preman Niles), Hong Kong and London, CCA-CWM, 2003, pp. 234–53, p. 253.

28 Cf. Paul Ricoeur, *Figuring the Sacred. Religion, Narrative and Imagination*, Minneapolis, Fortress Press, 1995, pp. 35–47.

29 Pandita Ramabai (1858–1922) defied the religious conventions of the time (which prohibited women from studying sacred texts) to study Sanskrit and the Hindu Scriptures. Converted to Christianity, she did not fall in line with the

negotiated the borders of Christianity and Hinduism, could draw from the Scriptures of both traditions and arrive at very refreshing interpretations for her own spiritual journey, and provide an innovative appropriation of both the traditions. Her explorations should not be an isolated instance, but should become more and more a general practice in a theology that is inspired by the spirit of genuine unity and catholicity.

In the intertextual interpretation, we need to be attentive so that it is not reduced only to classical texts of other religious traditions. There are any number of local texts – which unfortunately are not widely known – which have been produced by the subalterns like the Dalits. These texts provided them an interpretation of their identity and life-orientation. Often orally transmitted, the various forms of stories and narratives have acquired a 'sacred' character and have functioned as points of reference in the lives of the subalterns. Intertextuality applies as well to these subaltern texts, and the practice of intertextuality will be part of the methodology of various subaltern theologies.

In sum, intertextuality of sacred texts is important particularly in two respects: to develop a methodology of Indian theology that will be capable of addressing itself to our neighbours of other faiths and to promote a genuine interreligious dialogue that will be the matrix for the generation of a theology of religion that is sensitive to the self-interpretation of our neighbours.

Liberating process of knowledge: three interlocking purificatory stages

It may sound odd to speak of 'purification' – catharsis – when speaking of scientific knowledge. But that is precisely what is required today if we observe the way the system of knowledge, its production and dissemination function. Such a liberating purificatory process will be all the more necessary for theology because of the greater danger of

---

conventions of this tradition either. Through a practical hermeneutics of the Scriptures of both traditions, she could fuse together the riches for the cause of the emancipation of Indian women. In the process, she made a creative and controversial appropriation of Christianity. For a perceptive interpretation of her life and commitment, see Uma Chakravarti, *Rewriting History. The Life and Times of Pandita Ramabai*, Delhi, Kali for Women, 2000 (second impression of the work of 1998). On the controversies surrounding her interpretation of Scriptures and appropriation of Christianity, see Gauri Viswanathan, *Outside the Fold: Conversion, Modernity, and Belief*, Delhi, Oxford University Press, 1998.

distortion to which it is exposed. The various stages are part of the movement from *adhyasa* – illusion (which is a very important concept in the Indic epistemology) – to ever greater approximation to truth.[30] As in the human organism, the continuous purification of the system of knowledge is essential for the truth to be alive and flourish.

The first stage is the one of senses, their perception and the processing of data derived from them. As I noted earlier, this maintains the empirical character of theology and ensures its rootedness in everyday life and practice. Things would be fine if only our senses were to mediate the correct knowledge of things. Experience shows that senses can easily delude us. Hence the necessity of using instruments which can free us from such illusions. But how reliable are the instruments themselves to bring us closer to reality? In this connection, it is very instructive to recall the ecstasy and the despair use of the telescope brought to Galileo. While he hoped to demonstrate the actual state of the heaven, transcending the limits of the naked eye, what actually happened was different people saw different things through the same telescope! They could not agree upon what they saw, some seeing stars double and others seeing several moons.[31]

The first telescopic observations of the sky were indistinct, indeterminate, contradictory and in conflict with what everyone could see with their unaided eyes. And the only theory that could have helped to separate telescopic illusions from veridical phenomena was refuted by simple tests . . . Today we understand a little better why the direct appeal to telescopic vision was bound to lead to disappointment, especially in the initial stages. The main reason, one already foreseen by Aristotle, was that the senses applied under abnormal conditions are liable to give abnormal response.[32]

It is precisely here that the data of the senses, whether through their naked powers or through instruments, need to be checked, purified and explained. Here is precisely the need for a theory of light and refraction which would explain and help overcome the illusion of senses and instruments. We are in the *second stage* of the process. The process in social sciences and humanities could be a parallel one.

---

30 Cf. The classical Indic epistemological tradition identified many sources of illusion, including *pramana dosha* (defect in the subject) and *premeya dosha* (defect in the object). See the important recent contribution by Srinivasa Rao, *Perceptual Error. The Indian Theories*, Honolulu, University of Hawai'i Press, 1998; see also Swami Satprashananda, *Methods of Knowledge According to Advaita Vedanta*, Calcutta, Advaita Ashram, 1995.

31 Cf. Paul Feyerabend, *Against Method*, London and New York, Verso, 2002 (3rd edition).

32 Feyerabend, *Against Method*, pp. 86 and 89.

The process of theologizing also includes the organization of the interpreted data through theorizing. For example, if grace is explained a priori and if claims are made on that basis without relation to empirical realities, it would be in contradiction to the experience of everyday in which the reality of grace seems to be present and operative in the struggles of the Dalits, the tribals and of women for dignity and freedom. In this case, it is a theorizing which sees *grace itself as a historical reality* lived and experienced in the lives of individuals and groups, and the inappropriateness of an approach to grace which does not take into account the empirical and historical realities of life.

Rationalizing (*vichara*) implies also the process of the sifting of data and placing them within an ordered, sequential and logical whole. It also has a place in the construction of theology. However, it would be a gross mistake to equate logical order and system with objectivity and truth. This is what many Western forms of theologies would seem to think and presuppose. Here we need to remember that the epistemological order or the logical consistency has but a meiotic function; they are like the scaffolding or pedestal for the truth to make its manifestation, but not themselves the truth.[33]

The logical need not be so formal if it is seen constantly in relation to actual realities. In fact, it may be interesting to note that the logic of cause and effect has not been a formal abstraction in the Indic tradition. The genesis of the formal logic of interconnection between cause and effect seems to derive from the practice of *ayurvedic* medicine and medical diagnosis. The study of symptoms of illness leads to the cause through a process of exclusions. I think this is very helpful to theology lest the rational and formal lose their generative matrix of empirical realities and their observations.

The rationalizing and theorizing stage needs to be also purified by moving into the third stage of *prajna* or wisdom. At this level, there takes place a purification of the rationalizing process. For this latter process could be seriously conditioned by interests, passions and desire. The formal aspect of rational procedure, as I noted earlier, does not necessarily lead us to truth. It could be so oriented as to serve particular interests, ideologies, etc. The purification and corrective takes the form of attending to those dimensions of the real that get excluded at the level of rationalizing process. For example, the second stage of rationalizing and theorizing could conveniently leave out such crucial issues as gender, race, caste, etc. It is the stage of wisdom which will draw attention to all those neglected elements in the theologizing process.

---

33 *Katha Upanishad* I, ii, 9.

It is a stage in which intellect and will, reason and passion, desire and restraint are reconciled and not polarized. The stage of *prajna* is able to do that precisely because it is a stage of wholeness in which various layers and dimensions of the real are held together.

In a world of knowledge that is becoming progressively specialized in every sector, the difficulty with religion and theology is that it seems to be related to everything without any one thing in particular. This is, of course, a weakness, but also its strength and specific vocation. Theology has to function as the nodal point where different layers of reality meet and merge. It is difficult to find appropriate analogies.

Maybe the function of theology at this stage can be compared to that of a family. A family is an institution which has to be concerned about everything – from the most lofty experiences and ideals to the most mundane. The management of the house (economy), education, human relationships, the place of women and many other things are all treated under one roof and in a unique way. The issues of communication, truth, sincerity, love, freedom, all converge into one. When theology brings together the wide variety of experiences and layers of reality, it surpasses the realm of thought (*vichara*) and moves towards that of *wisdom* (*prajna*). It has always been said that theology is wisdom. Today we understand it better when confronted with the fragmentation of knowledge and experience which we share with everybody else. All human persons are in need of help to be able to learn the art of continuous and dynamic integration. And that is why a theology that helps to integrate the wide varieties of experiences could be addressed to all.

Now, the stage of wisdom itself needs to be purified and corrected. For wisdom could mean a *stasis* – a quietist state of contemplation of the whole. If, as we said, all theology is oriented towards change and transformation, it is at this stage that wisdom needs to be oriented towards that goal. In one sense, more than the end result, the very theological procedure will turn out to be transformative. There will be transformation of the self (individual and collective), the other and the world at large. In terms of the concrete question or issue, theology will tend to effect transformation and change and will also provide reasons for the same.

A second corrective which this stage needs is to guard against the danger of a wisdom centred only on the *present*. The transformative role should lead on to the projection of utopias and alternatives. The various scientific disciplines not only analyse and interpret a specific reality, but also project something for the future. What is projected is often based on the deduction from the analysis and interpretation made. This is true not only of natural sciences but humanities and social sciences as well. For example, a study of evolution could project something on the future shape of a particular species, or the study of present demographic situation will lead to future projections.

The projection will depend on the nature of the particular discipline. As for theology, projection towards the future is a very central issue, because the role of theology is not simply to state *what is* and to interpret what they mean (presence). It is the important task of theology to diagnose what is not (the absence) and to project *what ought to be* on the basis of faith. We are in the realm of *utopias*. Utopias are not illusions. They are imaginative and creative, but realistic possibilities for the future. They can contribute to a critique of the present and shaping of a future which may escape present calculations. In this sense, the kingdom of God is a powerful symbol in theology.

Finally the stage of wisdom, which could give the impression of being general and universal, needs constantly to refer back to the empirical, the concrete, the particular. It is this type of wisdom which theology needs to be. Wisdom and the particular are not opposed to each other. On the contrary, it is in relationship to the concrete that wisdom expresses itself.

It is important that these three stages I have tried to develop are not to be viewed as an ascent from the lower to the higher level, or to be placed in a chronologically sequential order. They should all be in operation at the same time and continuously in interaction. Like the various organs of the body need to be active and interactive with other organs, so also the various levels and their components need to be in communication for a healthy theology.

The methodological indication I have made is meant only to make ourselves aware of, in an analytical way, the various threads and strands involved in the theological methodology. Besides, not all these procedures and stages may be applied equally to all themes and issues. Further, all the steps and procedures indicated (including the study of empirical data) are to be considered as part of the theological process. Theologizing happens all through the process; theology is not, so to say, the cream we churn out. Theology is deeply embedded in the warp and woof of the reality and experience we analyse, study, interpret and relate to praxis. This does not mean that we are imposing a theological format on reality. Rather we move from the discovery of an unthematized theological stage to ever more thematized theological articulation and application with the help of a methodology.

Conclusion

The future trajectory I have tried to envisage and the corresponding development of method pose a great many challenges. I do not want to go into all of them. But by way of conclusion let me highlight the *challenge of language* that is being posed by the kind of theological trajectory and method enunciated.

Various theologies emerging in India with new methodologies will also bring about *new theological languages*. Already we see these languages in formation. But we need to become more conscious of this fact. Each one of these languages will be addressed to all, thus opening up the possibility of intense conversation and dialogue among various theologies within India. All the theologies may not speak the same way to all people; but it is important to listen to their different voices.

The plurality of languages is to be understood also in a different but related sense. Theology may not always find expression through literary and textual language, which generally enjoy a privileged status. Theology will express itself starting from orality,[34] which is very much embedded in the culture and tradition of marginal groups and peoples like the Dalits and the tribals. Further, the theological genre itself will have to be plural, giving scope for different kinds of experiences to come to expression. The unidimensional conceptual language generally used in theology needs to be replaced by a multidimensional language to be able to do justice to the richness offered by emerging new theologies. If all languages have a metaphoric dimension, this is true much more of the new theologies emerging in India.

The methodology proposed and the challenge of language calls for *a reorganization of the theological discipline*. From our foregoing reflections it is clear that the traditional treatise approach presupposes a different kind of methodology. It may not square with the concerns expressed in calling for a different methodology and language. The future scenario of Indian theology will be one in which there will be varieties of theologies (Dalit, tribal, feminist, etc.), and since each one of them will have its own accent and specificity with regard to various themes (Christ, human person, understanding of the world and cosmos, ultimate fulfilment, etc.), learning each of these theologies will add depth and new dimensions to any particular theme that will be studied. All authentic theologies will be open to other experiences and insights. This should be true also about Indian theologies which

---

34 Cf. Felix Wilfred, 'Orality and Literacy: Contrast, Convergence and Dialectics', in *South Indian Folklorist* (1999), Vol. 2, No. 2, pp. 7–16.

will interact with theologies being pursued in other parts of the world, especially in other Asian countries, in Africa, Latin America and the Pacific.

Theologizing in India is an exciting pursuit. It is a journey. There is so much of richness of human resources, religious and cultural heritage on the one hand and all imaginable and complex societal and political situations on the other, that at every step we meet with endless possibilities of understanding ever more closely the mystery of God, the human realities and the entire cosmos. Let me cite the words of Tagore to conclude how exciting the journey of Indian theologies could be:

When old words die out on the tongue
New melodies break forth from the heart
And where the old tracks are lost
New country is revealed with its wonders[35]

---

35 Rabindranath Tagore, *Gitanjali*, Delhi and New York, Macmillan, 1918, song 37.

16 Theology and Liberation:
Juan Luis Segundo and Three Takes
on Secular Inventiveness

IVAN PETRELLA

Richard Rorty once defined philosophy in the following way:

> We can pick out 'the philosophers' in the contemporary intellectual
> world only by noting who is commenting on a certain sequence of
> historical figures. All that 'philosophy' as a name for a sector of cul-
> ture means is 'talk about Plato, Augustine, Descartes, Kant, Hegel,
> Frege, Russell . . . and that lot.' Philosophy is best seen as a kind
> of writing. It is delimited, as is any literary genre, not by form or
> matter, but by tradition – a family romance involving, e.g. Father
> Parmenides, honest old Uncle Kant, and bad brother Derrida.[1]

Rorty is happy with this understanding of philosophy. But I cannot
be happy with transferring his definition of philosophy to liberation
theology. Is liberation theology no more than talk about Gutiérrez,
Boff, Assmann, Bonino, Dussel and others? Is it delimited only by
an appeal to a specific set of authors, a family heritage? Is liberation
theology just a kind of writing?

The easy answer to this question is, of course not. Liberation theology was born with the promise of being a theology that would not rest
with merely writing about liberation but would actually help liberate
people from material deprivation. Theology is a second step, commitment and participation in the struggles of marginalized communities
is the first step.[2] The writing emerges from and reflects upon those
struggles and is literally embodied in the blood of martyrs such as

---

1 Richard Rorty, *Consequences of Pragmatism (Essays: 1972–1980)*,
Minneapolis, University of Minnesota Press, 1982, p. 92.

2 This point is famously stressed in Gustavo Gutiérrez, *A Theology of
Liberation: History, Politics and Salvation*, tr. Caridad Inda and John Eagleson, Maryknoll, NY, Orbis, 1985.

Ignacio Ellacuría. Nobody is killed by death squads, or persecuted by the Vatican, for a writing that's just a kind of writing.[3] In that sense, liberation theology can be grouped with the Communist Manifesto or the Declaration of Independence, writings that seek to advance political and economic freedom and thus aim at much more than Rorty's family romance.

This easy answer, however, today seems a tad too easy. As is well known, liberation theology was born at the crossroads of a changing Catholic and Protestant Church and the revolutionary political-economic climate of the late 1960s and early 1970s.[4] Things have changed. Back then, Vatican II gave national episcopates greater freedom in applying Church teaching to their particular contexts; now, instead, the Vatican has all but eliminated supporters of liberation theology from its ruling clique. Back then the Cuban revolution gave hope that an alternative to US capitalism and Soviet communism was possible; now, however, Cuba's lack of political freedom makes it no model for emulation or admiration. Back then, dependency theory provided a framework for understanding the mechanisms of the global economy; today the social sciences are rarely incorporated into liberationist writings.[5] Back then, the poor were seen as an organized force taking the reins of history; now it seems that history has passed them over. Back then, liberation theology was opposed with bullets, persecution and defamation; today liberation theology operates at the margins of politics and has been co-opted into mainstream theological discourse.[6]

---

3 Ellacuria is co-editor of the work that attempts to systematize liberation theology's theological perspective. See Ignacio Ellacuría and Jon Sobrino (eds), *Mysterium Liberationis: Fundamental Concepts of Liberation Theology*, Maryknoll, NY, Orbis Books, 1993. For the account of one liberation theologian persecuted by the Vatican, see Harvey Cox, *The Silencing of Leonardo Boff: The Vatican and the Future of World Christianity*, Oak Park, IL, Meyer-Stone Books, 1988.

4 For an overview of liberation theology's early development in English, see Christian Smith, *The Emergence of Liberation Theology: Radical Religion and Social Movement Theory*, Chicago, The University of Chicago Press, 1991; for one in Spanish, see Enrique Dussel, *Teología de la Liberación: Un Panorama de su Desarrollo*, Ciudad de Mexico, Potrerillos Editores, 1995; for one in English from a liberation theologian, see José Míguez Bonino, *Doing Theology in a Revolutionary Situation*, ed. William H. Lazareth, Confrontation Books, Philadelphia, Fortress Press, 1975.

5 For a groundbreaking critique of liberation theology's abandonment of economics as an integral part of the theological task, see Jung Mo Sung, *Economía: Tema Ausente en la Teología de la Liberación*, San Jose, Costa Rica, DEI, 1994.

6 For a brilliant examination of the co-option of liberation theology's vocabulary see Franz Hinkelammert, 'Liberation Theology in the Economic and

The end result of these changes is that in addition to using an increasingly domesticated vocabulary, liberation theologians also lack a viable social movement and a viable vision of an alternative society. While today they do have academic support, in itself such support is a double-edged sword – a liberation theology that comfortably exists in the academy is one that will rarely pose a threat to the status quo.[7] Given these factors, if there ever was a time when liberation theology is just a kind of writing – that time is now. If that is the case, then the writing is a waste of time and it would be better if I just devoted myself full time to political activism and social work.

For me, however, it is in Juan Luis Segundo's work that I find a path toward retaining the socio-economic and political relevance of the production of liberation theology.[8] This essay, therefore, draws from his legacy to explore a way the writing of liberation theology can be more than just writing. I will suggest that his stress on the need for incorporating secular, that is, disciplines traditionally deemed non-theological into liberation theology, can give renewed edge to liberationist production. In particular, I will suggest that Segundo shows that liberation theology requires an intimate connection with the social sciences. The essay will be divided in two parts. In the first, I outline the central element of Segundo's thought – the inseparable link between faith and ideologies. In the second, I present three ways in which liberation theology should relate to secular disciplines and even merge into secular disciplines.

Segundo on faith and ideology

Segundo's elucidation of the relation between faith and ideology reveals liberation theology's intimate dependence on the social sciences. Without them, there is no liberation theology.[9] What is his argument?

Social Context of Latin America: Economy and Theology, or the Irrationality of the Rationalized', in David Batstone, Eduardo Mendieta, Lois Ann Lorenzten and Dwight N. Hopkins (eds), *Liberation Theologies, Postmodernity, and the Americas*, New York, Routledge, 1997, pp. 25–52. The original Spanish can be found at Franz Hinkelammert, *Cultura de la Esperanza y Sociedad sin Exclusión*, San Jose, Costa Rica, DEI, 1995.

7 For a powerful critique of liberation theology's move toward 'decency' see Marcella Althaus-Reid, *Indecent Theology: Theological Perversions in Sex, Gender and Politics*, New York, Routledge, 2000.

8 See my use of Segundo in chapter two of Ivan Petrella, *The Future of Liberation Theology: An Argument and Manifesto*, London, SCM Press, 2006.

9 Segundo develops his views on the matter most completely in *Liberation*

For Segundo, faith is the value or meaning structure that is an indispensable component of every human life. Every human being structures their life around a set of values. Faith, therefore, is an anthropological component of the person that need not be tied to any religious scheme. Ideology, for Segundo, is also an anthropological component of human beings. Segundo defines ideology in a neutral sense, as a system of means that are used to attain an end or goal. Faith is more strongly identified with a goal, while ideology focuses more on the means toward the goal. However, while Segundo separates faith and ideology for analytical purposes, he claims that in reality they are inextricably linked. It is not really possible to separate faith from ideology and ideology from faith. Now it seems obvious that ideologies – as defined by Segundo – cannot be separated from faith. Any system of means must be placed within a meaning structure; that is, every ideology is linked to a faith for the simple reason that any means is a means to a goal. Without a goal the means lose their reason of being. But Segundo also insists that faith itself cannot be separated from ideology 'because a faith without ideologies is, in fact, dead'.[10] A faith without ideology is dead because faith can only be expressed through its concrete manifestations. Faith needs to be embodied in deeds,

> which are the product of the envisioned ideals [that is, faith] plus techniques employed to turn them into reality [ideology]. While the ideals, in the abstract, may aspire to a certain ubiquity and nontemporality, every concrete realization of them and every technique used for this realization will bear the mark of the time and place in which they are to be realized.[11]

Take Jesus' commandment to love your neighbour.[12] Love in this case is the basic meaning structure of the individual. Segundo stresses that 'love' can be expressed in a variety of ways and thus can only be made meaningful through ideologies as the system of means by which values are realized in practice. It's not the same to believe that the love commandment should be expressed solely at an individual personal

---

of Theology, trans. John Drury, Maryknoll, NY, Orbis, 1979 and Faith and Ideologies, Maryknoll, NY, Orbis Books, 1982. Also helpful is 'Fe e Ideología', Perspectivas de Dialogo Nov 1974: 227–33. On Segundo, see Alfred Hennelly, Theologies in Conflict: The Challenge of Juan Luis Segundo, Maryknoll, NY, Orbis Books, 1979 and Marsha Hewitt, From Theology to Social Theory: Juan Luis Segundo and the Theology of Liberation, New York, Peter Lang, 1990.
10 Segundo, Faith and Ideologies, p. 126.
11 Segundo, Faith and Ideologies, p. 122.
12 See Segundo, Faith and Ideologies, pp. 129–30. See also Hewitt, pp. 48–9.

level as it is to believe that it needs to be expressed through societal structural reform. More deeply, however, Segundo suggests that unless one focuses on the ideological elements of faith then the latter cannot even be discussed because it is the means by which faith is made real – of realizing faith in practice – that give content to faith. He notes that it's not faith that separates individuals and groups but faith given different content through different ideological garb.[13] Such conflict is unavoidable for there is no non-ideological way to realize the love commandment. So 'Christians cannot evade the necessity of inserting something to fill the void between their faith and their options in history. In short, they cannot avoid the risk of ideologies.'[14] Even Jesus faced that task:

> When Jesus talked about freely proffered love and nonresistance to evil, he was facing the same problem of filling the void between his conception of God and the problems existing in his age. In short, we are dealing here with another ideology, not with the content of faith itself.[15]

Live faith is always faith related to a particular historical context. Live faith, therefore, is always faith plus ideology. People usually inherit a particular package taken for granted. But what if one wanted to *consciously* relate faith to ideology?[16] Segundo sees two options. The first is to turn to Scripture and pick and choose what seems most in accord with the current historical situation:

> If, for example, the relationship between the Exodus situation and our own time today seems closer than the situation of the Hebrews in the time of Christ and ours today, then the Exodus rather than the Gospel should serve as our source of inspiration in trying to find a present-day ideology that will dovetail with the faith.[17]

---

13 Segundo, 'Fe e Ideología', p. 229.
14 Segundo, *Liberation of Theology*, p. 109.
15 Segundo, *Liberation of Theology*, p. 116.
16 Here I see some affinity between Segundo's project and some strands of liberal North American theology. Shailer Mathews, *The Growth of the Idea of God*, New York, The Macmillan Company, 1931, for example, can be seen as providing concrete examples of how the ideologies that concretize faith change in different contexts. In addition, the notion that we must consciously relate faith to ideology is similar to the idea of theology as 'imaginative construction' developed in Gordon Kaufman, *In Face of Mystery: A Constructive Theology*, Cambridge, MA, Harvard University Press, 1993.
17 Segundo, *Liberation of Theology*, p. 117.

Segundo, though, rejects this option, there just seems be little sense in looking for similar situations in cultural contexts dating back over thirty-five centuries ago.[18] He prefers a second option:

> The other possible approach is to invent an ideology that we might regard as the one which would be constructed by a gospel message contemporary with us . . . The second approach does call for creativity here and now. But if we must try to imagine what the gospel message would be if it were formulated today, it is becoming more and more obvious to Christians that *secular* inventiveness and creativity is more appropriate and fruitful.[19]

Secular inventiveness and liberation theology

What shape might secular inventiveness take? Segundo's approach is to highlight the inescapably ideological trappings of faith in order to critique and revise its content in light of the goal of liberation. For this reason he suggests that 'a sociology of ideology, a sociology whose object would be the ideology prevailing in social behaviors – is precisely the one starting point that could constitute an *intrinsic* element of the theological task.'[20] A sociology of ideology, however, is not the only path secular inventiveness might take – it is not the only way the social sciences can be integrated into liberation theology. Here are three more ways.

Secular inventiveness and the critique of idolatry

The critique of idolatry is a central liberationist theme grounded in liberation theology's understanding of God as a God of life – not an abstract ethereal 'life' but material human life in the flesh. As Matthew's Gospel stresses:

> for I was hungry and you gave me food, I was thirsty and you gave me something to drink, I was a stranger and you welcomed me, I was naked and you gave me clothing, I was sick and you took care of me, I was in prison and you visited me. (Matthew 31.35–6; NRSV)

---

18 Segundo, *Liberation of Theology*, p. 117.
19 Segundo, *Liberation of Theology*, pp. 117–18.
20 Juan Luis Segundo, *Signs of the Times: Theological Reflections*, ed. Alfred Hennelly, Maryknoll, NY, Orbis Books, 1993, p. 8.

Liberation theology's God of life stands in opposition to the idols of death.[21] An idol is a God to whom lives are sacrificed. Traditionally, liberation theologians have signalled out the 'market', 'globalization' and 'capitalism' as such idols.[22] The incorporation of the social sciences as an integral part of liberation theology can help sharpen a critique that often remains vague.[23] For example, instead of criticizing an abstractly stated 'globalization', the analysis can be sharpened to show how a sacrificial model of globalization is being created by specific global institutions such as the IMF or the WTO. To do so, however, requires immersing oneself in a body of literature liberation theologians tend to ignore. When examining the WTO, for example, one can see how specific agreements lead to the sacrifice of the world's poorest populations.

Take TRIMS (Trade-Related Investment Measures Agreement) as an example. TRIMS requires that governments give foreign firms national treatment in the area of production and trade of goods. It thus eliminates tariffs and subsidies geared towards the creation of a local industrial base and restricts the use of tools – such as local content requirements, technology transfer, local employment, joint venturing and performance requirements – through which governments have sought to steer local benefits from foreign direct investment. Follow the sequence: since tariffs and subsidies are illegal, the government of a developing country is deprived of the ability to nurse infant industries; that is, it is no longer able to help foster a national industrial base. It must by necessity look externally to foreign direct investment from multinational corporations. But what can it offer? Why would a multi-

---

21 See Pablo Richard and Barbara Ellen Campbell, *The Idols of Death and the God of Life*, Maryknoll, NY, Orbis Books, 1983.

22 Jose Míguez Bonino explains: 'As the economist-theologian Franz Hinkelammert cogently argues, the human subject vanishes and only the "fetish" (capital? property? the economic laws?) remains in control. Repression, torture, disappearances, the withdrawal of social, educational and health services, the cultural or physical genocide of native Indians, the suppression of all expressions of public opinion – these are not the result of the whim or the cruelty of bloodthirsty tyrants: they are "the necessary social cost" of "freedom." It is the sacrifice that the highest god, "the economic laws," demands. I am aware that the logic of this "compressed" argument will not be self-evident to many readers from the affluent world . . . May I suggest, however, that a meditation on "the unavoidability of unemployment," "the mystery of inflation," the escalation of programs of defense, and the "need" to cut down on social and assistance programs could be a healthy exercise also for theologians?' Jose Míguez Bonino, 'For Life and Against Death: A Theology That Takes Sides', in James Wall (ed.), *Theologians in Transition*, New York, Crossroad, 1981, p. 171.

23 See chapter 5 of Petrella, *The Future of Liberation Theology*, for one development of this critique. Another can be found in Sung, *Economía*.

national want to set up shop in a developing country? The only thing a developing country can offer are low wages. Unfortunately, every other developing country is in the same boat, so low wages are not enough to entice foreign investment. Developing countries thus engage in a race to the bottom, offering tax exemptions, waivers of industry regulation, guarantees against expropriation, lax social, environmental and labour regulations, even lower wages and a military willing to crush social unrest. The poverty and degradation of the population becomes the allure and selling point.

The spread of export processing zones (EPZs) is the direct consequence of this logic. Naomi Klein describes her visit to Cavite, an EPZ in the town of Rosario in the Philippines: 'the economic zone is designed as a fantasyland for foreign investors. Golf courses, executive clubs and private schools have been built on the outskirts of Rosario to ease the discomforts of Third World life.'[24] The contrasts are glaring:

In Cavite . . . the workers are uniformed, the grass manicured . . . There are cute signs all around the grounds instructing workers to 'Keep Our Zone Clean' and 'Promote Peace and Progress of the Philippines.' But walk out the gate and the bubble bursts . . . The roads are a mess, running water is scarce and garbage is overflowing.[25]

Workers either live in bunkers within Cavite or in the slums that grow outside its door. The rented piece of land upon which Cavite stands, moreover, exists as a separate country, a denationalized piece of territory:

the Cavite zone . . . is under the sole jurisdiction of the Philippines' federal Department of Trade and Industry; the local police and municipal government have no right even to cross the threshold. The layers of blockades serve a dual purpose: to keep the hordes away from the costly goods being manufactured inside the zone, but also, and perhaps more important, to shield the country from what is going on inside the zone.[26]

Workers are primarily migrants living far from home with little connection to the place where the zones are located. The work itself is

---

24 Naomi Klein, *No Logo*, New York, Picador USA, 2000, p. 206.
25 Klein, *No Logo*, p. 208.
26 Klein, *No Logo*, p. 207.

short term and often not renewed. Wages are low, sometimes below the nation's minimum wage laws. Hours are long. Drinking water is often unavailable and ventilation is poor. Mandatory production quotas beyond achievable limits force employees to work overtime without compensation. Women are often beaten, sexually harassed and abused by their employers. Girls may be forced to take birth control pills or injections to avoid costly pregnancies. When 7,000 workers from Sri Lanka's Colombo EPZ marched peacefully to deliver a complaint to their prime minister they were attacked with truncheons and fired upon by the police. In the Mexican *maquiladoras* – the assembly plants in the free-trade zone on the Mexican side of the US border – workers have been denied the right to form independent labour unions. While in the midst of a two-month labour strike Ford Motor Company unilaterally nullified its union contract, fired 3,400 of its workers and cut wages by 45 per cent. When the workers rallied around dissident labour leaders and tried to form a union outside the state-sponsored labour apparatus, gunmen hired by the official government-dominated union shot workers at random in the factory.[27]

As Naomi Klein notes, the rationale behind EPZs is simple: '*of course* companies must pay taxes and strictly abide by national laws, but just in this one case, on this specific piece of land, for just a little while, an exception will be made – for the case of future prosperity.'[28] In the past, the strategy has worked and countries have climbed up the wage ladder, most notably in the case of the East Asian tigers.[29] But it worked when there were far fewer EPZs and before TRIMS outlawed the mechanisms by which the Asian tigers created linkages that ensured the transfer of technology and knowledge. Today, however, if a country fails to lower its labour and environmental regulations, it faces the risk of being bid out of the global economy. When a country lowers its regulations, however, workers are left unprotected from abuse and lack job security. The greater the competition to attract foreign firms the greater the incentives. Cameroon, for example, offers foreign investors a 100 per cent tax exemption for ten years and free repatriation of profits; in its EPZ, multinational corporations can fire workers at

27 Jim Yong Kim, Joyce Millen, Alec Irwin, and John Gershman (eds), *Dying for Growth: Global Inequality and the Health of the Poor*, Boston, MA, Common Courage Press, 2000, p. 190.

28 Klein, *No Logo*, p. 207.

29 The best examinations of the rise of the East Asian 'tigers' remain Alice Amsden, *The Rise of the 'Rest': Challenges to the West from Late-Industrializing Economies*, Oxford, Oxford University Press, 2001 and Robert Wade, *Governing the Market: Economic Theory and the Role of Government in East Asian Industrialization*, Princeton, NJ, Princeton University Press, 1990.

will without compensation and are exempt from the nation's minimum wage laws. The exploitation of the worker, environment and nation as a whole is not the exception; it is intrinsic to the EPZ as a path to development.

Secular inventiveness and historical projects

Drawing from Segundo, I focused on this route in *The Future of Liberation Theology*. A historical project is 'a midway term between a utopia, a vision which makes no attempt to connect itself historically to the present, and a program, a technically developed model for the organization of society'.[30] Much the same way that faith without ideology is empty, so are liberation theology's main concepts empty without a role for the social sciences in the construction of historical projects. There exists, I argued, an intimate link between thinking about ideals and thinking about institutions, which requires paying attention to both the religious (or secular) ideal and the concretization that might approach that ideal. Concepts such as the preferential option for the poor and liberation hide more than they reveal about the way life chances and social resources may be theoretically approached and institutionally realized. What exactly is meant by the preferential option for the poor? What exactly is meant by liberation? Leonardo Boff once cautioned:

> What sort of liberation are we talking about? Here we must be careful not to fall into the semantic trap of endowing the same word with several very different meanings. The liberation involved here has to do with economic, social, political and ideological structures. It seeks to operate on structures, not simply on persons. It proposes to change the power relationships existing between social groups by helping to create new structures that will allow for greater participation on the part of those now excluded.[31]

While Boff alludes to the danger inherent in not specifying the concrete meaning of liberation, he also remains vague. For liberation theology the incorporation of the social sciences as political construction is not a secondary moment in the theological task – coming after the clarification of our theological concepts – but is the very means by which

---

30 Bonino, *Doing Theology in a Revolutionary Situation*, p. 38.
31 Leonardo Boff, *Jesus Christ Liberator: A Critical Christology for Our Time*, Maryknoll, Orbis Books, 1981, p. 275.

those concepts are given a degree of analytical rigour, are clarified and understood. John Dewey knew this as well:

> As for ideals, all agree that we want the good life . . . But as long as we limit ourselves to generalities, the phrases that express ideals may be transferred from conservative to radical or vice versa, and nobody will be the wiser. For, without analysis, they do not descend into the actual scene nor concern themselves with the generative conditions of realization of ideals.[32]

While the development of historical projects gives content to liberation theology's terminology that is not their only or even primary purpose. The main purpose of historical projects is liberation. They are the key way that liberation theology can pursue liberation concretely. It is for this reason that the social sciences can be seen as feeding the prophet in the liberation theologian, allowing him or her to envision the building blocks for a new era. In my case, I focused on legal theory and comparative political economy as the preferred tools. I suggested that liberation theology could adopt the notion of 'alternative pluralisms', the idea that representative democracies, market economies and civil societies can take different institutional forms.[33] To do so, liberation theology needs to stress the artificial, contextual and haphazard nature of political and economic systems. This allows liberation theology to approach society as partial, fragmentary and incomplete, in an attempt to open up a space for alternatives (i.e. historical projects) that are excluded a priori from a picture of capitalism as a unified system encompassing not just the economic sphere but culture and politics as well.[34] So, for example, liberation theology could draw from the

---

32 John Dewey, *Individualism Old and New*, New York, Milton, Balch & Company, 1930, p. 147. For more on the connection between thinking about ideals and thinking about institutions, see Roberto Mangabeira Unger, *Democracy Realized: The Progressive Alternative*, New York, Verso, 1998, p. 16; Roberto Mangabeira Unger, *What Should Legal Analysis Become?*, New York, Verso, 1996, p. 4 and Roberto Mangabeira Unger, *False Necessity: Anti-Necessitarian Social Theory in the Service of Radical Democracy*; *Politics: A Work in Constructive Social Theory*, Cambridge, Cambridge University Press, 1987, p. 10.

33 I take the notion of 'alternative pluralisms' from Roberto Unger. See Unger, *Democracy Realized*, p. 27.

34 For examples of this way of thinking about the economy see Michael Piore and Charles Sabel, *The Second Industrial Divide: Possibilities for Prosperity*, New York, Basic, 1984 and Charles Sabel and Jonathan Zeitlin, 'Stories, Strategies, Structures: Rethinking Historical Alternatives to Mass Production', in Charles Sabel and Jonathan Zeitlin (eds), *World of Possibilities: Flexibility and Mass Production in Western Industrialization*, Cambridge, Cambridge

social science literature on flexible specialization regimes to argue for a market economy that saw productive property as a bundle of rights to be vested in governments, intermediate organizations, communities and firms. Such a system would distribute the benefits of property ownership more democratically by restricting the absolute claim any one group could make on its productive base. The end result is neither capitalism nor socialism, but a democratized market economy. In addition, liberation theology could also propose reforms to strengthen the state, making the state less prey to the interests of moneyed elites. One could imagine a democratic regime with rules of mandatory voting, proportional representation, free access to the media for political parties and public financing of campaigns. This could be coupled with a constitutional design that resolves impasse between branches of government by appealing, through plebiscites or referenda, to the general populace as well as anticipated elections.[35] These moves give specific content to the preferential option for the poor and liberation, terms that remain vacuous as long as one forgets the intimate link between thinking about ideals and thinking about institutions central to devising a historical project.

University Press, 1997. For an example in politics, see Ernesto Laclau and Chantal Mouffe, *Hegemony and Socialist Strategy: Towards a Radical Democratic Politics*, New York, Verso, 1985. For work that highlights the diversity of forms 'capitalism' takes in different contexts, see Herbert Kitschelt, Peter Lange, Gary Marks, and John D. Stephens (eds), *Continuity and Change in Contemporary Capitalism*, Cambridge, Cambridge University Press, 1999 and Colin Crouch and Wolfgang Streeck (eds), *Political Economy of Modern Capitalism: Mapping Convergence and Diversity*, London, Sage Publications Ltd, 1997.

35 See Unger, *Democracy Realized*, for a summary, pp. 264–6; also Unger, *What Should Legal Analysis Become?*, pp. 15–17 and 163–9 and Unger, *False Necessity: Anti-Necessitarian Social Theory in the Service of Radical Democracy*, pp. 444–76. Political science and political economy literature stress the importance of a 'hard' state for economic development. See Alice Amsden, *Asia's Next Giant: South Korea and Late Industrialization*, New York, Oxford University Press, 1989; Stephen Haggard, *Pathways from the Periphery: The Politics of Growth in the Newly Industrializing Economies*, Ithaca, NY, Cornell University Press, 1990. Hard states, however, have often been achieved through authoritarianism. What is most interesting about the reforms briefly outlined is that they may soften the tension between the radical changes often needed for development and the incrementalism that is part of democracy. This is the challenge that a 'democratic developmental state' must meet. See Adrian Leftwich, 'Forms of the Democratic Developmental State: Democratic Practices and Developmental Capacity', in Mark Robinson and Gordon White (eds), *The Democratic Developmental State: Politics and Institutional Design*, Oxford, Oxford University Press, 1998, pp. 52–83.

Secular inventiveness and regime change

At the foundation of liberation theology lies a challenge to the stand-point from which thinking is done. Liberation theology tries to think about religion generally, and Christianity and society more specific-ally, from the perspective of the majority of humankind, rather than the perspective of a small minority. Today the richest 20 per cent of humankind consumes 82 per cent of the world's resources, the remain-ing 80 per cent consumes 18 per cent and the poorest 20 per cent consumes 1.4 per cent of its resources. The rich North Atlantic nations are home to approximately one fourth of the global population but consume 70 per cent of the world's energy, 75 per cent of its metals, 85 per cent of its wood and 60 per cent of its food. Early on, libera-tion theologians argued that theology, like the distribution of global resources, was slanted toward the affluent. As such, the history of modern religious thought was not a neutral and universal history, but rather the history of questions and answers related to religion posed and answered by people living in a context of wealth. Liberation theo-logians claimed that when religion is thought about from a context of poverty the focus and goal of theology changes. Modern theology had the sceptic, the person who denies belief in God, as its main interlocu-tor, and giving reasons for religious belief as its main goal, while libera-tion theology has the non-person, the person whose humanity is denied by the prevailing social order, as its interlocutor, and liberation as its goal.[36] This shift in standpoint from the concerns of a rich minority to those of a poor majority is liberation theology's epistemological break from modern religious thought.[37] The epistemological break leads to a

---

36 A few examples of the focus of the bulk of modern religious thought: Friedrich Schleiermacher's *On Religion: Speeches to its Cultured Despisers*; the title itself points to the theologian's main interlocutor, the sceptic, the per-son who thinks that Christian faith is anachronistic or even dangerous; Karl Rahner's *Foundations of the Christian Faith*, which is directed toward a person who 'is living in an intellectual and spiritual situation today . . . which does not allow Christianity to appear as something indisputable and to be taken for granted'; and Gordon Kaufman's *In Face of Mystery*, which remarks that 'many in our time have become especially sensitive to how implausible, indeed unacceptable or even intolerable, is the understanding of God which we have inherited.' Quotations from Karl Rahner, *Foundations of Christian Faith: An Introduction to the Idea of Christianity*, trans. William V. Dych, New York, Crossroads-Seabury Press, 1978, p. 5 and Kaufman, *In Face of Mystery*, p. 3.

37 See Gustavo Gutiérrez, 'Two Theological Perspectives: Liberation Theol-ogy and Progressivist Theology', in Sergio Torres and Virginia Fabella (eds), *The Emergent Gospel: Theology from the Underside of History*, Maryknoll, NY, Orbis Books, 1978, pp. 227–58 and Gustavo Gutiérrez, *Teología Desde el Reverso de la Historia*, Lima, Peru, Ed. CEP, 1977.

kind of conversion within the discipline of theology in which the world is now looked at differently. Paradoxically, the new sight is different because it's mainstream. It is only from a North Atlantic perspective that thinking from the context of poverty seems unusual; from a global perspective poverty is the norm. Liberation theology, therefore, merely tries to do theology from the norm.

This shift in standpoint, however, urgently needs to be translated to other disciplines. No discipline possesses a neutral framework of analysis – economics, sociology, law, political science and others usually encounter the world with a set of preconceptions that are biased, much like modern religious thought, toward the wealthy. And it is these disciplines, not theology, that set the intellectual frameworks by which the world is most influentially analysed. Here, therefore, the liberation theologian must operate undercover as an economist or legal theorist and work from within to transform the discipline's presuppositions – regime change is in order. As far as I know there is no liberation theologian involved in this task (perhaps s/he is too well disguised, too far undercover) so the best example comes from the work of Paul Farmer, who rethinks medical anthropology from the perspective of liberation theology. Farmer is a medical anthropologist at Harvard Medical School, founder of Partners in Health, an organization that provides health care to poor communities around the world. His intellectual production, grounded in the reality of caring for tuberculosis victims in Russian prisons and AIDS victims in Haiti, focuses on health and human rights.

Farmer notes that 'diseases themselves make a preferential option for the poor.'[38] Yet the focus of medical research operates oblivious to the needs of the communities that are most threatened by disease. For example, from the perspective of the well off, the minority of humankind, tuberculosis is barely a threat, with a cure rate of 95 per cent. From the perspective of the majority of humankind, however, 'tuberculosis deaths *now* – which each year number in the millions – occur almost exclusively among the poor, whether they reside in the inner cities of the United States or in the poor countries of the Southern hemisphere.'[39] The organizational paradigm upon which the medical profession is based renders this fact invisible. Medicine, Farmer shows, is based upon a health transition model according to which as societies develop 'death will no longer be caused by infections such as

---

38 Paul Farmer, *Pathologies of Power: Health, Human Rights, and the New War on the Poor*, Berkeley, University of California Press, 2003, p. 140.
39 Farmer, *Pathologies of Power*, p. 147.

tuberculosis but will occur much later and be caused by heart disease and cancer.[40] A different standpoint reveals that

> For the poor, wherever, they live, there is, often enough, no health transition. In other words, wealthy citizens of 'underdeveloped' nations (those countries that have not yet experienced their health transition) do not die young from infectious diseases; they die later and from the same diseases that claim similar populations in wealthy countries. In parts of Harlem, in contrast, death rates of certain age groups are as high as those in Bangladesh; in both places, the leading causes of death in young adults are infections and violence.[41]

This model makes the present sufferings of the poor unimportant – they are in fact sacrificed for the development of remedies for diseases that afflict the wealthy.

Medical ethics, from the perspective of a preferential option for the poor, fares no better. He notes:

> What is defined, these days, as an ethical issue? End-of-life decisions, medico legal questions of brain death and organ transplantation, and medical disclosure issues dominate the published literature. In the hospital, the quandary ethics of the individual constitute most of the discussion of medical ethics. The question 'When is life worth preserving?' is asked largely of lives one click of the switch away from extinction, lives wholly at the mercy of the technology that works to preserve some. The countless people whose life course is shortened by unequal access to health care are not topics of discussion.[42]

Farmer's work as a doctor and medical anthropologist, therefore, parallels the work of a liberation theologian within theology. Both struggle to reshape their disciplines around the concerns and issues that affect the majority poor of humankind.

Conclusion

Segundo once remarked that 'unless we agree that the world should not be the way it is . . . there is no point of contact, because the world

---

40 Farmer, *Pathologies of Power*, p. 156.
41 Farmer, *Pathologies of Power*, pp. 156–7.
42 Farmer, *Pathologies of Power*, p. 174.

that is satisfying to us is the same world that is utterly devastating to them.'[43] The liberation theologian's task is to contribute to changing that world. No one saw more clearly than Segundo that the social sciences were a necessary ally to this task. They are necessary for at least the three paths I outlined above. The critique of idolatry begins with the realization that the most important theologies today – the ones that have a life and death impact on people – are found outside the traditionally theological realm and within areas governed by the social sciences. The WTO and spread of EPZs are just one possible example among many. Readers familiar with liberation theology will notice that the display of the mechanisms by which idolatry surfaces in the WTO is made much more concrete by the analysis of TRIMS. For the critique of idolatry to be effective it must be as specific as possible, otherwise it remains at the level of vague denunciations and may be dismissed as such. The construction of historical projects emerges from the fact that it is not enough to criticize, liberation theology must also propose. It is the second part of the critique of idolatry – the best way to unmask the idol is by showing it is not necessary, that alternatives are possible. Constructing alternatives, however, also requires the social sciences. They have the building blocks from which liberation theologians need to draw. In both the critique of idolatry and the construction of historical projects the liberation theologian needs to have a foot in at least two disciplines, theology and one of the social sciences. Finally, regime change is the most intriguing of the three paths. Liberation theology's epistemological break can be applied widely, not just to theology. As I suggested, getting other disciplines such as law or economics to adopt the preferential option for the poor – rather than rendering the poor invisible – is an urgent task. As Farmer's work demonstrates, the transformation in theology needs to be carried on elsewhere. Here the liberation theologian need not carry the label of 'theologian' and works best under a different disciplinary guise. Perhaps the future of liberation theology requires its dissolution as an identifiable body of production.

43 Cited in Robert McAfee Brown, *Liberation Theology: An Introductory Guide*, Louisville, Westminster/John Knox Press, 1993, p. 44.

17 A Theology for Another Possible World is Possible

JUAN JOSÉ TAMAYO ACOSTA

What follows are some outlines for a new theological paradigm, which must be taken further in the different sociocultural and religious contexts where we develop our theological reflection.

I will divide this paper into four parts. First, I will critically analyse the division of theology in geocultural and social areas. Then I will introduce some of the new sociocultural climates that condition the way we do theology. Third, I will trace the new horizons which will conform the new theological paradigm for 'Another World is Possible'. Finally, I will try to sketch out some of the new categories of that paradigm.

An inadequate division of tasks

During the last decades of the previous century, and coinciding with the emergence of new theologies, a certain tacit consensus among theologians was reached (and often transgressed, the truth be said), in the international theological panorama, which established a distribution of tasks, issues and horizons according to their different geocultural and socio-economic areas of origin. To the theologians from the First World corresponded providing answers to the challenges proceeding from modern culture, trying to give a reason for – and to make credible – Christian faith, or if you prefer, to demonstrate the rationality of Christianity in a society characterized by secularization and unbelief in its different manifestations: philosophical and scientific atheism, agnosticism, religious indifference, etc.

The aim of such a theology was not – as it had been in the past – anathematization, nor even confrontation between opposing ideological cosmo-visions, but rather a demanding and comprehensive dialogue, rigorous and fruitful, between religion and culture, Christianity and secularization, faith, science and reason, gospel and modernity, religious experience and existence in the world, Christian religion and other religions. This does not mean that modern theology was a stranger to the reality of poverty, but it did not constitute its main challenge nor was it approached as a theological problem as it did not believe it affected it directly. It was studied as a social issue and related to moral theology.

The main reference for the ecclesiastical magisterium guiding theological reflection was the Second Vatican Council, with its declarations, decrees and constitutions, particularly when referring to dogmatics, pastoral action in the modern world and revelation. The main relational disciplines were, among others, philosophy and anthropology. The people responsible for these reflections were principally professors of religious disciplines in faculties of theology and diocesan or religious seminaries.

According to the above-mentioned division of tasks, Third World theologians should focus on answering the challenges that emerge from a world of poverty and injustice, give testimony to the Christian faith and provide reasons of this faith among the impoverished popular majorities who present multiple and for ever more emaciated faces: street children, child prostitution, landless peasants, women who are twice or three times oppressed, excluded aboriginal populations, marginalized black people, the unemployed, etc. An accurate description of such a situation was offered in the Third Latin American Bishops Conference, which took place in the city of Puebla (Mexico) in 1979, and the Fourth, which took place in Santo Domingo (República Dominicana) in 1992. A very high percentage of these impoverished majorities are Christian and live their religiosity through multiple manifestations.

In this previously fixed division of tasks and topics, what assignment did Third World theologians receive? There was no need to worry about finding answers to the challenges proceeding from the world of unbelief, because these challenges neither affected their society nor did they have the means to study them, nor were they considered of their competence. They were supposed to accept at face value the results and conclusions of the First World theologies. They were expected, on the other hand, to ask themselves how to be Christian women and men in a world marked by social, ethnic, cultural and religious exclusion, which affects the popular majority of the Third World, and to consider the role that the churches and prophetic Christian movements play in such a situation.

In this context, theologians were asked to reflect on the intrinsic relationship between Christianity and liberation, faith and the struggle for justice, colonialism and dependency, human rights and the rights of the poor, theological hope and historical utopias, salvation in Christ and social transformation, love and solidarity, Christian community and fraternity–sorority.

The recurring biblical themes assigned in exegetical tasks were, among others: Exodus, prophetic denunciation, new heaven and new earth, the kingdom of God, the practice of Jesus, the death of Jesus, resurrection as utopia. The principal mediations were the human and social sciences.

The subjects of this theology, it was said, did not need to be professional theologians, rather ecclesial base communities, solidarity Christian movements, biblical study groups, prayer groups, catechists, ministers, missionaries, etc. The magisterium which served as references were the documents of the Latin-American Episcopal Conferences, celebrated in Medellín (Colombia), 1968, Puebla de los Ángeles (México), 1979 and Santo Domingo (Dominican Republic), 1992.

In the cultural and Christian environment of the First World, theology elaborated in the Third World, particularly liberation theology, was usually considered a minor theology, verging on catechism or preaching, and placed within the realm of pastoral theology. And this, when it did not outright deny its theological status, as was the norm in the academic ecclesiastical world, reduced it to Marxist catechism or social science. Those who cultivated liberation theology, in the words of a renowned Spanish bishop, formerly a famous theologian at the Pontifical University of Salamanca, *were not theologians of value*, because they did not work on the great Christian themes: God, Trinity, Holy Spirit, grace, etc. If one knows well the content of such theology, however, at once it will be recognized that these are central issues within liberation theology. What happened was that the orientation differed quite radically from most of academic theology and of First World ecclesiastical hierarchy.

It is true that the religious, cultural, sociopolitical and economic contexts of these theologies is different, but not so as to justify the division in horizontal planes as mentioned above, because it ends up carving up theology and dividing it into watertight and uncommunicating compartments. Such a division runs the risk of secluding each theology in its own camp of reflection, making it insensitive to the questions of the others. This division would end up in atomization, loss of global vision and lack of solidarity. We would be closer to the Tower of Babel than to Pentecost, closer to theological rationalities in monologue form than to a communicative and intersubjective rationality.

The aim of the following reflections is to search for *common horizons* from which it is possible to reflect and in which one may find the different theologies of the First and the Third World from the perspective of liberation, maintaining on the one hand the methodological precision of all religious discourse and its prophetic *pathos*, while on the other hand the hermeneutical creativity particular to each theology, conforming to the context in which it is carried out. In this sense, not only is theology universal, but also contextual, or if you prefer, it is universal in its contextuality. All this oriented towards the development of a new theological paradigm that bids farewell to the dogmatic paradigm still found within official Christianity and no few theological centres; a paradigm, which wants to contribute, even modestly, to the proposal of the World Social Forum and the other-world-movement of 'Another World is Possible'.

New sociocultural climates

During the last 50 years we have gone through deep and radical changes which influence the way we live our Christian faith, understand Christianity and do theology. Rather than an era of change we should refer to a change of era, which is characterized by a series of phenomena that truly can be called 'revolutionary'. I will particularly refer to those which respond in a special way to the theology for 'Another World is Possible'.

Globalization makes its presence felt in all areas of human relationships, most of the time negatively for the Third World, and for a large proportion of popular sectors of the First World. Globalization is not an objective description of reality, rather it is an ideological construction of neo-liberalism at the service of the market, which is omnipresent and omniscient. The response to such an excluding globalization is offered by the other-world movements with their proposal that Another World, Another Society, Another Culture, Another Economy, Another Politics are all Possible.

We are witnessing the violent awakening of an *imperialism* in possession of discourses and practices that veer towards fundamentalism. The empire, which introduces itself with euphemistic expressions such as 'empire of peace', 'empire of liberty', 'democratic empire', etc. incarnates the synthesis of all fundamentalisms: political, economic, cultural and religious; above all, this last one as was clearly manifested in the re-election of Bush as president of the United States of America. As Alfredo Goncalves has affirmed, 'in the political heart of the Empire you find the United States of America, Europe and Japan', who count on the assistance of the most powerful international organizations such as the World Bank, the International Monetary Fund and the World Trade Organization. In actual fact, the current empire belongs to global capitalism, its most faithful caretakers are the government of the United States of America and its armies, as has been demonstrated in the invasions of Afghanistan and Iraq, and its headquarters are in the USA. This was clearly understood by the terrorists who on 11 September 2001 attacked the neuralgic centres of power: the World Trade Centre and the Pentagon. As counter-current to all this, there has been an emergence all over the world of movements and organizations, political leaders and intellectuals, resisting the empire, and which have come out in non-violent protests against the imperial logic, against war and against capital.

The main result of neo-liberal globalization and imperialism is the reality of *structural poverty* which has been installed in humanity today. Facts are facts. In 1960, for each rich person in the world there were 30 poor; today the proportion has worsened to the point where for each rich person today there are 80 poor. Of the 6,200 million human beings who inhabit planet Earth, 46 per cent – this is 2,852 million – live in poverty, and of these 1,200 million live in extreme poverty. In Latin America 44 per cent of the inhabitants live in poverty and 94 per cent live below the poverty line. If we centre our attention on farmers, the data is as follows: over 90 million Latin Americans live in poverty and 47 million in extreme poverty.

Another revolutionary phenomenon is *feminism*, which questions the root of the androcentric character of human mental structures and the current patriarchal organization of social, political, economic and religious institutions, as well as philosophical and religious androcentrism, which discriminates against women. By contrast, feminism proposes a society model based on the community of equals, symmetric, interdependent, non-oppressive; but which is not a clone, but rather respectful of differences. Feminism is a non-cruel revolution, perhaps the first in history; to this revolution patriarchal structures are responding in an aggressive way, with gender violence as an instrument to maintain power.

We are witnessing a growth of *ecological consciousness*, which questions the techno-scientific model of development of modernism, anthropocentric and predatory of nature. Ecological consciousness proposes instead a model based on interdependence, non-oppressive, bi-directionally liberating between human beings and nature, a subject–subject relationship, and not a human-subject–nature-object one. The market and multinational response to this consciousness is one that increases depredation of nature so as to serve the economic model which destroys the fabric of life.

We live in times of *cultural pluralism*, which declares the end of ethnocentrism, and opposes the clash of civilizations which would turn the world into a colossus in flames, and which upholds an intercultural, interreligious and interethnic society. The Western cultural response to this is the reaffirmation of its superiority, the imposition of itself through powerful and expansive means of communication it owns, and the gradual elimination of minority cultures considered ancestral, old-fashioned and against all market logic of production and economic rationality. Minority cultures defend themselves against this form of imperialism, reaffirming their cultural identity as a fundamental reference of their ways of existence.

We live in times of *religious pluralism*, and not of an only religion. This implies an option for interreligious dialogue as an alternative to conflicts between religions. The answer of some majority religions to religious pluralism, particularly monotheistic ones, frequently consists of a rigid reaffirmation of the religious identity in its dogmatic, disciplinary and moral aspects, applying the old excluding principle 'outside one's own religion there is no salvation'. The result of this awakens religious fundamentalisms, sometimes violent, which deteriorate civil coexistence and provoke new religious wars.

We live in times of *biogenetic revolution*, which manifests through important advances: embryonic stem-cell experimentation with therapeutical motivation, euthanasia and death with dignity, birth control, assisted reproduction techniques, bioethics, etc. In most cases, these refer to advances which benefit humanity, improving the quality of life and alleviating pain. However, at the same time, they present no few existential, ethical and religious questions. Faced with such a revolution, Christianity cannot seek shelter in a closed universe, or repeat the condemnations uttered against other scientific revolutions of the past. It must analyse this deeply and consider the consequences, with no dogmatic preconceptions nor authoritative pretensions, and value the new possibilities and hopes in the life of human beings, supporting equality of all human beings, their freedom and uniqueness.

We lie immersed in the *human rights culture*, a culture which can quite well be considered universal both in its foundations and content, as in its normative development. It is a culture of consensus which has few detractors, though some critics of its conceptual formulations, its juridical regulations and its, sometimes excluding, selective application. At the same time, we live immersed in a culture of transgressions against human rights. These transgressions fall on the individual, structural and institutional levels. They benefit sometimes not only from the silence – a complicit silence – of the national, regional and international organizations which should normally watch over the fulfilling of human rights, but also from their collaboration, since in reality the majority of times they protect the interests of the empire and the multinationals under the umbrella of neo-liberal globalization. It would seem that human rights were still the incomplete subject, or in the words of José Saramago, the utopia of the twenty-first century. Neo-liberalism denies human rights all anthropological foundation, it deprives them of their universality, which then becomes mere rhetoric, and establishes a purely economic base for their exercise, that of property, purchasing power. Human rights are reduced to the right to property. Only owners, who hold economic power, are the subjects of rights. For human rights to cease to be this incomplete subject, they can neither be formulated nor constructed in abstract or outside of time, but must be part of a concrete time. This is the constituent of a sociological-juridical conception of human rights. At the same time, they must be continuously reinterpreted in relation to each historical context. And the context in which they must be considered today is that of economic and technical globalization, the social and cultural fragmentation of citizenship, of intercultural reality and religious pluralism.

Sexuality constitutes one of the pending subjects for Christianity, and particularly that of theology, which tends towards dualistic affirmations, and frequently adopts a repressive attitude towards the human body, which is far from the origin of Christianity. This is reflected with all clarity, in a brief poem by Eduardo Galeano. 'Says the market: the body is business; says the church: the body is sin. Says the body: I am celebration.'[1]

New theological horizons

The different paradigms with which Christian theology has been operating have been showing severe signs of fatigue and even in some cases exhaustion and anachronism, because they do not have the capacity to respond to the challenges presented by the phenomena indicated. Their positions seem to respond to the cultural, social and religious contexts of the past. Currently, theology in general and very particularly, the official theology, repeats itself, suffers multiple sclerosis, lacks imagi-

---

1 Eduardo Galeano, *Walking Words*, New York, W. W. Norton & Co., 1995.

nations and creativity. It was to this that Karl Barth provocatively drew our attention in his renowned *Introduction to Protestant Theology;* an emblematic book written over 50 years ago, which still keeps its validity and is an invitation to permanent creativity:

> Theological activity is distinguished from others – and this could be an example for all the activity of the spirit – by the fact that the person who wants to carry out this activity cannot do so in a relaxed manner, from issues that have been solved, from safe results, it cannot continue the building on foundations which have been laid already, it cannot live from gains of an accumulated capital of the past; on the contrary, it is forced, each day and hour, to begin again from *the beginning* . . . In theological science, 'to continue' means always 'to begin again from the beginning'. Faced with this radical risk, theologians should be strong enough, when the earth moves under their feet, to seek a new firm ground on which to stand, as if there had never been any before. If theology does not want to rush into arteriosclerosis, or boring arguments, its labour in no way can be routine, it cannot be done in automatic ways.[2]

The phenomena I have just analysed demand a re-foundation of the theology of liberation, or if preferred, a new theological paradigm for 'Another World is Possible', which must be placed in a series of new horizons which respond to the new challenges, which are summarized as follows:

The new *intercultural* horizon implies a step from a single culture to cultural pluralism and the enculturation of theology, which maintains the principles and theological categories of the dominating culture, an elaboration of an intercultural theology in a symmetric dialogue between cultures. The theology of liberation is not a matter of one culture. In all of them there are liberating elements which must be activated, as there are also alienating ones which must be eradicated.

The new *interreligious* horizon implies a step from a single or privileged theology to religious pluralism, which will lead to the elaboration of a theology of religions from an intercultural and interreligious dialogue, beginning from the victims and with a liberating praxis. The theology of liberation is not a matter of only one religion, rather of all. What

---

2 Karl Barth, *Evangelical Theology: An Introduction*, Grand Rapids, Michigan, Eerdmans, 1992.

it is all about then, is to create an interreligious theology of liberation which the emancipatory traditions present in different religions and spiritual movements.

The *hermeneutical* horizon constitutes the clue to all theology and tries to liberate the religious discourse from all traces of fundamentalism and implies the step from theology as a mere exegesis of texts to a theology hermeneutically in search of sense. Without hermeneutical mediation, theological discourse ceases to be and becomes a repetition of texts from the past, reproducing the official religious discourse, legitimizing religious institutions and a simple gloss of doctrinal declarations proceeding from the respective hierarchical magisterium. Hermeneutics is inherent to the human condition. As David Tracy correctly affirms: 'being human is to act reflectively, decide deliberately, understand intelligently, experiment fully. *Whether we know it or don't, being human is to be capable interpreter.*'[3] Theologians of all religions would do well to follow George Steiner's accurate observation: 'what interests me is the "interpretation", in as much as it provides the word with a life which overflows the instant and place in which it has been pronounced and transcribed'.[4]

The new *feminist* horizon questions the patriarchal character of belief and the androcentric structure of religious theory or theology, and elaborates a reflection in gender perspective, beginning from the experience of suffering and the struggles for liberation of women. It incorporates epistemological and socio-analytical categories from feminist theory, though articulated in other categories. This is how feminist theology emerges, which is not a regionally thematic theology, which caters for questions relative to women, and which only interests women and is elaborated only by women. It is a theology that: (a) *fundamentally* tries to give reason for faith in God not submitted to the patriarchal divine model; (b) *is liberating,* wanting to contribute to the salvation of all oppressed and the transformation of all religious structures of male domination; (c) *is critical,* and as such turns to historical-critical methods and the feminist theory, and uses a *hermeneutics of suspi-·cion* to read the founding texts of religions, which have mainly been produced from an andro-anthropocentric perspective, within a gender

---

3 David Tracy, *Plurality and Ambiguity: Hermeneutics, Religion, Hope,* Chicago, University of Chicago Press, 1994.

4 Toma la cita de Cl. Geffré, *El cristianismo ante el riesgo de la interpretación. Ensayos de hermenéutica teológica,* Madrid, Cristiandad, 1984, p. 17. No English translation available.

perspective; (d) in which women become aware they are moral and theological subjects, direct interlocutors with God without the mediation of men, and bearers of grace and salvation. Feminist theology is developing in the majority of religions.

The new *ecological* horizon implies the step from an anthropocentric theology, which legitimizes the scientific-technical development model of modernity, to a theology in ecological perspective. This is an invitation to overcome anthropocentrism, which has characterized modern theology and a good part of the theologies of liberation, and as Leonardo Boff affirms, to hear the cry of the Earth that seeks its liberation together with the oppressed human being. A theology with an ecological perspective must be open to the contributions of science and all disciplines which study life and the cosmic reality: bio-logy, bio-chemistry, cosmo-logy, geo-logy, bio-ethics, etc.

The new *ethical-practical* horizon implies the consideration of ethics as a first theology and not as the application of some general principles, and of praxis as a first act of all reflection. Theology does not move within the horizon of pure reason, but rather within that of practical reason, and is reconstructed through historical process beginning with the new subjects: marginalized women, oppressed races and ethnic groups, submerged cultures, suffocated religions, people, countries, entire continents inundated by the hurricane of neo-liberal globalization. It must awaken from the dogmatic dream and a state of quadruple innocence in which it has been living for centuries: social innocence, which forces it to assume what is true in the critique of religion and in theology itself as an ideological superstructure and the false conscience of history; historical innocence, which demands it place itself on the historical stage, not as an a-critical spectator who contemplates the spectacle of humanity from afar, but rather an actress who compassionately intervenes on the stage of eco-human suffering, provoked by human injustice and raises its voice in favour of victims; ethnical-cultural innocence, which obliges to overcome ethnocentrism and Christian centrism, and stands on a wider horizon, the one of human reality in all its complexity, multidimensionality and multiversality.

The new *utopian* horizon part of the hope-principle and the encyclopaedia of utopias which is the Bible reformulate theology as *spes quarens intellectum*.[5] Theology must learn to reconcile the interrogative way,

---

5 Ernst Bloch, *El principio Esperanza*, Madrid, Trotta, 2004.

which leads to unmasking false securities and stereotypes, with the utopian way, which dreams the still un-existing and asks itself, as the serpent does in Bernard Shaw's *In the Beginning*, 'why not?', paving the way for what one day may be reality and is not so, yet. Utopia, today considered a forgotten category and considered mythical, must regain, in a theology for 'Another World is Possible', the centrality it had in the beginnings of liberation theology; though it must also be liberated from its pejorative connotations and naïve inclinations. Thus, as Moltmann points out, the 'Hope-principle can encourage theology to seek new interpretations of its primitive hope to revalue it faced with all accommodating senses which pretend to distort its true sense'.[6] It is not a question of a blind hope, rather a *docta spes*, as Bloch mentions, which remits and appeals to reason. The relation between theology and hope is the same as that Bloch establishes between reason and hope: 'only when hope begins to speak, does a hope begin to flourish, in which there is no falseness'.[7] In this sense I think that, at the end of the 1960s, Max Horkheimer provided a good definition of theology: 'theology is the hope that the injustice which characterises the world will not prevail, that injustice can not be considered the final word'.[8]

Inseparable from the utopian horizon is the *anamnetic*, which contributes to recuperating the apocalyptical inheritance, it centres on the subversive memory of victims, who seek their rehabilitation and consider obedience to those who suffer the constitutive element of moral conscience. It is the remembrance knowledge of which Metz talks about, which must not be confused with Platonic amnesia, nor with the contemplation of eternal ideas, rather it remits us to the biblical memory, which destabilizes the present, questions the dominating evidence of current canons, and the law of lineal progression, and defends the lost cause of the defeated, whose hopes were crushed by power.

The *symbolic* paradigm in which the new theological paradigm is placed, questions the despotic absolutism in which dogmatic language often falls and recuperates symbol as the more proper language of religions and theology. Dogma, which is a language convention, becomes dogmatism when imposed, in its literal formulation, without interpretation, leaving out the cultural distance between the time of its formula-

---

6 Jürgen Moltmann, *Hope and Planning*, New York, Harper & Row, 1971.

7 Ernst Bloch, *The Principle of Hope*, Vol. III, Cambridge, MIT Press, 1986.

8 Max Horkheimer, *Anhelo de justicia*, Madrid, Trotta, 2000, p. 169. No English translation available.

tion and the new historical context. Dogmatism impoverishes symbol. What in symbol is polysemic in dogma becomes univocal. One should not forget that, as Paul Ricoeur once said 'symbol leads to thinking', while dogma tends to close the horizon of thought.

The *interdisciplinary* horizon demonstrates that theology is a literary genre which has its own rules; following Wittgenstein's terminology, 'it is a language game', it has its *Sitz im Leben* and its own grammar. Yet, at the same time, it is part of a wider network of communication with other disciplines. It lives within a regime 'of dependency in relation with the social conditions of production, this means to say, with the economy of cultural goods, on which theologians are called to exercise a permanent ideo-political surveillance'.[9] This explains the importance of philosophy, anthropology, sociology, economy, political science, ecology, etc. as necessary mediations of the theological discourse.

The horizon of *religious science* implies the step from theology as the only or privileged knowledge of God to a theology of dialogue with other discourses and methods which occupy the study of the religious phenomena both diachronically and synchronically, particularly the sciences of religion: sociology of religion, phenomenology of religion, psychology of religion, philosophy of religion, cultural anthropology, history of religions, ecology of religion. In this horizon, it is necessary to redefine the articulation between theology and the above mentioned disciplines.

Corresponding with religious and cultural pluralism it is necessary to construct an *interspirituality* or an interreligious spirituality, which transgresses the frontiers that each religion has raised in its history to distinguish itself from others. Following the Christian *sannyasi* theologian Wayne Teasdale, by interspirituality I understand the elimination of barriers that have separated religions and the elimination of ancient antagonisms that have confronted them, while at the same time creating a fertile exchange and a dynamic participation in the respective spiritual treasures of these religions. Eliminating barriers and overcoming religious antagonisms will prepare the way for weaving links of friendship and communication between believers of different creeds. As the Dalai Lama has often said, without friendship, interreligious

---

9 Clodovis Boff, *Teología de lo político. Sus mediaciones*, Salamanca, Sigueme, 1980, p. 61. No English translation available.

dialogue is not possible; neither can the religions work together for peace.

The new *political imperial* horizon demands, in the accurate words of Jon Sobrino, an 'anti imperialistic spirituality', which must be translated into a liberating praxis, inclusive of all people, including the continents the empire oppresses and excludes. It is an interreligious spirituality that resists the empire and the world disorder it generates; a spirituality that contributes to the construction of another world without empires is possible. 'Christianly speaking', writes Pedro Casaldáliga,

> this is a transparent concept (and also a very demanding one), and Jesus of Nazareth is the one who issued it, turned it into message, and life and death and resurrection. Against the oppressive politics of the Empires, the liberating politics of the Kingdom. This Kingdom of the living God, which is of the poor, and all those who are hungry and thirst for justice. Against the agenda of the Empire, the agenda of the Kingdom.[10]

The *economic* horizon invites questions on the significance, function and social place of theology in times of globalization, and to go beyond political neutrality and theological ingenuity to be firmly placed in the world of the poor and excluded, and the struggle with the other-world movements.

The option for those who are excluded by neo-liberal globalization is a theological truth before it is an ethical attitude, because it is rooted in the mystery of God who is revealed in history, a God of the poor, and in Christianity, a Christological truth because it is deeply rooted in the mystery of Jesus the Christ, who freely, consciously and in active solidarity with the poor, assumed impoverishment, and he did this not for poverty, which he considered a social stigma that should be combatted, nor for ascetic or romantic reasons, but rather because of solidarity with the poor.

This is a truth often overlooked by theology and which the Roman Catholic ecclesiastical magisterium tends to diminish. The president of the World Council of Churches, Visser't Hooft, when considering this, said: 'The member of the Church who refuses to take on the responsibility for the disinherited is as guilty of heresy as those who

---

10 Pedro Casaldáliga, *Agenda Latinoamericana 2005*, p. 8. No English translation available.

reject this or that article of faith.'[11] I know many Catholic theologians, over 500 over the last quarter of a century, condemned, processed and retired from their academic chairs under the accusation of rejecting one article of faith or another, generally the divinity and resurrection of Christ. On the other hand, I don't know of any theologian who has been sanctioned for denying the truth of the option for the poor.

The social, political and geographical place of the new theological paradigm cannot be Davos, where the globalists of the world gather under the neo-liberal cry 'proprietors of the world unite' and in this way elaborate their particular neo-liberal theology, which was revealed to Hayek by the god of the market religion; rather it should be Porto Alegre, where liberating religious movements meet with other-world movements, and elaborate the theology for 'Another World is Possible', trying to contribute the best solidarity, emancipatory, fraternal-sorority traditions of the different religions; traditions which can be summarized in the following ethical decalogue:

- Ethic of liberation: in a world dominated by multiple oppressions; the moral imperative is: *Free the poor, the oppressed!*
- Ethic of justice: in a structurally unjust world, the moral imperative is: *Act with justice in all relations with others, and work towards the construction of an international just order.*
- Ethic of gratuity: in a world in which calculations, interests, benefits, business rule, the moral imperative is: *Be generous! All you have, you have received gratis. Do not turn gratuity into business.*
- Ethic of compassion: in a world in which the principle of insensitivity rules, creating human and environmental suffering, the moral imperative is: *Be compassionate! Have gut-feeling with those who suffer. Share to alleviate their suffering!*
- Ethic of otherness: in a world where strangers, refugees and the undocumented are marginalized, turned away and 'disappeared', the moral imperative is: *Recognize, respect and receive the other as other, as different! Difference enriches you!*
- Ethic of solidarity: in a world where the rule is to enclose, endogamy, the moral imperative is: *Be a citizen of the world! Work for a world in which all have a place!*
- Ethic of fraternal-sorority community; in a patriarchal world, in which gender discrimination predominates in every sphere of life,

---

11 Willem Visser't Hooft, cited in J. J. Tamayo-Acosta, *Para comprender la teología de la liberación*, Estella, Verbo Divino, 2000, 5th edn, pp. 139–40. No English translation available.

the moral imperative is: *Share in the construction of a community of women and men who are equal, not clones!*

- Ethic of peace, inseparable from justice: in a world of structural violence caused by the injustice of the system; the moral imperative is: *If you want peace, work for peace and justice through active non-violence!*
- Ethic of life: in a world where the lives of the poor, the oppressed and the non-human are constantly threatened, the moral imperative is: *Defend the life of all living creatures. Live and contribute to life!*
- Ethic of incompatibility between God and money: in a world in which faith in God and belief in idols, in which adoring divinity and the golden calf are so easily combined, the moral imperative is: *Share your goods! Your accumulation causes the impoverishment of those who live around you!*

New categories

A theology for 'Another World is Possible' requires a categorical change. Some of the principal categories to be incorporated in the theological field are the following.

- From the field of science of religions: secularization, de-secularization, return to religion, market religion, empire religion, new religious movements, goddess religion, fundamentalisms, interreligious dialogue, dialogue of civilizations, interspirituality, laity, sacredness, monotheism–polytheism.
- From the field of life sciences: bioethics, biogenetics, biology, biotechnology.
- From the fields of politics and economy: politics, economy, market, emancipation, liberation, neo-individualism, globalization, otherworldness, people movements, victims, dependency, solidarity, exclusion, marginalization, justice, structural sin, global resistance movements, liberation, otherness, closeness.
- From the field of gender: god–goddess, patriarchy, gender, autonomy, nets, gender violence.
- From the field of ecology: ecology, Earth, cosmos.
- From the field of intercultural studies: culture, intercultural, multiversity, indigenous, afro descendants, ethnic, race, etc.

To conclude, I believe that the new theological paradigm we want to construct in this World Forum must avoid falling under the condemnation of the banality of philosophical discourse produced by Epicurus: 'vanity is the word of the philosopher which does not contribute to the healing of suffering of human beings',[12] and instead assume the beneficial functions that Marx applies to religion: 'the sigh of the oppressed creature, the heart of a heartless world, as the spirit in a situation lacking spirit'.[13] This is the true place for a theology for 'Another World is Possible'.

12 Epicurus, cited in Denis Huisman, André Vergez and Serge Le Strat (eds), *Historia de los filósofos ilustrada por los textos*, Madrid, Tecnos, 2000, p. 70. No English translation available.

13 Karl Marx, 'Introduction to a Contribution to the Critique of Hegel's Philosophy of Right', in K. Marx and F. Engels, *On Religion*, New York, McGraw-Hill, 1974.

Afterword
The Future of the World Forum
on Theology and Liberation

The 'World Forum on Theology and Liberation' held in Porto Alegre on 21–25 January 2007 was not a one-time event. It will continue to be celebrated in the future and will be closely linked to the World Social Forum. We committed ourselves to this project, and hope to carry it through as one more piece of evidence that the hurricane of neoliberal globalization has not destroyed liberation theology and its practitioners. Liberation theology continues to be alive and active 40 years after its birth. Today it is found in every continent, and placed within different neocultural, social and political contexts. It has many names and faces and tries to respond with humility and creativity to the great challenges of the changes we are presently living and participating in.

Liberation theology does not move in the horizon of pure reason; it moves in that of practical reason. It is not an 'eternal theology', instead it is built and rebuilt within historical processes connected to social movements, especially those seeking an alternative globalization found with the World Social Forum. To follow emancipatory movements, to learn from them, to contribute the best religious and spiritual traditions to defend peace, justice, and solidarity is the best guarantee of liberation theology's continued vitality.

As the talks published in this volume demonstrate, we have taken an immense step at the Porto Alegre World Forum. Until now, liberation theology was divided by regions and continents. Now, however, we can speak of a world liberation theology, one that includes all the continents represented in the Forum and this work.

The next step has already begun – the elaboration of an intercultural and interreligious liberation theology that recognizes and promotes religious and cultural pluralism as an expression of the diversity and richness of religions and cultures. Such a theology must identify the most urgent human and ecological problems, discover and analyze the causes of eco-human suffering in alliance with the social sciences, and examine different religious expressions with the goal of activating their ecological, pacifying and humane elements, as well as help give an answer to the challenges posed by poverty and religious/cultural pluralism. Such a theology must also create bridges of communication and find meeting places for liberation theologies of different religions, reread the sacred texts and rethink their themes and moral principles from the perspective of a world of exclusion, the option for the poor, while integrating ethnicity, race, gender, and religion. Indeed, religions have a public dimension that cannot be renounced, and as such they cannot limit themselves to the private and cultural spheres

This requires dialogue between cultures and religions from a liberationist perspective. We thus have much work ahead, but there are many theologians and believers committed to this task.

Index of Names and Subjects